The
EVERYTHING
Catholicism Book

Dear Reader:

The decision to write this book was not easy to make; both of us had conflicting emotions about undertaking this project. We were excited about exploring the history, structure, beliefs, and practices of Catholicism. However, we felt somewhat daunted. To explore Catholicism is to come to grips with the history of Western civilization over two millennia. To explain dogmas and doctrines is to delve into the thorny and challenging concepts of theology and cosmology of the Catholic Church. To describe current Catholic practices requires a study in sociology.

Though raised as Catholics, we realized that much had changed since our days in Catholic school. However, we were fortunate to have great friends, contacts, and resource facilities, including two excellent Catholic libraries: the John M. Kelly Library at St. Michael's College (University of Toronto) and the Odette College Library at St. Michael's College School (high school).

We hope that this book shows the heart and soul of Catholicism, a faith that has given hope, inspiration, and daily guidance to millions of people. For Catholics, may it serve as a refresher course and new inspiration; for non-Catholics, may it lead to greater understanding. And for would-be converts, may it be a useful stepping stone.

Helen M. Keeler   *Susan Grimbly*

For your reference, the version of the Bible we used to quote from is the New American Bible. You can find this text online at *www.nccbuscc.org*, by clicking the Bible link.

The EVERYTHING® Series

Editorial

Publishing Director	Gary M. Krebs
Managing Editor	Kate McBride
Copy Chief	Laura MacLaughlin
Acquisitions Editor	Bethany Brown
Development Editor	Julie Gutin
Production Editor	Khrysti Nazzaro

Production

Production Director	Susan Beale
Production Manager	Michelle Roy Kelly
Series Designers	Daria Perreault
	Colleen Cunningham
Cover Design	Paul Beatrice
	Frank Rivera
Layout and Graphics	Colleen Cunningham
	Rachael Eiben
	Michelle Roy Kelly
	Daria Perreault
	Erin Ring
Series Cover Artist	Dave Winter
Interior Photographs	©2001 Brand X Pictures

Visit the entire Everything® Series at everything.com

THE
EVERYTHING®
CATHOLICISM
BOOK

Discover the beliefs, traditions, and
tenets of the Catholic Church

Helen Keeler and Susan Grimbly

Adams Media Corporation
Avon, Massachusetts

To Julia Keeler, Cathy and Julia Grandison, and
Ian Pearson, for all your support

An Everything® Series Book.
Everything® and everything.com® are registered trademarks of F+W Publications, Inc.

Published by Adams Media, an F+W Publications Company
57 Littlefield Street, Avon, MA 02322 U.S.A.
www.adamsmedia.com
ISBN 13: 978-1-58062-726-9
ISBN 10: 1-58062-726-9
Printed in the United States of America.

J I H G F E

Library of Congress Cataloging-in-Publication Data
Keeler, Helen.
The everything Catholicism book / by Helen Keeler and Susan Grimbly.
p.   cm.   (An everything series book)
Includes index.
ISBN 1-58062-726-9
1. Catholic Church–Doctrines. 2. Catholic Church–Customs and
practices. I. Grimbly, Susan. II. Title. III. Series: Everything series.
BX1754 .K325   2003
282–dc21   2002014954

This book is available at quantity discounts for bulk purchases.
For information, call 1-800-289-0963.

Contents

Acknowledgments

Special thanks to Susan Noakes, Catherine Grandison, and Julia Grandison for your support and helpful research.

Top Ten Catholic Heroes and Heroines

1. Jesus Christ, God the Son
2. The Virgin Mary, Mother of God
3. St. Peter, the Rock of the Church
4. St. Paul, a convert and missionary to the Gentiles
5. St. Stephen, the first martyr to the Christian faith
6. St. Augustine, a great Catholic intellectual
7. St. Patrick, the man who brought Catholicism to Ireland
8. St. Joan of Arc, the defender of France
9. St. Thomas Aquinas, one of the greatest Catholic Theologians
10. Mother Theresa of Calcutta, a woman who dedicated her life to the poor of Calcutta

Introduction

▶WITH ADHERENTS WORLDWIDE, Catholicism is one of the world's major religions. It has had a profound impact on Western civilization for two millennia. It is, in a sense, the original form of Christianity, a tree from which the many branches of the Protestant denominations have grown.

Catholicism has had a huge impact on the world. As it has acquired millions of converts, it has also developed doctrines, dogmas, devotions, and a fairly rigid organizational structure. The Church as an institution became a dominant force. Popes and other clergy influenced nations and politics, and politics, in turn, had an impact on the Church.

Catholicism was the religion of medieval Europe, and it influenced the development of European art, architecture, education, and social structures. Though much good came from the Church, it sometimes abused its powers and dominance. The horrors of the Inquisition were visited on dissenters. Religious offices were bought and sold. Superstition and faith grew side by side.

The separation of the Eastern church and the rise of Protestantism as a reaction against abuses in the Church brought many changes, and the Catholic Church also undertook its own reforms. But the Catholic faith continued to grow in the midst of these upheavals. Catholicism spread to other continents and to the New World, where missionaries joined early explorers to bring the faith to all indigenous peoples.

In the last couple of centuries, the Catholic Church has struggled with the sweeping social changes wrought by the Enlightenment, the Industrial Revolution, the rise of democracy, and a move toward individualism—developments that have, for good or for ill, run counter to Catholic ideology.

Since the Second Vatican Council (1962–1965), the Church has resolved to modernize, look outward, reform itself from within, and find more common ground with other Christian faiths. Its emphasis has shifted from hierarchy to community, but the hierarchy still holds firm. The primary dogmas and doctrines remain unchanged, though the atmosphere is more open to healthy debate.

To the Church's credit, it has tried over the past fifty years to look at itself honestly. Recently, it has apologized for some of its past policies and transgressions. The Church also faces ongoing crises in religious vocations and in allegations of sexual abuse among its priests. How it deals with these challenges will influence how it changes in the twenty-first century. If its history is any indication, the current crises will certainly challenge the Church, but they will not damage the bedrock faith of its community.

Why is it important to learn about Catholicism? A working knowledge of this major religion is important for everyone, no matter what his or her religious background. Learning about other religions helps promote respect, tolerance, and cross-cultural and interfaith understanding. Understanding Catholicism means gaining a grasp of the Catholic belief system as well as a deeper insight into world history and modern Western society.

Anyone raised in a Catholic home knows the truth of the saying, "You can take the man out of the Catholic Church, but you can't take the Catholic Church out of the man." Embodying a theological view of the universe, a belief system, prayers and practices, and a veritable world outlook, Catholicism makes an indelible impression on anyone raised in the faith. The importance of good works, God's immensity, and the mercy of Jesus remain even with those no longer practicing their religion. Many who do lapse return to the Church at critical times in their lives.

For members of the Church, students of the Catholic faith or history, and those contemplating conversion, this book is a user-friendly guide to the essentials of Catholicism—the origins, history, doctrine, sacraments, liturgies, devotional practices, and organizational structure of this major world religion. Ⓔ

Chapter 1

What Is Catholicism?

Catholicism is founded on the teachings of Jesus Christ, which have evolved over 2,000 years into the religion we have today. It is important for us to understand Catholic beliefs. Non-Catholic Christians can see how many of their own beliefs are mirrored in or developed from Catholicism; non-Christians can gain an understanding of one of the world's great religious movements.

A Community, a Way of Life, a Religion

Catholics form a diverse community of varied ethnic and national groups that share a sense of belonging to the formal institution of the Catholic Church. The Second Vatican Council defined the Church as "a kind of sacrament or sign of intimate union with God, and of the unity of all mankind." In joining the Church, each member joins a community that comprises the Body of Christ on earth.

The local congregation, ministered to by a priest, is the basic unit of Catholic community. Each congregation is part of a larger diocese (the territory under a bishop's jurisdiction), and all the dioceses in the world answer to the Curia in Rome. All these units make up one living, breathing entity that prays and worships in the same way, forming a huge community of souls.

The senses of community and mutual responsibility are reinforced through thousands of service organizations that the Church sponsors around the world. Service to others is elemental to Catholicism. Out of love for the Lord, the Church is expected to serve mankind compassionately, both through its service institutions and through the work of individual Catholics.

In Devotion to God

The religious aspect of Catholicism is its belief in and an understanding of God. Catholics learn how to live their lives based on their devotion to God, and Catholicism offers them a way of life that is based on specific doctrines, faith, theology, and a firm sense of moral responsibility. These elements, based on the Scriptures or "divine revelations," later evolved through tradition. Other religions may contain some or many of these elements, but these specific liturgical, ethical, and spiritual orientations give Catholicism its unique character.

Tradition is key to understanding Catholicism. According to Catholic thought, the Bible is considered to be a product of traditions, pulled together from numerous sources and over a long period of time.

What It Means to Be Catholic

No study of Catholicism would be complete without an understanding of the word *Catholic*. The word itself comes from the Greek *katholikos,* meaning "general" or "universal," which appeared in Greek writings before the rise of Christianity.

Writing in A.D. 110, St. Ignatius of Antioch was one of the first to use the phrase *katholike ekklesia* (literally, "catholic church"), but the force behind the phrase's meaning came from St. Cyril of Jerusalem in 386: "The Church is called Catholic because it extends through all the world and because it teaches universally and without omission all the doctrines which ought to come to human knowledge."

We know from the New Testament, particularly Matthew 24:14, that Christ intended his Word to extend beyond Jewish Palestine to all nations. By the end of the first century, at least 100 communities of Christians were established in and around the Mediterranean.

Since then, the Word has spread farther still, to nearly one billion people, across state lines and over cultural boundaries. What's more, these various cultures have adapted Catholic rites and created variations that the Church fully accepts today.

Catholicism and Other Christian Religions

Christians have many ways of practicing their faith—through the Catholic Church, the Eastern Orthodox church, and the many Protestant denominations such as the Baptists, Lutherans, Methodists, and Presbyterians. All Christians share their belief in and acceptance of Jesus Christ, but they also differ in many important ways.

The Church first underwent a split into the Western and Eastern Church in the Great Schism of 1054. (For more details on the Great Schism, see Chapter 4.) Much later, in the sixteenth and seventeenth centuries, the Protestant movements split the Western Church further into the Roman Catholic and Protestant denominations.

The word *Protestant* comes from "protest." The Protestant faiths splintered from the Catholic Church because ordinary people protested against the Catholic institution and some of its conduct and practices.

The head of the Catholic Church has been situated in Rome for many centuries. However, the word *Roman* was first appended to the Catholic Church during the Reformation. The followers of Martin Luther, the group that made the first major split from the Church, also considered themselves Catholic. They described the Church as "Roman" to indicate the distinction between themselves and followers of "Romish" or "Papist" Catholics.

The Protestant Faiths

In some ways, the Protestant churches are similar to the Catholic Church. Most believe in the importance of the Bible, the resurrection of Jesus Christ, the Triune God (Father, Son, and Holy Ghost), the sacraments of Baptism and the Eucharist, and other Christian doctrines and practices.

The main distinction between Catholicism and Protestantism is that Catholicism is a religion of sacraments (seeing the spiritual enfleshed in the secular world) while Protestantism is more a religion of the bodiless Word of God. Sacramentality is the idea that everything reveals God. Over time, Protestantism has retained only parts of this concept. Protestants don't believe, as Catholics do, in the special significance of Mary. They don't believe in transubstantiation (that the Eucharist is after declaration by a priest, the Body and Blood of Christ). They believe that priests and ministers are merely members of the laity, trained in the practices of that particular religion, and not that members of the ordained ministry are actually mediators of God's grace. Finally, they see religious statues and icons more as forms of idolatry than as windows to the spiritual world.

Another fascinating difference is in approaches to the Bible. Catholics believe that the Church—as the authentic moral and theological authority—should be their guide in interpreting the Bible. Peter, who was the first Bishop of Rome, wrote, "There is no prophecy of scripture that is a matter of personal interpretation" (2 Peter 1:20). Protestants challenged this relationship. Many Protestant faiths accept personal interpretation of the Bible as they do a personal (unmediated) relationship between each person and God.

The Protestants also denied that the pope, as the head of the Church hierarchy in matters of faith and morals, was infallible in matters of faith and morals, a belief known as the Petrine Primacy or apostolic succession. In Catholic ideology, the pope is infallible because he is the representative of Christ on earth. He follows a line of succession back to St. Peter, the first bishop of the early Church, who received his appointment directly from Jesus.

There was also a difference in how Protestants and Catholics worshiped. Until recently, Catholics celebrate the Mass with a highly structured, formal ceremony conducted in Latin (today, most Catholic churches in the United States and many other countries have made a switch to having services in the vernacular). Protestant forms of worship were simpler: Believers prayed in their native tongues and there was more preaching. In some denominations, the service was completely unstructured, allowing the congregation a greater degree of participation.

The Grace of God

The Catholic Church is a living, growing entity. Open to changes that come with the times, it also adheres to some basic doctrines it has always held to be true. The most basic of the Church's doctrines is the idea that man achieves salvation through divine grace, where divine blessings are an expression of God's love.

The Two Mysteries

God's grace is expressed through the dual nature of Christ (man and God) and the trinity of persons in God. These two mysteries are fundamental to Catholic belief and the Church's teachings about God. On his deathbed, just before receiving the Holy Eucharist, the Church's most precious sacrament, St. Thomas Aquinas, considered to be one of the fathers of the Church, said: "If in this world there be any knowledge of this sacrament stronger than that of faith, I wish now to use it in affirming that I firmly believe and know as certain that Jesus Christ, True God and True Man, Son of God and Son of the Virgin Mary, is in this Sacrament."

St. Thomas affirms Christ's humanity, that Jesus was born and died a man, with a man's physical strengths and weaknesses. The Catholic

Church teaches that it is our great gift that Christ walked among us, was one of us, and that he took on the burden of atonement for our sins. St. Thomas also affirms Jesus' divinity, that the man who walked among us 2,000 years ago was indeed a divine person, a person of God, who made himself over into our image for a brief time.

QUESTION?

What is "incarnation"?
Incarnation, which literally means "made into flesh," describes what happened when Jesus assumed a bodily form and the human condition. Understanding the concept of the Incarnation is essential to the Catholic belief system.

Catholics believe that the world is essentially good but that it has fallen from grace, or the "divine presence," into original sin. As a result of this falling away, the world had to be redeemed by God in Christ.

The Eucharist

The Catholic belief in God as a real, living presence is best exemplified in the Eucharist, another of the mysteries fundamental to the Catholic faith. Celebration of the Eucharist, the Mass, is the centerpiece of Catholic worship.

During this ceremony, the assembly partakes of bread and wine that, through consecration, are converted into the Mystical Body and Blood of Christ. The process through which the bread and wine are converted is known as "transubstantiation." Through transubstantiation, the bread and wine are literally changed into Christ's body and blood. In sharing this sacrament, the entire Catholic community is united in communion with Christ. For this reason, the Mass is also known as the Holy Communion.

The Four Tenets of the Church

The Catholic Church has four basic tenets: tradition, universality, reason, and analogy. Tradition includes all the teachings contained in the Bible.

Universality—remember, the word *Catholic* comes from the Greek word for "universal"—is the openness to all truth, unfettered by any particular culture and unrestricted to all human beings. The last two tenets, analogy and reason, are both used in our quest to understand the Catholic mysteries. Analogy is a common logic device that helps us understand God through our knowledge of the created world; reason and philosophy are both pre-eminent in the Church's thinking.

FACT

St. Augustine, one of the great fathers of the Church, had this to say about the important relationship between faith and reason. The right use of reason is "that by which the most wholesome faith is begotten . . . is nourished, defended, and made strong."

Human powers of reason aside, God does not leave the faithful to figure out his mysteries on their own. The Bible reveals God's wisdom and teachings and is an essential part of divine revelation. Catholic doctrine holds that neither the Gospels nor the Bible's other books are self-explanatory. To understand these texts and see the truths they contain, people need the guidance of the Church. The highest authority in interpreting the Scriptures is the pope.

Sacramentality, Mediation, and Communion

The concepts of sacramentality, mediation, and communion are essential to the Catholic faith. Besides providing guideposts for the faithful in their response to the Lord, these concepts illustrate how Catholics see themselves in relation to the Divine.

Sacramentality: The Presence of God

Sacramentality is the principle that says everything in creation—people, movements, places, the environment, and the cosmos itself—can reveal God. Under this principle, the division between sacred and secular is erased: Everything is sacred, because all comes from the Lord.

Beyond sacramentality as a general concept, Catholicism recognizes seven specific sacraments that confer grace (the seven sacraments will be discussed in greater detail in Chapter 8). Additionally, objects, words, or ceremonies used in conjunction with the sacraments and which confer holiness are known as the sacramentals. When a priest blesses an object—such as giving a blessing upon the dedication of a church or upon holy oils and vestments—the blessed object is sanctified and becomes a sacramental.

Mediation: Intercession Between Man and God

Catholics believe that God and man can be brought to a greater common awareness through the power of certain intercessors that are venerated by the Catholic Church. An angel, saint, holy person, or a priest can plead a believer's cause to God or, in other words, be a mediator between the believer and the Lord.

Mediation is a process that bridges the divide between the human and the divine. The saints, especially the Virgin Mary, take their spiritual power from Christ, the ultimate mediator, and can intercede with God to confer his grace on man.

In the very essence of his being, Christ conjoins the human and the divine, and is therefore considered to be the most effective mediator. The second most perfect advocate for us is the Blessed Virgin Mary. She was born without original sin and was never estranged from God.

Communion: A Communal Faith

The principle of communion stresses the communal aspect of Catholic life. Regardless of one's personal relationship to God, the only way to him is through the community of the faithful, especially as it is embodied in the sacraments of the Church.

Chapter 2

The Birth of the Church

Christianity began with Jesus Christ, and to this day, Catholics trace their beliefs to Jesus' last three years of life and the teachings and practices of the Twelve Apostles. This chapter will explore the origins of Christianity and the Catholic Church, which formally considers its beginning to be the first Pentecost after Jesus' crucifixion.

The Story Begins with Jesus

The story of the Catholic Church must begin with Jesus Christ and his human life. Catholic doctrine teaches that Jesus had a dual nature: He was both human and divine. Jesus the Son of God was made man as a perfect expression of God's love.

How do we know that Jesus was a real, historical human being? Catholic scholars and laypeople rely on the main written source, the Bible, but books by early Roman historians also mention his existence. The most important such source is *Jewish Antiquities,* a historical work written by Flavius Josephus, one of the world's earliest historians.

The search for the facts proving Jesus' existence didn't really start until the 1700s, the age of early science. The quest for the historical Jesus is not essential for authentic Catholic faith.

Flavius Josephus was born in Jerusalem in A.D. 37 to a priestly Jewish family. Although he was involved in the First Revolt against Rome, he later switched sides and moved to Rome, where he wrote his historical accounts under the auspices of the Roman emperor. The *Jewish Antiquities* is a collection of twenty books that discuss the history of the Jewish people; while we no longer have the original text, the earliest extant versions of the manuscript include the following reference:

> Now, there was about this time Jesus, a wise man, if it be lawful to call him a man, for he was a doer of wonderful works— a teacher of such men as receive the truth with pleasure. He drew over to him both many of the Jews, and many of the Gentiles. He was [the] Christ.

According to the Bible, Jesus Christ was born to the daughter of Anne and Joachim, Mary, who was chosen by God to bear his Son. The Blessed Virgin Mary, the Mother of God, is one of the most important figures in Catholic liturgy. She embodies the great maternal impulses of kindliness and wisdom. As such, Mary is venerated around the world. And yet very little is known about her actual life. What we do know mostly comes from canonical Scriptures, especially the Gospels.

The Annunciation

A rare and important reference to Mary in the New Testament concerns her visit from the Angel Gabriel. He appeared to her and announced: "You will conceive in your womb and bear a son" (Luke 1:31; Luke 1:26–38 tells the story of the Annunciation). In a state of grace, Mary accepted God's will.

Mary was betrothed to an older man, the carpenter Joseph. The social stigma of bearing a child outside of wedlock was enormous. Indeed, Joseph intended to quietly divorce her. But an angel also appeared to Joseph to explain that he would be head of a household in which Mary would bear the coming Messiah. And so Joseph too accepted his role.

FACT

Under Jewish law, a marriage took place in two stages: the betrothal and the marriage. Mary and Joseph were betrothed, but they were not yet living together as man and wife.

The Magnificat

The next significant "Marian" event in the Bible takes place five months later (in Luke 1:39–56). Mary visits her kinswoman Elizabeth, who is also pregnant with the child who will become John the Baptist. Mary greets Elizabeth with a song of praise called the Magnificat. The Bible tells us that at the meeting of the two women, Elizabeth's baby leaped in her womb. Elizabeth also tells Mary that Mary "is twice blessed."

Jesus Is Born

Although Mary and Joseph lived in Nazareth, and Jesus is often known as Jesus of Nazareth, he was actually born in Bethlehem. According to the Gospel of Luke, Mary and Joseph had to travel to Bethlehem for the census. The town was full of people and the only place where the couple could find a place to sleep was in a manger. It was there that Jesus was born and where he was visited by the three wise men, the Magi (as depicted in Nativity scenes every Christmastime).

When Herod heard from the Magi that the King of the Jews was born, he sent out soldiers to kill all Jewish boys two years old and younger. To save their son, Joseph and Mary fled to Egypt. When Herod died, the family returned to their home in Nazareth.

Preaching the Word of God

Jesus was a man of conviction, an eloquent and passionate speaker—his mother, Mary, found him in the Temple conversing with the elders when he was only twelve. According to the Bible, his formal ministry began with his baptism in the River Jordan by John the Baptist, also known as the Precursor. Because Jesus was without sin, his baptism was a highly symbolic undertaking in which his message of love was expressed in the triune acts of repentance, forgiveness, and the washing away of sins.

Immediately after his baptism, Jesus retired to the desert of Judea for a forty-day fast. Here, according to the Gospel of Mark and the Gospel of Luke, Satan subjected him to three assaults, or temptations:

1. That to relieve his hunger, he change the rocks to bread
2. That he cast himself off a parapet to see if the angels would catch him
3. That in exchange for worship, he receive dominion over all the kingdoms of the earth

Jesus' time in the desert is considered a ritualistic preparation period for his ministry. In his ministering, Jesus traveled for three years around Galilee. A small province of ancient Palestine, Galilee was part of the Roman Empire. According to the Gospels, Jesus also came to preach in and around Jerusalem.

Jesus' preaching alarmed the local authorities almost immediately—first the Pharisees (those who practiced strict adherence to Jewish religious laws) and then the Romans. When the people proclaimed Jesus as the King of the Jews, both the Jewish religious leaders and the Roman government saw him as a threat.

ALERT!

Jesus of Nazareth was Jewish. He was born into a Jewish family and raised in the Jewish tradition—an important point to keep in mind when studying the origins of Catholicism.

A Message of Love

Jesus was not preaching a new religion. He brought people the Word of God, and he taught that every person can receive salvation. He reminded them that following the letter of the Law was not as important as living a good life on earth.

Jesus taught his message of love with clarity and simplicity. He taught God's infinite love for the humble and the weak, and he taught that each person should strive to follow God's example.

The Beatitudes

Jesus addressed his largest audience in the hills of the Galilee with the Sermon on the Mount, where he gave his followers eight blessings, known as the Beatitudes (Matthew 5:3–11):

Blessed are the poor in spirit, for theirs is the kingdom of heaven.
Blessed are they who mourn, for they will be comforted.
Blessed are the meek, for they will inherit the land.
Blessed are they who hunger and thirst for righteousness, for they
 will be satisfied.
Blessed are the merciful, for they will be shown mercy.
Blessed are the clean of heart, for they will see God.
Blessed are the peacemakers, for they will be called children of God.
Blessed are they who are persecuted for the sake of righteousness,
 for theirs is the kingdom of heaven.
Blessed are you when they insult you and persecute you and utter
 every kind of evil against you (falsely) because of me.

FACT

Jesus also used stories, or parables, to illustrate his lessons. Parables about nature and harvest, weddings and feasts, and fathers and sons all appear in the Bible. The two best known are probably the parables of the good Samaritan and the prodigal son.

The Twelve Apostles

Jesus had many disciples and devoted followers. From them, he picked twelve men to travel with him. These disciples came to be known as the apostles, from the Greek word *apostolos*, "to send forth." Jesus taught them, so that they would one day go out into the world to spread his message.

These were the Twelve Apostles:

- Peter and his brother Andrew
- James and John, also brothers. (This John is not to be confused with John the Baptist, who had a separate role as the Precursor—the one who announced that the Son of God was coming.)
- Philip, Bartholomew, Matthew, Thomas, James (son of Alphaeus), Thaddaeus (son of James), and Simon
- Judas Iscariot, who would betray Jesus for thirty pieces of silver

Paul would join the Christians later and become an "honorary" apostle, making their number twelve again.

It was the apostles' special privilege to stay close to Jesus and receive his training and wisdom. As witnesses to Jesus' life on earth and students of his teachings, the apostles became founders of the Church and the authors of the Gospels (first passed down orally and eventually written down). The Gospels, apostolic letters, and other writings were later compiled into what we know as the New Testament.

Peter, the Rock of the Church

Peter was a married fisherman who lived in the Galilee. Peter's name was originally Simon; later, Jesus came to call him Cephas ("rock," in Aramaic). Later still, this name came into Greek as Peter (*petros* being Greek for "rock"). The new name denotes Peter's central function in Jesus' inner circle: "And so I say to you, you are Peter, and upon this rock I will build my church" (Matthew 16:18).

Jesus' choice of a fisherman and the name he gave him are both symbolic. Jesus chose Peter to be a fisher of men, the first in the apostolic line of popes who would later follow him.

Paul, the Twelfth Apostle

The story of Paul is different from that of all the other apostles. Saul (as he was originally called) never knew Jesus during his lifetime. A practicing Jew, Saul saw the Christian faith as heresy. In fact, he was a zealous persecutor of the new Christian faith. (He acted as a witness at the stoning of the apostle Stephen, the first Christian martyr.)

One day, on the way to Damascus to rout out Christians, Saul received a revelation from the Lord that blinded him for three days. Once he recovered, he took his Roman name, Paul, and became an enthusiastic convert to Christianity. From that day, Paul devoted all of his energy to spread the message of Jesus Christ and help new converts to interpret it.

Recognizing the Messiah

Jesus of Nazareth was not the only man who traveled around the countryside preaching sermons and instructing the people in the Way of God. How, then, did his followers come to know he was the Christ? They knew because of the prophecies of the Old Testament and the miracles that Jesus worked when he walked among them.

QUESTION?

What are the meanings of "Messiah" and "Christ"?
The word *messiah* comes from the Hebrew for "anointed" (as king); Jews expected the arrival of the "anointed," sent by God, as prophesized by the prophets of the Old Testament. "Messiah" translates into Greek as *khristos,* or Christ. Jesus of Nazareth was understood to be God's messenger, the Messiah, and is therefore known as Jesus Christ.

Jesus' identity was established at his baptism. When he arose from the waters of the Jordan, the heavens opened, "and the Spirit as a dove [descended] upon him. And a voice came from the heavens, 'You are my beloved Son; with you I am well pleased'" (Mark 1:11). At this moment, Jesus was proclaimed the Messiah.

Signs and Miracles

It is recorded that Jesus performed thirty-five miracles; of these, seven were "sign miracles" (those miracles that were signs that Jesus was the Christ) as recorded in the Gospel of John, Chapters 1–11. The first of the sign miracles—and therefore the most important one—was the miracle at the wedding feast at Cana.

Jesus and Mary were at a wedding celebration when the party ran out of wine. Jesus changed water into wine, performing his first miracle. This transformation illustrated that a Christian's life on earth is like a wedding feast, full of bounty and joy as well as community—the coming together of loved ones. The running out of wine is a symbol of the hurdles that life puts before us.

The honeymoon that comes after the wedding represents our eventual return to God's presence. In more religious terms, Jesus compared the soul to being the bride of Christ.

The other six of Jesus' sign miracles were the following:

- Healing a royal official's son
- Healing a paralytic man who had been unable to walk for thirty-eight years
- Feeding 5,000 people with only five loaves of bread and two fish
- Walking on the sea to calm his disciples, who were frightened that their boat was sinking
- Healing a blind man by placing mud mixed with his saliva over his eyes and telling him to wash in a pool
- Raising Lazarus from the dead

The miracles demonstrate both Christ's compassion and the power of the living God. They are potent symbols that demonstrate how Jesus helped his followers understand what he was doing. His miracles helped persuade the disciples that Jesus was God's son on earth. Raising Lazarus from the dead won over many religious leaders, who began to follow Jesus and his teachings.

FACT

Performing miracles sometimes led to trouble with the authorities. When Jesus healed the blind man at Siloam, the Pharisees accused him of breaking God's commandment to keep the Sabbath as a day of rest.

The Passion of Christ

Jesus' brief life—thirty-three years in total—culminated in Jerusalem. The last events of his life, from the Last Supper to his crucifixion, are known collectively as the Passion. Each stage of the Passion provides an essential element in the fretwork of Catholic belief.

The Passion begins with the Last Supper, a Passover meal that Jesus ate with his apostles. During this meal, Jesus invited his followers to enjoy communion with him forever by literally partaking of his Body and Blood through consecrated bread and wine. Catholics and many Protestant denominations still celebrate this important ceremony, now known as the Eucharist. To Catholics, the Eucharist is the heart of the Mass, or Catholic service of worship.

The Arrest and Crucifixion

After the Last Supper, the apostles left Jesus to a lonely vigil in the Garden of Gethsemane, where he prayed. He was betrayed by Judas. Pontius Pilate's soldiers found Jesus in the garden and arrested him. Jesus was tried and taken to Golgotha with two other men, and they were crucified.

The Crucifixion is also known as the Agony: Jesus died on the cross to atone for our sins. It is also considered a sacrifice: God sacrificed his Son for us. After he died, Jesus' mother and other followers laid his body in a tomb cut in the rock. The tomb was sealed with a large stone.

Resurrection: The Best Miracle of All

The physical resurrection of Jesus Christ is fundamental to Catholic and all Christian belief. Resurrection is literally a crucial event in Christianity, the most important of all Jesus' miracles. Resurrection is what Catholics celebrate at Easter. It is a symbol of renewal, and it brings us the message that even though we are all sinners, we can be reborn in Christ, our Savior.

Two days after the crucifixion, Mary Magdalene—another follower of Christ—discovered that Jesus' tomb was empty. Jesus Christ had risen from the dead. According to the Gospels, Mary met Jesus on the road. Later, Jesus communed with his disciples, and then he ascended into Heaven.

If you are a Catholic, don't forget your Easter duty! Good Catholics are required to go to confession before Easter Sunday so that they may receive the Eucharist in a state of grace on the holiest of days.

The Spiritual Birthday of the Church

Catholics consider Pentecost Sunday, which ends the season of Easter, as the birthday of the Catholic Church. That first year, only a few weeks after the Ascension of Christ, the apostles had gathered in Jerusalem with Mary, the Mother of God, to observe *Shavuot,* the Feast of Weeks—a Jewish holiday held fifty days after the Passover Sabbath to celebrate the midseason grain harvest. (Pentecost, "the fiftieth day," is a Greek translation of the Hebrew *Shavuot.*)

It probably wasn't much of a celebration. Jesus' disciples were confused, unsure of what to do next. They probably grieved their teacher, and they were likely anxious about their personal safety. Yet what happened during this feast day transformed them:

> And suddenly there came from the sky a noise like a strong driving wind, and it filled the entire house in which they were. Then there appeared to them tongues as of fire, which parted and came to rest on each one of them. And they were all filled with the holy Spirit and began to speak in different tongues, as the Spirit enabled them. (Acts 2:2–4)

FACT

Around the world, there are many traditions that commemorate this momentous event. In Italy, people scatter rose leaves from the church ceiling to recall the miracle of the fiery tongues. In France, they blow trumpets during the Divine Liturgy service to recall the sound of the mighty wind that accompanied the Descent of the Holy Ghost.

Blessed with the Holy Spirit

The apostles were filled with the Holy Spirit, which cemented their belief and gave them courage and the gift of tongues. This gave the apostles the ability to speak so that people of different languages could comprehend their meaning. They went out, and they began to preach.

Peter, filled with the Holy Spirit, preached with such joy that 3,000 were baptized that very day. These converts were Jews from Mesopotamia,

Judea, Cappadocia, and many other places. Visiting Jerusalem for the holiday, they took Peter's message with them back to their homes. Peter's central role in the expanding circle of Christ's followers was thus clearly defined, and the Church was made public.

The apostles proceeded to spread the word in and around the Mediterranean region, drawing in people from all races and religions, and establishing Christian communities wherever they went. This was their mission, and it came with great tests of faith. Sometimes they were welcomed. At other times, they placed themselves in great personal peril.

Jesus said: "The kingdom of God may be likened to a king who gave a wedding feast for his son" (Matthew 22:2). Everybody is invited, and the only requirement is that the guests be "dressed in a wedding garment" (Matthew 22:11)—in other words, that they have Jesus in themselves.

Earliest Church Practices

At the beginning, the Christians did not have formal practices. They were guided by the teachings of Jesus Christ and the writings of the apostles. The one essential belief or practice that they performed was the celebration of the Eucharist, or Holy Communion, at various assemblies. These assemblies were the first church gatherings. In fact, the English word *church* is a translation of the Greek word for "assembly," *ekklesia*.

Birth of the Sacraments

Catholics believe that the sacraments, or the rites of the Catholic Church, are the sacred base of a good Catholic lifestyle. The sacraments also remind us that we carry Jesus through our daily lives. The seven sacraments, which have been given to us by Christ, include Baptism, Confirmation, the Eucharist, Penance, the Anointing of the Sick, Holy Orders, and Matrimony. (For a detailed description of the sacraments, refer to Chapter 8).

Celebration of the Eucharist symbolizes the Last Supper and commemorates Christ's death and Resurrection. Partaking of the Eucharist—

literally the Body and Blood of Christ—is at the very essence of Catholicism. That is because through the Eucharist, believers partake of the Divine, coming as close to God as they can.

The practice of baptism, the cleansing away of sin, began when John the Baptist baptized Jesus at the River Jordan. Converts to early Christianity underwent baptism as a symbolic cleansing of sins and a public demonstration of their faith. Not until the Middle Ages did infant baptism become an accepted practice: Infant mortality was high, and many parents feared their unbaptized babies would not get into Heaven.

FACT

Before the Middle Ages, Confirmation was part of the baptismal rite, not a separate sacrament. Originally, immersion in water (Baptism) was followed by the ceremony in which a bishop anointed the new believer with oil (Confirmation). Eventually, though, there were too many people to be baptized and the bishops could not officiate at every baptism. At that point, the sacrament of Confirmation broke off and was performed separately.

Another new sacrament was Penance, also called reconciliation or confession. In the early days of persecution, some people denied Christ to save themselves from death by torture. Catholic communities accepted the apostates' public reconciliation, following in the spirit of Christ's message of forgiveness and compassion. Later, confessions became private.

Catholicism adopted the sacrament of Matrimony from the Jewish tradition. Formalizing the sacraments of Anointing the Sick and Holy Orders came later, as the Church grew and developed.

Origins of the Catholic Liturgy

The Catholic liturgy originated in private gatherings. Christians read from the missives of the apostles, which were copied and passed from one community to another. (By A.D. 200, Church leaders agreed on which writings were most authoritative.) The assembly might discuss these readings. Then, the early Christians prayed, sang, and celebrated the Eucharist.

Chapter 3

The Church Grows and Develops

From the days of the Twelve Apostles, the Church continued to grow and develop, despite the many obstacles it encountered along the way. Early Christians faced persecution from non-Christians, but a greater challenge was disagreement over Christian belief among believers themselves. Despite the obstacles, the early Christians persevered, inspired by the Holy Spirit and the Word of God.

Spreading the Word

The first great step in Christian history was the spreading of the Word from ancient Palestine throughout the Mediterranean. Primarily, the faith spread by word of mouth and letters of the apostles, who were charged with educating the people about the life and teachings of Jesus Christ.

Paul's Journeys

After his conversion, Paul became an ardent missionary. He took three important journeys through the Mediterranean, mainly on foot. On his first trip, with Barnabas, he traveled through Palestine and then north, as far as Antioch, seeking converts among the non-Jewish peoples. On his second trip, he ventured farther afield. He traveled to Thessalonica, in ancient Macedonia; the seaport of Philippi (the first European city to accept Christianity, thanks to Paul's efforts); and on to Corinth. On his third trip, Paul ventured into the Roman Province of Asia (what is now western Turkey) and continued his missionary work along the coast.

During his second trip, Paul wrote his first epistle to the Thessalonians, which became a book of the New Testament (Thessalonians). In his zeal to foster more Christian communities, Paul wrote many more letters that aspired to illuminate Christian ideals. These epistles—along with the letters of Peter, James, John, and Jude—were handed around and discussed during prayer sessions.

Paul's missionary activities are described in the New Testament in the Book of Acts. In Rome, St. Paul's Outside the Walls marks Paul's burial place. And St. Paul's Cathedral in the Vatican is considered one of the great Catholic churches.

The Early Letters

Most epistles were written to particular churches struggling with particular issues. Early Christians prized and venerated these apostolic writings. They were passed along, informally, for about 150 years after Paul's death. Eventually, the thirteen letters of Paul and the many letters of the other apostles that survived were compiled, along with the four Gospels, into the New Testament.

Interestingly, most of the books and epistles of the New Testament were not completed until the second half of the first century. Following Christ's death, many of his followers believed he would return quickly, according to the urgent prophecies of the Second Coming, and there was no time or need to write down a record of his life. However, when the first generation of believers began to die, people realized the need for a written history of the Church's beginning. These writings became the basis of the New Testament.

The Four Gospels

The word *gospel* means "good news." The four Gospels that bring to us the news of Jesus Christ's life and teachings are the Gospels of Mark, Matthew, Luke, and John. The four Gospels recount the same story, but each author concentrates on different aspects and a different message:

- The Gospel of Mark (A.D. 65–70) focuses on Jesus' suffering, which persecuted Christians could identify with.
- The Gospel of Matthew (A.D. 80–100) explains how Jesus, as the Messiah, fulfills Jewish prophecies.
- The Gospel of Luke (A.D. 85) points out how Jesus, as Savior, does not discriminate on the basis of race or class.
- The Gospel of John (circa A.D. 90) formulates the difficult notion of Jesus as a divine being.

FACT

The New Testament was formalized by the bishops who assembled at Carthage in two councils, one at the end of the fourth century and the other shortly after. They agreed on the twenty-seven books that would be proclaimed as divine Scripture—from that point on, only these books would be read during Church services.

Tests of Faith: The Martyrs

When Christianity spread beyond Palestine and through the rest of the Roman Empire—which covered most of the Mediterranean—it naturally got as far as Rome. The Roman emperors did not appreciate the new religion that rejected their almost-divine status, all other Roman deities, and their religious holidays. (Celebrating these holidays was supposed to bring the gods' favor to Rome, and it was considered patriotic duty; rejection of the gods was therefore considered treason.)

Still, Christians lived in Rome with relative peace until A.D. 64, when a terrible fire swept the city's cramped streets. The causes of the fire remain unknown. Some believe that Emperor Nero was at fault, but Nero blamed the Christians and reprisals followed. Christianity was proclaimed anti-Roman and outlawed around the year 100.

Practicing or preaching Christianity was punishable by death, and yet many early Christians chose to stand behind their beliefs. They preferred to die as martyrs rather than renounce their faith. Their courage and willingness to cling to their faith despite everything impressed the people of Rome. Christianity continued to attract converts and to spread.

The First Martyr

Tradition names Stephen as the first Christian martyr. One year after the Crucifixion, Stephen was preaching to the crowd in Jerusalem. Most were skeptical of his message. To convince them, Stephen tried to compare his position (as a representative of Jesus) to that of Moses, reminding the people that the Israelites had even at one point rejected Moses. Offended by the comparison, the Jews accused him of blaspheming against Moses and God.

ALERT!

Stephen's martyrdom is especially significant. Saul, who approved of the execution, was there at the moment of Stephen's stoning. This moment is considered instrumental in Saul's later conversion and his becoming the apostle Paul.

Stephen's speech was so inflammatory—he also accused his listeners of not keeping the law given them by the angels—that he was dragged outside Jerusalem and stoned to death. Later, he was canonized by the Church and became a saint.

Martyrdom of Peter and Paul

The apostles Peter and Paul met their deaths under the Romans. Peter, who had established a Christian community in Rome, was arrested there and sentenced to crucifixion. According to one story, Peter requested to be crucified upside down, so that his death would not reflect that of his Lord.

Paul was arrested and tried twice. The first time, he was charged with inciting a riot and was held in Rome for two years, although he enjoyed relative freedom, living in hired lodgings and preaching. He was eventually acquitted of the false charges. The second time, he was arrested near Ephesus, the capital of the province of Asia. He was taken to Rome and beheaded, rather than crucified. Beheading was considered a more dignified form of execution, and Paul was accorded this honor as a Roman citizen.

Rome adopted crucifixion as a form of punishment from the Persians and used it in the repression of its subjugated peoples. We know from the Roman writer Cicero (106–43 B.C.) that crucifixion was used against slaves and non-Roman citizens, particularly against those who had fomented rebellion or committed other treasonous acts.

Leaders of the Early Church

Christianity shifted its center from Jerusalem to Rome around A.D. 70, when the Romans suppressed a Jewish rebellion and destroyed Jerusalem. Peter, proclaimed by Jesus to be the rock of the Church, had worked and died in Rome. He left behind a line of apostolic succession of bishops (or popes) who would maintain the Roman bishopric as the spiritual center of the Catholic Church.

As the Church continued to grow, a number of strong, forceful characters helped shape its development. Whether they were bishops or laypeople with a strong religious bent, the Church would not be what it is today without them.

Clement of Rome

Clement became the third Bishop of Rome around the end of the first century. Some evidence—though no proof—suggests that he worshiped with Peter and Paul. If so, he was very close to the source of divine inspiration, and its influence on him would have been great.

Clement's fame comes mainly from one masterful letter in which he establishes the inviolable authority and primacy of the Church of Rome, which descends from Peter through apostolic succession. Clement wrote his letter to the church of the Corinthians, who had been led into sedition, and he demanded their return to obedience.

Here is what a peer of his time, a man named Eusebius, wrote of him in his *Ecclesiastical History:* "Clement has left us one recognized epistle, long and wonderful, which he composed in the name of the Church of Rome. In many churches this epistle was read aloud to the assembled worshipers in early days, as it is in our own."

Clement may have suffered a martyr's death. According to a story that surfaced in the fourth century, the Emperor Trajan was miffed that Clement had converted so many pagans to Christianity and banished him to a quarry, where he performed a miracle and slaked the thirst of thousands. Trajan then ordered Clement to be weighted down with an iron anchor and tossed into the sea near Crimea. When the waves subsided, Clement was entombed in marble by angels.

FACT

Around the year 868, St. Cyril discovered a mound with bones and an anchor in Crimea. He was certain that he had found Clement's remains. He took the bones to Rome where they were placed in the altar of the Basilica of St. Clement.

Ignatius of Antioch

Ignatius, the third bishop of Antioch, lived from the first to second centuries. He was a good pastor and gave his people courage when the Emperor Domitian began persecuting Christians.

Ignatius was a strong and impassioned writer. He sent epistles to various churches—to the Ephesians, Magnesians, Trallians, Romans, Philadelphians, Smyrnaeans, and to Polycarp. In his letters, Ignatius warns against heresies and explains that they are a threat to unity.

He continued to write while under arrest and on his way to Rome. Ignatius of Antioch was sentenced to be torn apart by lions at the Flavian amphitheater in Rome. He died a martyr.

Irenaeus of Lyon

Irenaeus grew up in Smyrna, where he remembered hearing the great bishop Polycarp, another father of the Church, talk about the apostle John. Irenaeus was ordained in Lyon. There, he witnessed the horrifying martyrdom of Greek-speaking Christians, including Lyon's bishop. Irenaeus traveled to Rome to tell the bishop, who asked Irenaeus to return to Lyon, take over the duties of the martyred bishop, and help rebuild the Christian Church. (By "Church," the pope meant the Christian community, not a physical building.)

In his writings, Irenaeus argued against the Gnostics, who did not accept the humanity of Jesus Christ because they saw the body as evil. Irenaeus also fought for and helped perpetuate the idea of apostolic succession.

Clement of Alexandria

Clement of Alexandria was a second-century teacher who traveled among the Greek-speaking communities before settling in Alexandria to start a school. He is known for three important philosophical works expressing his ideas: *The Protrepticus, The Paedogogus* ("The Tutor"), and *The Stromateis*. One of his ardent beliefs was that a Christian life should be devoted to the perfect knowledge of truth.

Rome Embraces Christianity

For its first 300 years, Christianity was viewed with great suspicion. Christian communities grew, but people joined them at great personal peril. Believers worshiped in secret. Christians were harassed and persecuted throughout the Roman Empire; they had no political power. The empire itself was under stress from without and within. Roman territories were under barbarian attack, while at home the Roman aristocracy was growing weak and corrupt. Under siege and without great leaders, Rome was falling apart.

The First Christian Emperor

In 312, the Roman army stationed in Britain elected Constantine the next Roman emperor. He returned to Rome, knowing that he would have to fight for his position when he got there. As Constantine rode through France with his army, he had a vision of a cross. He took this as a sign and ordered his soldiers to paint the Greek letters for the word *Christ* on their shields. Constantine defeated his rival and entered Rome victorious, as the new emperor. Although he did not convert to Christianity until shortly before his death many years later, both he and Rome officially supported Christianity.

The Nicene Creed, handed down from the Council of Nicaea, states belief in the divinity and humanity of Jesus. It is recited at the celebration of the Eucharist during every Mass.

Constantine was the author of the Edict of Milan, which allowed Christians the freedom to worship openly and freely. His actions in support of the Church didn't stop there. He moved the capital of the Roman Empire east to Byzantium (modern-day Istanbul), renaming it Constantinople. This new Rome gave Christianity a fresh new start. Moreover, Constantine summoned the Council of Nicaea, a congregation of 300 bishops who formalized the doctrines of Christian faith. From that point, the Roman state became formally involved in Church affairs.

Eradication of Pagan Practices

The second Roman emperor to exert great influence over Christian affairs was Theodosius the Great, a military leader who lived from 346 to 395. Theodosius was baptized in 380 after he became sick and nearly died.

Theodosius, the last emperor to rule both the eastern and western Roman empires, tolerated pagan practices early in his reign. Toward the end of his life, he became much stricter, slowly eroding pagan power and rights to worship, until he passed an edict that outlawed pagan practices altogether.

As part of this edict, Theodosius banned the Olympic games and forbade the practice of pagan holidays, which he converted into workdays. He also allowed the destruction of the beautiful and impressive Egyptian temple of Serapeum at Alexandria.

Theodosius also streamlined the unity of the Church by suppressing the Arian and Manichean heresies in Constantinople. He is also known for calling the second General Council of Constantinople, in 381, to provide for a Catholic succession in the patriarchal see of Constantinople.

QUESTION?

What is a heresy?
A heresy is a challenge to an accepted belief. Two heresies that arose during the fourth century were Arianism and Manichaeism. Arianism, taught by an Alexandrian priest named Arius, denied Jesus' divinity. According to Arius, Jesus was made by God and is therefore subordinate to God. Manichaeism, a synthesis of different religious systems, taught that one god created good and another evil, and that mortals were not responsible for their sins.

The Rise of the Papacy in Rome

In the fourth century, the power of the bishop in Rome continued to grow. Pope Damasus I (366–383) as well as those who followed him—Siricius, Anastasius I, Innocent I, Zosimus, Boniface I, Celestine I, Sixtus III, and Pope Leo the Great—each made the Church more powerful and established the idea that when they spoke a papal utterance, they were speaking through the mouth of Peter. After Rome fell in 410, during the papacy of Innocent I, the office of the pope moved in to fill the vacuum of leadership.

These popes all wrote about the glory of the Church in Rome, and this is where the formal title, Holy Roman Catholic Church, comes from. "The entire Catholic Church spread over the globe is the sole bridal chamber of Christ," writes the influential fourth-century pope Damasus. (As you remember, *catholic* means "universal" or "all-embracing.") "The Church of Rome has been placed above all other churches not by virtue of conciliar decree, but by virtue of the words of the Lord: 'Thou art Peter!'"

Pope Leo the Great

Pope Leo the Great, who held the papal office from 440 to 461, was a man of enormous personal strength and of great eloquence: He persuaded Attila the Hun to turn from the gates of Rome when the Barbarians planned to sack the city. Leo's most significant achievement was forcefully asserting the primacy of the Roman bishop's position. He coaxed Emperor Valentinian to officially recognize the status of this role. As a result, in 445, Valentinian issued an edict proclaiming the papal supremacy of the Bishop of Rome, for all time.

In 451, Pope Leo participated in and greatly influenced the Council of Chalcedon, where doctrine on Jesus' dual nature was firmly established. (That Jesus the Christ was both fully human and fully divine is a critical Catholic doctrine.) The council also voted that the Bishop of Rome had higher authority than the patriarch of Constantinople. This proclamation festered over five centuries of bickering and led to the eventual schism between the Eastern Orthodox and the Roman Catholic (Western) Church.

Gregory the Great

Over time, the Church became increasingly involved in secular (and especially political) affairs. Rome and the papal office were becoming the center of the world. Three men—Gregory, Boniface (a monk), and Gregory VII—were instrumental in shaping the papal office. Pope Gregory I, who was born in about 540, started his career as a civil servant in Rome trying to feed the poor. He gave up his job and established a monastery, living a quiet life. When the pope died of the plague, the people elected Gregory to the office, at the age of fifty.

He accomplished many things during his tenure, demonstrating what could be accomplished in the world at large and in the spiritual world. He tried to look after the poor. He helped rebuild the aging churches, established education for priests, and wrote extensively on matters of theology. One of his most important contributions was the beautiful liturgical music of the Gregorian chant. He also spread the faith to Britain.

The Birth of the Papal States

One man who contributed to centralization of power in the Western Church's hands was an English Benedictine monk named Boniface. His great mission was to preach to the Germanic states, for which he was made a bishop. He established monasteries and was trusted by the German (then called Frankish) rulers.

The Church has come a long way from the first wandering missionaries. With the establishment of the Papal States, the Church not only found a home, but a country, of its own. The papacy held on to its lands for a long time, until 1870.

In 751, with the approval of the pope, Boniface crowned Pepin the Short as king of the Franks. This relationship between the papacy and the French monarchy let the pope appeal to the Franks for help when a barbarian tribe threatened Rome. Pepin defended Rome and then gave the pope a huge strip of land in Italy as his own territory. The office of pope was now a territorial ruler too: The Papal States were born. This cozy arrangement of popes crowning kings and kings helping popes lasted for quite a while.

The Rise of Monasteries

While the bishops—and the Bishop of Rome, in particular—were getting more involved in worldly affairs, some believers wanted to distance themselves from secular life and wholly devote themselves to God. Thus, the fourth century also saw the rise of monasticism, a movement pioneered by hermits who wished to emulate Jesus' sojourn in the wilderness and lead a quiet, simple life, away from worldly temptations.

The earliest monasteries originated in Egypt. The word *monastery* comes from the Greek word *monos,* meaning "alone" or "single," because the early monks lived alone and gathered only for prayer in a common chapel. From these early groups of loosely collegial hermits sprang full-fledged communities, with well-defined and centralized systems and doctrines.

FACT

The bishop and monk Basil, who established an order in Cappadocia, Asia Minor, was the first to stress the importance of scholarly work (in addition to prayer) in monastic life. Until then, most monks were poorly educated and shunned study.

St. Augustine of Hippo

St. Augustine (354–430), one of the early monks, played an important role in Church theology through his development of a theological tradition.

As a young man, Augustine was not pious. However, he later found his faith with the help of Bishop Ambrose, whom he met in Rome. He then returned to North Africa, where he set up a small monastery.

After Rome fell to the Goths in 410, everyone wondered how God could allow it. Augustine wrote *The City of God,* his most important work. It is still read today—if you ever wonder how people can hold onto their faith during times of great injustice, this is a text to turn to.

Augustine's most renowned work is *The Confessions,* which is an autobiographical account of his life and how he had found his faith. In this deeply philosophical and personal account, St. Augustine shows how God's grace is available to everyone, even "prodigal sons" who started their lives in idleness.

St. Benedict of Umbria

Another very important character in early monastic development was St. Benedict (480–547). Sickened by the crimes and sin around him, St. Benedict introduced the ascetic tradition (a tradition of self-denial that included poverty and chastity) within the monastic setting.

The Benedictine order he founded, on a mountaintop halfway between Naples and Rome, eventually established a style of self-sufficient monasteries, which included vineyards, orchards, a church, a library, and sleeping cells. The Benedictine monastery was the model for others—to become, in essence, a complete economic unit—for hundreds of years.

Spread of Monasticism

By the fifth century, monasteries had been established all over the populated world: through Africa, the dwindling Roman empire, France, Germany, and even Ireland, where St. Patrick worked to convert the Irish to Christianity.

During the Middle Ages, these monasteries became oases of peace and order, providing food, clothing, and shelter. The times were terribly hard on poor people, who were vulnerable to rampant diseases and warring feudal factions. The monasteries kept the flame of Christianity alive during that difficult period of European history.

Both the male and female adherents of the monastic life performed important functions. They ministered to the poor and sick, and they welcomed travelers. They established libraries and some rudimentary education for children. Monasteries also deserve the credit for preserving the literature of antiquity, which had to be transcribed by hand. The monks spent hours laboriously copying and painting the most important sacred works into beautifully illuminated manuscripts.

Chapter 4

During the Middle Ages

The history of the Roman Catholic Church is full of twists and turns, successes and failures. This chapter will take you through the highs and lows of this increasingly powerful—and now institutionalized—religion as it developed during the major events of the Middle Ages: the Great Schism, the Crusades, the Inquisition, and other movements within the Catholic Church.

Rome and Byzantium Part Ways

The separation of the Greek-speaking Eastern church (the church known as Eastern Orthodox) from the Roman Catholic Church began officially with the Great Schism of 1054, but the actual division didn't happen overnight. It came about gradually, as Rome and Constantinople struggled for political power and religious authority.

Controlling the Spread of Christianity

Often tensions occurred because the two factions of the Church competed to get more converts to accept their way of practicing Christianity as a way of establishing political and cultural alliances. Such was the case with the conversion of the Slavic people of Eastern Europe.

By the end of the first millennium, Serbians, Russians, and Bulgarians worshiped according to the Eastern rites, while Croatians, Czechs, Magyars, Moravians, Poles, and Slovaks joined the Roman Church.

Many Slavic languages are written in the Cyrillic alphabet. The alphabet is named for St. Cyril, to whom the invention of this alphabet was incorrectly attributed. The introduction of the Cyrillic alphabet promoted literacy and allowed the Slavs to translate the Bible and other Christian writings into their own languages.

Rising Tensions

As you might remember, Emperor Constantine moved the capital of the Roman Empire from Rome to Constantinople in 450. When Charlemagne, the king of France, was crowned Emperor of the Holy Roman Empire by Pope Leo III in 800, there had been no Western emperor for over 300 years. The Eastern emperor had—in name anyway—been ruler of the West, once the line of Roman emperors collapsed. This appointment signaled that the West was pulling away, and the East was not happy about it.

A Permanent Rupture

Finally, in 1054, the Eastern and Western churches reached a point of no return. Michael Cerularius, who was Constantinople's patriarch, decided to take a stand. He proclaimed that the two churches could not work together any more.

Pope Leo IX did not want to see a schism between the Christians, and he sent Cardinal Humbert to Constantinople to negotiate as the pope's appointed representative. However, there were a lot of religious and political disagreements to deal with, and the two sides could not come to terms. When Pope Leo passed away, Cardinal Humbert decided to take aggressive action and excommunicated Michael. Michael reacted with a condemnation of this excommunication, arguing that the cardinal was not acting with papal authority. Michael then declared that he was taking control of the Eastern church.

The Struggles Between Church and State

After the Great Schism, the power of the Roman Catholic Church continued to grow in the West. As Europe was moving from a feudal system to unite into states and kingdoms that were ruled by monarchy, the popes increased their involvement in the politics of surrounding territories, often exerting a lot of influence through their religious authority.

Pope Gregory VII, also known as Hildebrand, played an important role in centralizing the power of the Church. In 1073, Gregory decided to introduce reforms in how bishops and abbots were to be appointed to their clerical positions. In the past, such appointments were made by high-ranking laypeople. That meant the Church was subject to local rulers—a distinctly compromising position.

To introduce the reform, Gregory declared a ruling against "lay investiture," or clerical appointments by Church outsiders. Understandably, the Holy Roman Emperor Henry IV of Germany, who virtually controlled the Western world, did not agree with this ruling. Unfazed, Gregory excommunicated Henry from the Church.

To be reinstated, Henry humbled himself before the pope, but the tensions between them did not end there. When civil war broke out in Germany, Gregory called for peace in the empire. When Henry refused to cease fighting, Gregory proclaimed Henry to be deposed. Henry responded by setting up an antipope, Clement III, and managed to win the war. He then turned around and attacked Italy—unsuccessfully, at first, in 1081, and again in 1083. Upon the second foray, he also wooed the Romans with his generosity, and they betrayed Gregory. The pope escaped to Salerno and died a year later.

The conflict continued until Henry V and Pope Calixtus II reached an agreement, known as the Concordat of Worms (1112), that all bishops would be consecrated by the Church. The emperor had the right to be present at the ordination and to invest secular powers upon the clergy.

This reform, as well as many others introduced by subsequent popes, was complemented by reform in the lower clergy and in Catholic customs and practices. The Church decreed that priests had to attend a Catholic college before they could be ordained and introduced the practice of priestly celibacy.

Finally, the Church formally established the seven sacraments, as we know them today:

- Baptism
- Confirmation
- The Eucharist
- Penance
- Anointing of the Sick
- Matrimony
- Holy Orders

Cathedrals and Universities

The power and influence of the papacy and the Catholic Church was further enhanced and solidified by the monumental architecture that the wealthy Church championed.

At the same time, the Church led the way in education. The first universities grew from small schools that had been set up in conjunction with Catholic cathedrals into large organizations offering students great learning and scholarship. Universities in Italy, France, England, and Germany attracted good teachers and ambitious students and taught subjects such as medicine, philosophy, mathematics, and logic.

The Crusades

The Crusades are an unfortunate chapter in Catholic history. The Crusades served different political, social, and religious purposes. Of course, war in the name of religion deeply disagrees with Jesus' message of peace, but at the time, people saw the Crusades as acts of faith and religious duty.

QUESTION?

How many Crusades were there?
Much depends upon the historian's definition of what constitutes a Crusade. Although historians disagree on the exact number, most claim there were at least seven, and all agree on four of the major Crusades.

The first Crusade, in the eleventh century, was a reaction to the takeover of Jerusalem by the Turkish Muslims. One important issue was safe travel for pilgrims visiting the Christian holy sites. Afraid that the Muslims would destroy the sites, and believing the Holy Land should be liberated in the name of God, Pope Urban II called for a Crusade. Armies of knights were sent to recover the Holy Land. This became the first in a series of similar campaigns, which were undertaken throughout the eleventh, twelfth, and thirteenth centuries, usually with little result except misery for everyone involved.

When you look at the progression of the four major Crusades, it's not difficult to see that each one was less noble than the one before. The knights in the First Crusade did manage to enter Jerusalem, a victory that resulted in a massacre of Muslims and Jews. However, the Christians could not hold Jerusalem for long, despite the reinforcements that arrived during the Second Crusade. The Third Crusade, led by Richard the Lion-Hearted, recovered some land, but the knights were more interested in booty than a divine cause. During the Fourth Crusade, the knights sailed to Constantinople and ransacked it—in other words, Christians were fighting Christians!

The Rise of Mendicant Orders

As previously noted, monasticism has a long history within the Catholic Church. First individually and then in groups, men and women congregated apart from society so that they could become closer to God. This tradition grew stronger during the Middle Ages, which saw the introduction of new religious orders that still exist today.

Those who joined the mendicant orders kept on the move, preaching and begging for alms in order to survive. The mendicant friars were poor, but they were rich in spirit, because they followed the example of Christ. The two great mendicant orders were the Dominicans and the Franciscans.

What are the mendicant orders?
Mendicant orders are religious orders whose members take the vow of poverty ("mendicant" comes from Latin *mendicare,* which means "to beg"). All members of the mendicant order hold property and goods in common.

The Dominicans

The Dominicans took their name from Dominic de Guzman, born in 1170. Dominic's mission was to convert heretics back to the Christian fold, and he persuaded a number of men to help him in his teaching all over Europe. That's how the Dominican order got started. The Dominicans are also known as Black Friars, because of the black cloaks they wear over their white robes. Eventually, members of the Dominican order settled down into communal houses; one of the great achievements of this order is the fostering of scholarship.

One of the most well known Dominicans is St. Thomas Aquinas (1224–1274), who disobeyed his wealthy family's wishes when he joined the order. Aquinas studied with learned Dominican teachers like Albert the Great and became a great scholar. His greatest achievement was applying the philosophical reasoning of Aristotle to the wisdom of the Bible in his *Summa Theologica,* a work that would be used for any official decrees the Church issued.

The Franciscans

It is very likely that you have heard of St. Francis of Assisi, especially if you have pets! There are many pictures of him surrounded by animals because he was so simple in his lifestyle and so in tune with nature that he could coax the birds from the air and animals to his feet.

Like Thomas Aquinas, Francis turned his back on wealth and comfort, but his personal vow of poverty was more severe than most. Francis cared for the sick and the lame—even the lepers whom no one would go near. Eventually he attracted many followers who also adopted his simple style of living and good works, and he took them across Europe. One of the people he attracted was a woman named Clare, who started a convent called the Poor Clares for nuns who wished to spend their lives in prayer.

The Inquisition

The Papal Inquisition began in 1232, under the auspices of Pope Gregory IX, as a reaction to the heresies that threatened to break up the unity of the Church. The purpose of the Inquisition was to ferret out heretics and force them to accept Catholicism as practiced and taught by the Church.

Public inquiries were set up town by town. People were encouraged to report heretics, and because their identity was kept secret, many came forward with names. Heretics who confessed received a penance (a kind of religious fine), which could be anything from reciting prayers to a flogging. Those who refused to accept the charges against them and "repent" were punished. Some were burned at the stake or hanged.

The Papal Inquisition lasted through most of the thirteenth century. It was conducted mostly in the south of France, northern Italy, and northern Spain. It reappeared in fifteenth-century Spain in its most virulent form. The Spanish Inquisition still horrifies us, even to this day.

The Spanish Inquisition

In Spain, the inquisition was initiated by the monarchy—that is, it was a political as well as a religious institution. King Ferdinand and Queen Isabella (the monarchs who funded Columbus's voyages) needed a cause under which they could unify the Spanish people into a powerful nation. They also needed money.

They chose the unifying force of Catholicism and asked the pope for permission to begin the Inquisition, whose purpose was to "purify" the land. Muslim and Jewish converts to Catholicism, Protestants, nonbelievers, and Christians who did not see eye-to-eye with any aspect of the Catholic dogma all needed purifying. Conveniently, the state appropriated all possessions that belonged to the executed heretics.

The Papacy in Trouble

The 1300s were a ghastly time. The bubonic plague, or Black Death, ravaged Europe and wiped out a third of its population. No one, from royalty to peasants, was safe. The Church was not spared either. New priests were hastily ordained to replace those who perished while taking care of their parishioners.

Meanwhile, England and France began a conflict that would last for more than a century—the Hundred Years' War. Caught up in the struggle, they were not paying much attention to the Church, and the papacy began to lose its power.

The Move to Avignon

The fourteenth century had barely begun when power over Europe began to shift back to the secular world. King Philip IV of France drew the papacy into battle by levying taxes on the clergy for defense of the realm. Pope Boniface VIII fought him valiantly but unsuccessfully. After Boniface's death in 1303, Philip secured the election of a Frenchman, Bertrand de Got, as pope. He was "crowned" in Lyons as Clement V, and shortly thereafter he took up residence in Avignon, in the south of France.

Although this move was meant to avoid political tension among the Italian city-states, Clement left the papacy vulnerable to the French monarchy. After Clement died, the next pope made Avignon a permanent seat for the papacy and surrounded himself with church and government officials to do his bidding. Seven French popes would rule from Avignon before the seat returned to Rome.

St. Catherine of Siena was so concerned with the papal seat returning to Rome that she visited the last Avignon pope, Gregory XI, and pleaded with him to return the papal seat where it belonged. In 1377, he did just that.

The Great Papal Schism

The papacy's troubles did not end with the pope's return to Rome. Upon Gregory's death, under pressure from Roman leaders, the College of Cardinals elected an Italian pope, Urban VI, who proved to be weak and undiplomatic. Unhappy with this choice, the French cardinals returned to Avignon and elected a pope of their own, Clement VII. Some countries gave their allegiance to Urban, while others preferred Clement VII, dividing the papacy and all of Europe. This calamity, which became known as the Great Papal Schism, lasted for thirty years.

It took the efforts of the Holy Roman Emperor Sigismund to end the Church's ignoble behavior. He called the Council of Constance, which settled the Great Schism in 1417 and resulted in the election of a Roman pope, Martin V.

FACT

It was during Martin's pontificate that the extraordinary story of Joan of Arc took place. Now the patron saint of France, her brief life ran from 1412 to 1431. Joan claimed the divine inspiration of angels to unite her country against England. In the end, she was burned at the stake for heresy.

The Church was united again under one pope, but papal power had been damaged. Peasants and the growing middle class were shocked and appalled. The monarchs of various countries grew stronger and more powerful and the papacy could no longer control them. These changes set the stage for the Renaissance, a formidable flowering of the arts, but also the Reformation, the Protestant movement that threatened to destroy the Catholic Church.

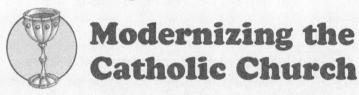

Chapter 5

Modernizing the Catholic Church

Times change, and the Catholic Church has changed as well. Over the last four centuries, the Church has struggled with its own corruption, the rise of Protestantism, and—perhaps most difficult of all—its need to adapt to the democratic and social movements that have swept the Western world.

From Protests to Protestantism

At the dawn of the sixteenth century, the Holy Roman Catholic Church found itself beset with internal problems. Its hierarchy was corrupt and disorganized. Wealthy families staffed the leadership positions of churches, bishoprics, and the Roman curia. These members of the clergy bought and sold clerical positions. Bishops controlled huge territories on behalf of the Church that increased their own revenues, and Church officials bought and sold indulgences. Meanwhile, the local clergy was not properly educated and did not make much effort to take care of their flocks. They seldom preached, instructed the young, or ministered to the other needs of their parishioners. Worse, they set a bad example. Some had drinking problems, and others kept mistresses.

QUESTION?

What is an indulgence?
An indulgence is a partial reduction of the punishment that is still due for sin after confession and absolution. You earn an indulgence by acts of repentance, such as prayer or fasting, so that you may spend less time in Purgatory. In the late Middle Ages, clergy took advantage of people's desire to speed the souls of their deceased relatives to Heaven by selling them indulgences, a practice that reformers strongly denounced.

Religious orders were no better off. War, political strife, and the Black Death had stymied the growth of monasteries. Discipline in monasteries had waned, and members were no longer concerned about social and cultural conditions in the country. Common worship and common meals had given way to the desire for private property.

The Renaissance popes, wealthy patrons of the arts and shrewd statesmen, saw the sorry state of affairs, but they were enjoying the status quo too much. The Lateran Council, which concluded in 1517, called for reforms that included adequate training of clergy; however, the pope at the time, Leo X (1475–1521) failed to support them.

Luther Leads the Way

The need for reform paved the way for Martin Luther (1483–1546), the founder of the Reformation movement that led to the birth of many Protestant faiths. A thoughtful, loyal Catholic and scholar, Luther became an Augustinian monk, studied theology, and eventually became a professor at the University of Wittenberg in Germany.

Introspective and depressive, Luther felt he was not worthy of being saved. But in 1513 he had a spiritual insight: Our faith in God's love is what qualifies us for salvation. Good works are secondary. Man is a sinful vessel, saved only because he is cloaked in God's love.

Luther preached his new vision, but he didn't make an impact until he began his campaign against the selling of indulgences, which—for the right price—promised the rich redemption from Purgatory. One of Luther's arguments was that the pope could not possibly have control over souls in Purgatory.

Luther's Ninety-five Theses, each addressing a different aspect of the selling of indulgences, became the talk of Germany. An innovative theologian and skilled orator, Luther quickly won the hearts and minds of many people who were ready for a change.

Principles of Protestantism

In addition to the concept of salvation in faith alone, Luther's other theological principles have remained central to most Protestant denominations:

- **Scripture alone.** The Bible, especially the New Testament, is the only infallible source and rule of faith; each individual should interpret the Scriptures as he or she sees fit. Nothing written after the New Testament by Christian saints and theologians can claim to have the same authority as the Bible.
- **The universal priesthood of believers.** No person needs to depend on mediation of a clergyman between him or her and God. Neither the papacy nor the hierarchy of the Church has any more divine authority than an ordinary Christian.

- **Preaching of the Word.** A primary responsibility of ministers is to preach the message of the Scriptures so as to best reach their audience. As a consequence of this thesis, Protestants condensed the liturgy to an exegesis of the Scriptures and communion and began to conduct services in their native tongues (rather than in Latin).

Luther's movement spread rapidly through Europe, where Protestant churches began to come under the protection of the secular government. Another reformer, John Calvin, built on Luther's credos and sent missionaries throughout Europe to preach and to organize communities. Switzerland, Scotland, parts of France, and the Netherlands all embraced Calvinism. Calvin's teaching upheld the objectively real presence of Jesus in the Eucharist and stressed this sacrament as a way for believers to relate to God. By the time Calvin, Luther, and other reformers had finished their preaching, half of all Europe was Protestant.

The Counter-Reformation Movement

The Catholic Church managed to survive the Reformation and to renew itself from within. The sixteenth and seventeenth centuries were a time of the birth and rebirth of religious orders, of saints and mystics, of dedicated popes, and sweeping reforms ushered in by the Council of Trent (1545–1563).

Among religious orders, the new Oratory of Divine Love, founded in Genoa, Italy, in 1475, involved regular devotions and works of mercy for personal spiritual renewal. Composed of both laypeople and the clergy, it included members of the Curia. Important Christian humanists and reformers, including Gian Pietro Carafa (later Paul VI), came from the ranks of this order.

The Capuchin order branched out from the Franciscans as a result of the struggle against the Reformation. The Augustinians and Dominicans both undertook reforms, and the Dominican Antonio Ghislieri became Pius V (1566–1572), bringing greater integrity to the papal office.

FACT

The Carmelite order underwent reforms thanks to two saints, St. Teresa of Ávila (1515–1582) and St. John of the Cross (1542–1591). Both saints were known for their mysticism and exceptional writing. St. Teresa wrote the inspirational *Autobiography;* St. John authored the famous *Dark Night of the Soul*.

This time period also saw the founding of the Jesuit order by St. Ignatius of Loyola, a soldier who experienced spiritual enlightenment while recovering from his wounds. Active and practical, the Jesuits worked for propagation and defense of the faith. Members were recruited carefully and received proper training.

Other men and women who distinguished themselves by reforming or founding a religious order during the Counter-Reformation include the following:

- **Philip Neri** (1515–1595), who founded the Oratorian Priests. Neri was a cheerful, zestful man with deep spiritual qualities. He was prominent in Rome during the latter part of the sixteenth century; as confessor of popes and cardinals, he no doubt influenced the transformation of the Curia.
- **Saint Francis de Sales** (1567–1622), founder of the Salesians, managed to persuade the people of the Chablais district to return to the Catholic faith. His writings are held to be classic guides to the spiritual life.
- **St. Jane Frances de Chantal** (1572–1641), a protégé of Francis de Sales, founded the order of the Sisters of the Visitation.
- **St. Vincent de Paul** (1580–1660) founded the Congregation of the Mission, which did much to improve the French clergy. With Louise de Marillac, he established the Sisters of Charity in 1633. The nuns of this order were not cloistered. Instead, they went out to work among the poor and the sick and were instrumental in founding many hospitals.

Papal Reformers and the Council of Trent

Pope Paul III speeded up papal reform by appointing reformers to the College of Cardinals and by finally convening the Council of Trent (1545–1563), which accomplished a great deal.

The Council of Trent reaffirmed the primacy of the pope. It upheld the importance of tradition. It reminded Catholics that salvation requires hope and charity—manifested in good works—as much as it does faith in God's love. Additionally, it rejected Protestant beliefs on the number and nature of the sacraments.

The council strengthened the authority of the bishops and required each bishop to reside in his diocese. It passed regulations on the granting of indulgences and forbade the practices of simony (the buying of sacred things and offices) and pluralism (the holding of more than one diocese). Seminary education and clerical dress became mandatory for the diocesan priests, along with the practice of celibacy. The council encouraged the priests as well as the laity to be active in acquiring virtue and to meditate. The Council of Trent concluded under the reformer Pope Pius IV.

The next pope, Pius V (1504–1572), issued new editions of the Index of Forbidden Books, Catechism, the Breviary (the devotional book of priests), and missal. The new missal transformed the Roman Catholic Mass and made it uniform throughout the Church. With all the Catholic churches around the world adopting the same way of conducting the Mass, the faithful could go anywhere in the world and still find the same services familiar from home.

Catholic Missionaries in the New World

The age of maritime voyages and discoveries of new lands ushered in a new missionary era. While the Church's battle with Protestantism raged in Europe, the Catholic fold was increasing in the New World. In 1493, Pope Alexander VI divided the lands discovered by Columbus between two Catholic countries, portioning half to Portugal and half to Spain. In return, Spain and Portugal had the exclusive right and responsibility to convert inhabitants of the New World to Catholicism.

That such a mission was linked to political conquest was unfortunate; however, it was the greatest and most rapid expansion of Christianity the Church had seen. Catholicism would spread to Central and South America, North America, and parts of Asia and Africa.

FACT

Previously, most missionary work had been done in Europe. Medieval missions to Muslim territories were largely unsuccessful, except in the states held by the Crusaders. Attempts to establish missions in the Far East were short-lived, although in 1542 the Jesuit Francis Xavier would land in Goa (in modern-day India) and preach successfully to thousands.

Mission Control

The monarchs of Portugal and Spain used their missionary mandate to further their own political aims while cleverly freeing up their own armies and civilians. While the secular explorers searched the New World for its mythical treasures and conquered its territories, the Catholic clergy went to teach the natives the Christian faith at Catholic missions.

Priests from a variety of orders brought the faith to the vast regions and many peoples of the New World, including the following:

- Spanish Mercedarians, Dominicans, Franciscans, and Jesuits, followed by Augustinians and Salesians, successfully converted the natives of Peru, Colombia, Ecuador, Venezuela, Bolivia, and Chile.
- Portuguese Jesuits, Franciscans, and Carmelites brought the faith to the huge territory that would become Brazil.
- Spanish Franciscans and Jesuits converted hundreds of thousands of natives in Mexico and Central America.
- The efforts of Spanish Dominicans, Franciscans, and Jesuits brought Christianity to the so-called borderlands of Florida, New Mexico, California, Texas, and Arizona. Fray Junipero Serra is perhaps the most famous Franciscan to work in this huge territory.
- French Jesuits, Recollets (French Franciscans), Sulpicians, Capuchins, and Carmelites, as well as diocesan priests, risked their lives to spread Catholicism throughout New France, an area that included Nova Scotia, Acadia, New Brunswick, Quebec, Maine, New York, Illinois, and Louisiana.
- The English missionary effort spread out from the state of Maryland, first settled by George Calvert, an English Catholic who sought freedom of religion in the New World.

While some natives accepted conversion peacefully, others did not. In both the eastern and western territories of the United States, many priests endured great hardship. They suffered and died believing it was their duty to bring the Word of God to the people of the New World. Missionaries who were martyred for their faith include the martyrs Isaac Jogues, S.J. (1607–1646), and Jean de Brebéuf (1593–1649).

Rejection of New Ideas: Vatican I

From the mid-seventeenth to the mid-nineteenth centuries, the Church in Europe struggled to cope with new ideas, new ideals, and a changing political order. Freedom of thought, rationalism, and liberalism all challenged the way the Church had always operated.

The Church has never been known for hastily changing its beliefs and practices to keep up with political and cultural trends. It therefore isn't surprising that conservative Catholic clergy denounced new ideas and new approaches to interpreting the world. When books such as *The Evolution of Species* by Charles Darwin challenged long-held views of Creation, the Church hierarchy refused to modify its stand on the literal truth of the creation story in the Old Testament.

The French Revolution, the demise of monarchies, and the rise of democratically elected governments throughout Europe undermined some of the protection that both Catholic and Protestant churches had enjoyed.

In France, the Revolution shattered the Church; the French government demanded that priests take an oath of loyalty to the state. Clerics throughout Europe became salaried state functionaries. The Church had lost its protected status and its independence.

Liberalism and freethinking, which were replacing blind obedience to authority, challenged the individual's adherence to the Church. Society was becoming more liberal, less dogmatic, more freethinking, and more secular.

As a result, the Catholic Church came to be associated with the old world order, and some governments even adopted an anti-Catholic stand.

Many individuals lost their belief in God, leading lives that lacked faith and spirituality. By the middle of the nineteenth century, Catholics in Europe were a fractured and insecure group.

Pope Pius IX Rallies the Church

Something had to be done, and Pius IX took control of the task at hand. Pius IX was a strong pope, and he succeeded in bringing significant changes to the Church throughout his long tenure (the longest of any pope in history) from 1846 to 1878.

Pius was not an intellectual, and he alienated those who wanted the Church to open to new scholarly methods and to recognize the new democratic and social movements, including freedom of religious practice. However, he was a pious, personable, charitable, and—above all—charmingly persuasive man committed to the solidarity of the Church.

FACT

In 1864, Pius IX published a paper, *Syllabus of Errors,* in which he criticized liberal trends point by point. This paper was an embarrassment to many enlightened thinkers in the Church.

Pius IX worked hard to help bishops deal with their governments, to relocate many religious orders to Rome, and to hold on to the land of the Papal States, despite the efforts of the newly formed Italian republic to take it away. He had the courage to stand up to political leaders and to his opponents, and many in the Church rallied around his strength.

Vatican I

In 1867, Pius IX called together a general council, known as Vatican I, to reaffirm the doctrine of papal infallibility. Despite the protests of liberal prelates who believed the Church should focus on modernization, the conservative views of the pope and his supporters prevailed, and papal infallibility passed the vote.

By the time of Pius's death, the Church was virtually at war with society. However, Pius IX had strengthened the Church internally. The community had regained its piety, and its religious order once again thrived. The importance of the sacraments, the reaffirmation of Christ as both God and man, and a true sense of the supernatural would continue to enlighten the interior life of most Catholics.

Entering the Modern Age

The reactionary attitudes established by Vatican I could not help the Church deal with the social and political upheavals of the late nineteenth and twentieth centuries. In response, the Church had to form new policies and groups to deal with the issues of the day.

The Industrial Revolution

The Industrial Revolution of the nineteenth century, said to be one of the movements that catapulted Western civilization into the modern age, created many problems. One was the oppression of the working class, the people whose hard work had made the Industrial Revolution possible.

As the need for industrial labor increased, entire families left farms and small towns to work in mills and factories. Living conditions in large cities became horrendous as large populations were cooped up in slums, and the working conditions were no better. Workers had no rights and no protection. Child labor was common.

The Church worked to alleviate the suffering of the workers by providing social services, bringing religion to their lives, and by publicly supporting the workers' rights. In 1891, Pope Leo XIII issued *Rerum Novarum,* an important encyclical on workers' rights that upheld the right of the individual to private property and defined the family as the primary social unit. It stated that workers had a right to a living wage and the right to organize in order to improve their lot. The *Rerum Novarum* made it clear that the Church was in favor of trade unions.

The World Wars

In the twentieth century, the popes tried to steer a neutral course through the political maelstroms of fascism, communism, and the Great

Wars. Benedict XV was totally opposed to World War I and found it completely unjustifiable. However, he maintained neutrality and did not publicly come out against the war for fear that Catholics would be hurt by emulating his stance. As a result of his neutrality, all sides were angry with him at the end of the war.

Pius XI saw the rise of Hitler and Mussolini and their dictatorships, which posed a threat to the Catholic Church. In the encyclicals he issued, Pius XI denounced the Nazi regime as well as racism and anti-Semitism, but he passed away in February of 1939, before the events of World War II really began to unfold.

Pius XII, his successor, maintained neutrality during World War II. Although he is criticized today for not speaking out strongly enough against the atrocities committed by the Nazis and other fascist regimes, he did work on relief efforts for the Jews. The Vatican also carried on a massive and expensive war relief effort and launched a huge program to find missing persons.

The New Era: Vatican II

The most drastic changes that the Church had recently experienced and that finally modernized it took place thanks to Pope John XXIII, who was elected in 1958. John ushered in a new era of tolerance, openness, and dialogue in the Church by convening a general council that ran for four sessions, from 1962 to 1965. This council is known as Vatican II.

By the time Vatican II concluded, 2,500 Church leaders had engaged in vigorous debate during the four 3-month sessions. As a result, the council issued sixteen documents that would introduce sweeping changes; their repercussions are felt to this day. At last, the Church was moving into the modern world.

John XXIII set the tone of the council by expressing optimism and belief that all members of the Church, particularly the bishops, could open up dialogue within the Church, with other Christian faiths, and with nonreligious groups everywhere. The goal of all this dialogue was to find areas of common ground and to tackle common problems.

John XXIII asked the bishops from all over the world to set the agenda for the council and to have a share of influence as great as or greater than the Curia in determining issues and exploring directions. At this council, for once, the liberals prevailed. Even though Pope John XXIII died before the council was finished, his successor, Paul VI, carried on in the same spirit.

Here are some of the primary changes that the Vatican II Council made possible:

- Liturgy is now conducted in the vernacular language of each church's parishioners and not in Latin, so that the service is accessible to all laypersons who are given the opportunity to fully participate.
- For centuries, the writings of the Church focused on who had what power over whom. The Church emphasized the importance of hierarchy: pope over bishops, bishops over clergy, clergy over the laity. Since Vatican II, the power lies in the common priesthood of the faithful, and the clergy's role is defined as service to the community of the Church.
- The Church also changed its outlook toward other Christian denominations. It is no longer the Church's goal to try to convert Protestants back to Catholicism. Instead, the Church recognized the status of all Protestant communities, apologized for contributing to Christian disunity and the mistakes made during the Counter-Reformation, and urged all Christian communities to work together to solve social problems.
- Writings that were once accepted as divine revelation to an individual and that were rigidly adhered to received new interpretations. The Church accepted that written works are always influenced by historical context and may not have as much relevance for succeeding generations.
- Rather than expressing skepticism, or even condemnation, of new forms of government or new social movements, the Church is now more open to accepting and embracing them. Its new position is one of service to humanity, and it has become committed to working with all groups for human rights and dignity.

The Church Today

Since Vatican II, the Church has experienced a tidal wave of change. The new liturgy, the questioning of the Church's authority, the changes in the role of priests and other clergy, and the rising sense of importance of the individual conscience have all rocked the ecclesiastical boat.

Controversies around priestly celibacy, birth control, divorce, and the ordination of women have fired up ecclesiastical discussions. One thing is for certain: Dialogue is alive and well in the Church today.

Quite frankly, changes to the Mass shocked many Catholics. They hated the new liturgy, and they thought fondly back to the old days when the priest intoned Latin phrases with his back to the congregation. Some people felt uncomfortable having the priest so close or having to turn and shake hands with the congregants around them. Some people fled the Church altogether, while others went even further. They found a sympathetic group and did their own thing, chose their own readings, and shared some bread and wine.

A Shift in Authority

Vatican II also touched off a major revolution within the Church. In the old days, the word passed down from the top of the hierarchy was law. Now, the Catholic clergymen were questioning that authority. Forces within the Church wanted decisions to be more democratic. However, there has not been enough support for these kinds of changes.

FACT

For example, Cardinal Suenens of Belgium felt the pope should make his decisions in union with bishops, not on his own. Suenens suggested that bishops should elect the pope. He believed that the laity should elect bishops.

Along with questioning authority, more Catholics have come to realize the importance of individual conscience and of the moral responsibility people have in making decisions that affect their actions. Many arguments have centered on issues of divorce, remarriage, and birth control. Is it fair that Catholics cannot remarry after a divorce as long as their first spouse is still alive? Is it wrong to practice birth control when a couple has had as many children as they feel they can handle? The Church as a whole now has more sympathy for people in these positions.

A Decline in the Ranks of the Clergy

One of the problems that the Church faces as a result of the changes is the decline in vocations of priests, nuns, and brothers that began in the late 1960s and early 1970s. The reason for the decline is not obvious—it's not the vow of celibacy. In fact, there is evidence that the problem lies in the shifting relationship between the clergy and the laity.

After Vatican II, the Church proclaimed the priesthood of all the laity. While this new attitude was beneficial to lay Catholics, who now felt they were more involved with the Church, the clergy lost some of their special status as mediators between the laity and God. The increased participation of all the faithful in the sacraments began to impinge on the clergy's ministerial roles.

However, the shift in roles has also been beneficial. The Church began to realize that priests are not superhuman. They need vacations, pension plans, friends they can rely on, and personal interests that invigorate them and allow them, like other human beings, to do a better job. The recognition of priests' humanity and need for support, as well as a strong attempt to help men discern whether they are suited for the priestly role, have helped reduce the isolation experienced by many priests. It has also promoted a healthier, more realistic view of clergy among the laity.

Ecumenical Dialogue with Other Religions

Another change brought about through the efforts of the Vatican II council is the movement toward ecumenical dialogue and greater understanding among Catholics and people who practice other religions, Christian and non-Christian alike.

The Vatican II goal to move the Church toward dialogue with other faiths demonstrated their recognition that Catholics live alongside people of other faiths and that there must be understanding among them. The Church continues to assert that it is the one true religion, but it also acknowledges that God may make his grace known to other peoples of the world who have not yet embraced the truths of Catholicism.

FACT

"The Catholic Church rejects nothing which is true and holy in these religions. She looks with sincere respect upon those ways of conduct and of life, those rules and teachings which, though differing in many particulars from what she holds and sets forth, nevertheless often reflect a ray of that Truth which enlightens all people" (from the *Declaration on the Relationship of the Church to Non-Christian Religions,* Vatican II).

The U.S. branch of the Church established a Commission for Ecumenical Affairs, which met for the first time in March 1965. It appointed personnel to begin making contact with Lutheran, Anglican, Presbyterian, and other Protestant denominations. The commission joined the Division of Christian Unity of the National Council of the Churches of Christ in the United States and the Commission on Faith and Order of the National Council. It began dialogue with various branches of the Eastern, or Orthodox, churches. Eventually, this ecumenical dialogue would grow to encompass relations with Jewish, Muslim, Buddhist, and other non-Christian communities.

The commission was renamed the Bishops' Committee for Ecumenical and Interreligious Affairs in 1966. The committee now has nineteen bishops serving as members and consultants and more than ninety Catholic theologians and other experts participate in the ongoing dialogues and consultations. Worldwide, the Church participates in the World Council of Churches through the Pontifical Council for Promoting Christian Unity for the Catholic Church.

With other Christian religions, the Church already shares many of the same values and sacraments. Vatican II decries the divided church and urges prayer for unity. It is keen to work with other Christians on issues of social justice and morality, and on spreading the gospel message. It has held in-depth discussions on scripture, salvation, sanctification, and the Eucharist with several different faiths.

FACT

At the 1991 World Council of Churches conference, Protestants and Catholics agreed on twelve elements that were common to all their faiths in the celebration of the Eucharist. These included a confession of faith, an invocation of the Holy Spirit, the Lord's Prayer, and consecration of the faithful to God.

Some of these discussions, such as the dialogue with the Anglican Church, resulted in much common ground. With some other faiths, such as the Southern Baptists, there are larger areas of disagreement, but dialogue has resulted in an understanding of one another's position. A 1991 dialogue from the World Council of Churches resulted in a document outlining areas of agreement on the Eucharist. The goal is to eventually reach an understanding on how to share in a common communion, including experiencing the Eucharist together. Ⓔ

Chapter 6

One God, Three Persons

A central belief of the Catholic Church, and one that distinguishes it from other Christian faiths, is the concept of the Holy Trinity—the triune nature of God as Father, Son, and Holy Ghost. This chapter will examine the nature of God in his three persons as understood and taught by the Catholic Church.

The Holy Trinity

The Catholic Church regards the mystery of the Holy Trinity, that of three persons in one God, as one of the central mysteries of the faith. It is the mystery about the nature of God himself and the source of all other mysteries of faith, because God is the source of all Creation.

QUESTION?

What is a mystery?
The Catechism of the Catholic Church describes a mystery as something that is "hidden in God, which can never be known unless . . . revealed by God." It is something that is difficult to comprehend: "that is inaccessible to reason alone," according to the Catechism, yet it is a central article of the Catholic faith.

Many religions have an image of God the Father, and the Catholic Church is no exception. It teaches that God is the origin and Creator of all, and he provides protection and loving care for all his children. According to the Scriptures, Creation is the work of the Holy Trinity.

Not only is God the Father in the sense that he is the father of Creation, he is the Father in relation to his only Son, Jesus. The first ecumenical council at Nicaea decreed that the Son is "consubstantial" with the Father; that is, he is one God with him. Jesus is the "only-begotten" Son of God, "true God from true God, begotten not made" (Nicene Creed).

The Gospel of John is rich with images of the Spirit as Paraclete. The term is derived from the Greek *parakletos,* which means "one called alongside," a term of law used to refer to a defense counselor or advocate.

Jesus is considered to be the first Paraclete (advocate), pleading with God on behalf of mankind. Before he returned to Heaven to join the Father, he told his followers that a second Paraclete, the Spirit, would be sent down to dwell with the apostles in order to guide them and would remain with mankind until Judgment Day. Existing since creation, the Spirit is the third person of God.

The Church recognizes God the Father as the source of all divinity. Therefore the Holy Spirit, the third person of the Trinity, is one with and equal to God the Father and the Son; they are all of the same substance and have the same nature. In 1438, the Council of Florence explained, "The Holy Spirit is eternally from Father and Son; he has his nature and subsistence at once from the Father and the Son. He proceeds eternally from both as from one principle and through one spiration."

The Dogma of the Trinity

From the earliest days of the Church, the apostles referred to the Holy Trinity of God. Over time, this belief came to be enshrined in the central worship of the Church, the Eucharistic liturgy. At every Mass, the priest gives this blessing: "The grace of the Lord Jesus Christ, the love of God, and the fellowship of the Holy Spirit be with you all." The Church fathers aided the early Church councils to clarify the theology of the Holy Trinity; eventually, a dogma of the Holy Trinity was declared.

The dogma of the Holy Trinity consists of three parts:

1. The Trinity is One. The Church does not believe in three gods, but in one God in three persons. These persons do not share one divinity—each of them is God, completely and utterly.
2. The divine persons are really distinct from one another. Father, Son, and Holy Spirit are not simply names for different aspects of God. Rather, they are distinct persons with distinct origins and special roles. God the Father is Creator or Source; God the Son is Redeemer; God the Holy Spirit is Advocate and Teacher.
3. The divine persons are relative to one another and are distinguished by the ways in which they relate to one another. According to Lateran Council IV (1215), it is the Father who generates, the Son who is begotten, and the Holy Spirit who proceeds. "The Father is related to the Son, the Son to the Father, and the Holy Spirit to both" (Council of Florence, c.1438).

The One God of the Scriptures

The knowledge of God's oneness was imparted through divine revelations to men, as recounted in the Old Testament. God told Israel, his chosen nation: "Hear, O Israel! The LORD is our God, the LORD alone! Therefore, you shall love the LORD, your God, with all your heart, and with all your soul, and with all your strength" (Deuteronomy 6:4–5).

FACT

In the Old Testament, God speaks through the prophets, calling all nations: "Turn to me and be safe, all you ends of the earth, for I am God; there is no other. . . . To me every knee shall bend; by me every tongue shall swear, Saying, 'Only in the LORD are just deeds and power'" (Isaiah 45:22–24).

God revealed himself to the people of Israel progressively, over time, but one of the most important revelations for the Old and New Covenants was when he told his divine name to Moses as he appeared to him in the burning bush: "I am who I am. . . . This is my name forever" (Exodus 3:14–15). The divine name is mysterious, and the Church believes it expresses God as infinitely beyond anything man can comprehend.

The qualities of God as revealed in the Old Testament are mercy and graciousness: "I will not give vent to my blazing anger. . . . For I am God and not man, the Holy One present among you" (Hosea 11:9). When the Israelites Moses led out of Egypt fell to worshiping the gold Calf, God heard Moses' prayer and agreed to walk amid the unfaithful to demonstrate his love. "The LORD, the LORD, a merciful and gracious God, slow to anger and rich in kindness and fidelity" (Exodus 34:6).

The Church believes that God is unique and that he made Heaven and earth. He transcends the world and history, and he is enduring and unchanging. He remains ever faithful. Following the Hebrew Scriptures and tradition, the Church believes that "God is the fullness of Being and of every perfection, without origin and without end. All creatures receive all that they are and have from him. But he alone is his very being, and he is of himself everything that he is" (Catechism of the Catholic Church, 1, II, 213).

The God of Truth and Love

The God of the Scriptures is also known for his truth and his love. As the Psalms proclaim, "Your every word is enduring; all your just edicts are forever" (Psalms 119:160). The Church teaches that God is truth itself and that he can never deceive, so believers can fully trust in his word on all matters. God's truth is synonymous with his wisdom, which he can impart to man through revelation. God, who created Heaven and earth, knows about everything he created. Anything he reveals is true instruction, and he sent his Son into the world "to testify to the truth" (John 18:37).

The Church teaches that God's sole reason for establishing a covenant with the people of Israel was his pure, unsolicited love. Because of this love, God never stopped saving and forgiving the Israelites. The Scriptures characterize God's love for his people as boundless. It is compared to a father's love for his son; it is stronger than a mother's love for her children or a bridegroom's love for his beloved. God's love triumphed over the worst infidelities. His love for us is why God gave us his most precious gift: "God so loved the world that he gave his only Son" (John 3:16).

The Church teaches that not only does God love us, God consists of love. God is an external exchange of love between Father, Son, and Holy Spirit, and man is destined to share in that exchange.

God's love is also everlasting. "With age-old love I have loved you," God tells his people through Jeremiah (31:3). The New Testament goes even further when it affirms that God's very being is love. According to the Gospel of John, "God is love" (1 John 4:8, 16).

Man and His Creator

The Church teaches that God created an ordered universe, and since it came out of his goodness, that it was good. Therefore, man is entrusted to respect and defend the goodness of Creation, including the physical world in which he lives.

Having created his work, God is present to all his creatures. "In him we live, and move and have our being," wrote Saint Augustine. God is with us to uphold and sustain us, enabling us to act and helping us to achieve salvation. Catholics believe that recognizing our total dependence on our Creator is a source of wisdom, joy, and confidence.

Creation is not perfect. The Church speaks of it as being a journey. God guides his creatures on his journey by means of divine providence, his way of governing creation. Scripture teaches that this providence is concrete and immediate, and that God cares for all, from the greatest to the smallest, here and now. Jesus taught his followers not to worry: "So do not worry and say, 'What are we to eat?' or 'What are we to drink?' or 'What are we to wear?' . . . Your heavenly Father knows that you need them all. But seek first the kingdom [of God] and his righteousness, and all these things will be given you besides" (Matthew 6:31–33).

A Gift of Free Will

God also granted us the free will to act on our own, to make our own decisions, to interact with each other, and to advance his plan. He entrusted us with having dominion over the earth. In return, our job is to complete the work of creation and to perfect it for the good of all.

Physical evil, suffering, disease, and natural calamities exist because the world is still in flux and is not yet perfect. Moral evil, which is considered to be far worse than physical evil, also exists since men and angels, both intelligent creatures with free will, have the power to make choices and, hence, to go astray. However, the Church teaches that God, through his providence, can bring good from evil, even a moral evil caused by his creatures. From the murder of Christ, caused by the sins of all men, God brought about his glorification and the redemption of man.

The Catholic faith accepts that God's power is mysterious, and we don't always understand his ways. God allows evil and suffering in the world, and he allowed his own Son to suffer and be crucified. But through the Resurrection, God showed that he could conquer suffering and evil. Paradoxically, it requires humility and faith to begin to feel or to draw close to God's power. The Virgin Mary modeled this faith with her words, "Nothing will be impossible with God."

God the Father

In the Old Testament, God is called the Father because he created the world. In the imagery of the Book of Exodus, God the Father made a covenant and gave his Laws to Israel, his firstborn son (Exodus 4:22).

For the Catholic Church, God is Father because he is the origin of everything and the supreme authority; also, he displays loving care for all his children. Additionally, God is a Father in relation to his Son, Jesus Christ.

In the Catholic creed, God is referred to as "the Almighty." This adjective refers to his omnipotence, or universal power and might—God created everything, he rules everything, and he can do everything. His power is loving and mysterious. God reveals his loving power in the way he takes care of his children, and by his mercy, for he displays his power not by vengeance but by forgiveness.

God the Son

Catholics believe that Jesus of Nazareth, the carpenter who was born in Bethlehem during the time of King Herod the Great and who was crucified under the procurator Pontius Pilate, is also the second person of the Trinity. The Gospel of Matthew relates that St. Peter once told Jesus, "You are the Messiah, the Son of the living God" (Matthew 16:16). Catholics believe that Jesus was the Son of the Father; he suffered and died for mankind, arose, and lives with men forever. That message is at the heart of all the Church's teachings.

ALERT!

In the context of the Old Testament, the chosen people (and also the angels) are "sons of God." However, Jesus *is* the true Son of God, not only metaphorically. In the Gospels, God calls Jesus his "beloved Son," and Jesus refers to himself as the "only Son of God."

The Significance of the Name

Jesus comes from the Hebrew for "God saves." The Church teaches that God was not content only to save the Hebrews from literal slavery or domination by another nation. He also wanted to save them from their sins. His Son's death atoned for the sins of mankind. The Catholic Church teaches that men must be aware of their need for salvation and must call on their Redeemer. The name of Jesus is at the heart of all Catholic prayer.

The title *Christ* is the Greek equivalent of the Hebrew *Messiah*, the "anointed one." In Israel, those consecrated to God—including kings, priests, and prophets—were anointed with oil. Jesus was all three: the King of Kings, a priest, and a prophet of the New Kingdom. Many Jews hoped that Jesus was the long-promised Messiah who would free them from literal, or political, bondage, but Christ's kingdom was not a temporal one. As Jesus said to Peter, "The Son of Man did not come to be served but to serve and to give his life as a ransom for many" (Matthew 20:28).

Jesus was also known by the title *Lord*, in recognition of his divine power. The Church teaches that Jesus became a man to save men by reconciling them with God, so that men might know God's love, and also to be a model of holiness. Through imitating Christ and getting close to him, men could also partake in the divine nature. God's taking of a human form is known as the Incarnation.

Both Human and Divine

Taking human form did not mean that Jesus was not true God as well, nor is it true that by being God he was any less human, as various heresies taught. The fact that the Son of God was both God and man is one of the central mysteries of the Catholic faith.

The Church explains that through the Incarnation, "human nature was assumed, not absorbed" (*Gaudium et spes,* 22:2). Christ had a human body, soul, intellect, and will, which belonged to the divine person, the Son of God, who assumed them. With a truly human soul and knowledge, Christ would have to learn from inquiry and experience like other men. The Church teaches that he loved all mankind with his human heart, which has led to veneration of the Sacred Heart of Jesus.

As divinity, Christ knew and manifested everything that pertained to God. For example, Jesus could know what was in someone's heart (Mark 2:8; John 2:25).

The Mysteries of Jesus' Life

As Jesus was a being both human and divine, the Church accepts and believes mysteries of Christ's life that cannot be fully explained. The mysteries of the Incarnation, which have to do with Jesus' early life, include conception by the power of the Holy Spirit, and birth to a virgin, Mary, who is venerated as the Holy Mother of God. The so-called Paschal mysteries, which have to do with the end of Jesus' life, include the passion, Crucifixion, death, burial, descent into hell, Resurrection, and Ascension. These two sets of mysteries, revolving around Christmas and Easter, illuminate the purpose of Jesus' earthly life: the revelation of the Father and the redemption of mankind.

The Church teaches us that Jesus' whole life, and not just his death, was dedicated to man's redemption. By becoming poor, he enriched mankind; as an obedient son, he made up for man's disobedience. His words purified the ears of his listeners; his cures and driving out of unclean spirits was his way of taking on men's weaknesses; and his Resurrection justified man's existence. He existed only for man's salvation and to be a model for him.

The prophets had foretold the arrival of the Messiah and the manner of his life and death. The most immediate prophet was John the Baptist, who advised people to make way for the coming of Christ.

Jesus' birth, life, and death are so important that God spent centuries preparing for them. God prefigured his Son's coming through all the symbols, rituals, and sacrifices of his first covenant with the Jews (for instance, the sacrificial lamb) and symbolic stories such as Jonah being swallowed up by a whale for three days (as Jesus lay in the tomb for three days).

The mysteries of Jesus' early life contain important lessons for the Church:

1. Jesus' birth in a lowly stable. One of the conditions for the faithful to enter the Kingdom of God is to humble themselves as children of God.

2. Jesus' circumcision, eight days after his birth. Jesus was circumcised under the covenant of Abraham and was therefore subject to the Law that God had given to the Hebrews. The circumcision prefigured Baptism, a sacrament that reminds Catholics they are subject to the Law of God and the teachings of Christ.

3. The feast of the Epiphany (the arrival of three wise men bearing gifts to the baby Jesus). The wise men represented neighboring pagan nations who would take up the good news of the Messiah, as was predicted in the Old Testament.

4. The presentation of the infant Jesus in the Temple, where Simeon and Anna recognize that he is the Savior. Simeon and Anna prefigure all the others who will hear Jesus' words and recognize him as God.

5. The flight of the holy family into Egypt and the massacre of the innocents by Herod. This tragedy characterizes the opposition of darkness to light and the kind of persecution Jesus faced all his life and that his followers would share with him.

6. Mary finding Jesus in the Temple at the age of twelve, discussing Scriptures with the wise men. This event foretold his mission—that he must be about his father's business (Luke 2:49).

FACT

The Church does not hold any specific individuals, groups, or races responsible for the death of Christ. The Church teaches that all sinners are responsible for Christ's death: "We must regard as guilty all those who continue to relapse into their sins. Since our sins made the Lord Christ suffer the torment of the cross, those who plunge themselves into disorders and crimes crucify the Son of God anew in their hearts" (Roman Catechism I, 5, 11).

Why Jesus Had to Die

Central to the Catholic faith is the paschal mystery of Christ's death and resurrection. Jesus had to suffer and die so that mankind could be saved.

The earthly cause of Jesus' death is attributed to the enmity of some religious Jews (who thought that Jesus was acting against the Law and the Temple) and the Roman rulers in Palestine (who feared insubordination and rebellion among the Jews and wished to make the death of the so-called King of the Jews an example).

Pharisees accused Jesus of demonic possession, blasphemy, and false prophecy—although Jesus made it clear that he came not "to abolish the law or the prophets . . . but to fulfill. . . . Whoever breaks one of the least of these commandments and teaches others to do so will be called least in the kingdom of heaven" (Matthew 5:16–18). Jesus also showed respect for the Temple, the dwelling of his Father, a holy place. He was angered that it had become a bargain warehouse, and he drove out the money-changers. "My house shall be a house of prayer, but you are making it a den of thieves" (Matthew, 21:13).

But there was another reason that events unfolded the way they did. The Church teaches that Jesus' death was part of God's plan, long foretold by the Scriptures, especially by the prophet Isaiah, who referred to him as the suffering Servant (Isaiah 53:7–8). Jesus took on man's sin and the suffering attached to it. As the sacrificial Paschal Lamb, he offered his life to the Father for our sins, out of pure love for us. His death was the sacrifice of the New Covenant, which helped restore man to communion with God.

The Resurrection

Three days after his death, Jesus was resurrected and appeared among his followers. The Resurrection is highly significant for the Church. It fulfilled the promises of the Old Testament and those made by Jesus during his life, and it confirmed his divinity. Jesus had said, "When you lift up the Son of Man, then you will realize that I AM" (John 8:28).

Men are Christ's brothers through grace, because through this grace they can share in his life. The Resurrection will allow our own resurrection as well. Men who live in Christ and hold him in their hearts live in hope of their own future glory.

The Resurrection is important for another reason. By suffering and dying, Christ redeemed man from sin. By rising, he opened the way to new life for mankind. This new life justified man. It gave him victory over death, which is caused by sin, and allowed him to be filled with grace.

Following his Resurrection, Jesus spent forty days and forty nights with his apostles, living with the appearance of an ordinary man. Then, he ascended into Heaven in a glorious fashion, rising up body and soul.

The Ascension

The Ascension also has great significance for Catholics. It reaffirms that Jesus came from the Father and has returned to him. Through Christ, mankind now has access to the Father's house, by growing close to Christ and following him. The Church teaches that Jesus is in the presence of God on our behalf, exercising his priesthood in order to intercede for those who follow him. He is the high priest of the liturgy that honors the Father in Heaven.

The Church holds that, as Jesus sits at the right hand of God, and as one with God, he shows forth his power and might. He exercises his dominion over the Kingdom of God, a "kingdom that will have no end," "the kingdom of Christ is already present in mystery," "on earth, the seed and the beginning of the kingdom" (Nicene Creed). However, the final fulfillment will come when Jesus returns to earth, which is why Catholics pray for the Second Coming of Christ. And meanwhile, mankind must endure the trials of physical and moral evil with the guidance of the Spirit.

The Holy Spirit

The Holy Spirit is the last person of the Holy Trinity to be revealed (this revelation is made through the story of Christ in the New Testament). The Church teaches that people can only draw close to Christ if they have been touched by the Holy Spirit, who gives his grace through the sacrament of Baptism.

The Spirit works invisibly. He inspired the prophets, and now he inspires other aspects of the faith, such as the sacraments, which put the faithful into communion with Christ; prayer, where he intercedes for the faithful; ministries and missions; and the saints, through whom he shows his holiness.

The Holy Spirit has a joint mission with Christ. The world has seen Christ, but it is the Spirit who revealed him. Christ was anointed, but it was the coming upon him of the Spirit that was his anointing. Christ and the Spirit are inseparable. When Christ ascended to Heaven, he sent the Holy Spirit to dwell among mankind to unite all to Christ as adopted children. At Pentecost, the Spirit descended on the apostles, and he has remained with the Church ever since. The Church completes the mission of Christ and the Holy Spirit because in a mysterious way the Church is the Body of Christ as well as the Temple of the Holy Spirit.

The Spirit is at work in several ways:

1. It prepares men through grace to draw them to Christ.
2. It manifests the Risen Lord to men by spreading his word and helping them to understand the mysteries of the faith.
3. It makes Christ present, especially in the Eucharist.
4. It brings men into closeness with God.

Thus the Holy Spirit helps the Church carry on the mission of Jesus and the Holy Spirit: to draw all to Christ.

ALERT!

The Church teaches that the Holy Spirit is the channel through which God's love pours into our hearts. Those who receive that love will bear "the fruit of the Spirit . . . love, joy, peace, patience, kindness, faithfulness, gentleness, self-control" (Galatians 5:22–23).

Holy Spirit in the Scriptures

In the Old Testament, there were two streams of prophecy: one for the Messiah and one for the Holy Spirit. The Spirit spoke of himself through the prophets: "But a shoot shall sprout from the stump of Jesse, and from his roots a bud shall blossom. The spirit of the LORD shall rest upon him: a spirit of wisdom and of understanding, A spirit of counsel and of strength, a spirit of knowledge and of fear of the LORD" (Isaiah 11:1–2).

The last prophet through whom the Holy Spirit spoke was John the Baptist. John said of Christ, "On whomever you see the Spirit come down and remain, he is the one who will baptize with the holy Spirit" (John 1:33–36). After baptism, Christ entered into his joint mission with the Holy Spirit. He alluded to the Spirit as he preached to the crowds, as he spoke to Nicodemus and the Samaritan woman, and as he talked to his disciples about prayer and their future testament to him.

Names and Images

Titles of the Holy Spirit include *Paraclete*, which is commonly translated as "consoler," "advocate," or "he who is called to one's side." He is also known as the Spirit of Truth, the Spirit of the Promise, the Spirit of Adoption, the Spirit of Christ, the Spirit of the Lord, and the Spirit of God.

These are some of the symbols connected to the Holy Spirit:

- **Water.** Man's birth takes place in water; the water of Baptism signifies rebirth.
- **Anointing with oil.** This action relates to Jesus's anointing with the Holy Spirit. Jesus was the Anointed One, revealed and anointed with the power and presence of the Holy Spirit.
- **Fire.** Fire symbolizes the transforming energy of the Holy Spirit, who at Pentecost rested on the heads of the disciples as tongues of fire.
- **Cloud and light.** In the Old Testament, images of cloud and light depicted the Holy Spirit revealing and obscuring God in his apparitions to Moses.
- **The seal.** A symbol of the effect of anointing with the Holy Spirit, an indelible character printed on the soul.
- **The hand.** A reference to the laying on of hands in healing and teaching, where the Holy Spirit is an agent.
- **The finger.** By the finger of the Holy Spirit, Jesus casts out demons and writes on the human heart.
- **The dove.** At Jesus' baptism, the Holy Spirit comes over him in the form of a dove.

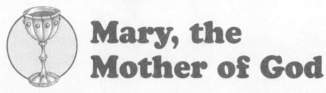

Chapter 7

Mary, the Mother of God

Over the centuries, the Church has worked to understand Mary's theological role in Catholicism, and it has proclaimed five Marian dogmas (or truths) that devout believers uphold. The dogmas state that Mary is the Mother of God; that Mary is a perpetual virgin; that she was born by Immaculate Conception; that she was assumed into Heaven and did not suffer mortal decay; and that she is the Mother of the Church.

Mary and the Gospels

In the Gospels, Mark, Luke, and John all take a very different approach to Mary's role in the life and works of Jesus Christ. (The fourth Gospel, the Gospel of Matthew, is fairly similar to the Gospel of Luke.) The differences among their portrayals of Mary have implications for how the Church understands her and on the Marian devotions practiced by believers. Many Catholics tend to favor the images of Mary from the Gospel of Luke, which describes the Annunciation and includes a passage that extols Mary's virtues.

Luke describes how the Angel Gabriel appears to Mary and greets her: "Hail, favored one! The Lord is with you!" Mary must have shown her fear, because the angel says, "Do not be afraid, Mary, for you have found favor with God." The angel tells Mary that she will conceive and bear a son, the Son of God.

Understandably, Mary is confused. She asks: "How can this be, since I have no relations with a man?" The angel replies, "The Holy Spirit will come upon you, and the power of the Most High will overshadow you. Therefore the child to be born will be called holy, the Son of God" (Luke 1:28–35).

QUESTION?

What is the Virgin Conception?
Mary conceived of Jesus while remaining a virgin, through the power of the Holy Spirit. The concept of the Virgin Conception has been a stumbling block for many believers, and some scholars believe that Mary went on to have more children—siblings of Jesus.

The Magnificat

When Mary goes to visit her cousin Elizabeth (who is pregnant with John the Baptist), Elizabeth greets Mary with these words: "Blessed are you among women, and blessed is the fruit of your womb! And why is this granted me, that the mother of my Lord should come to me? . . . Blessed is she who believed that there would be a fulfillment of what was spoken to her from the Lord."

Mary replies with the passage that has come to be known as the Magnificat: "My soul magnifies the Lord, and my spirit rejoices in God my

Savior, for he has regarded the low estate of his handmaiden. For behold, henceforth all generations will call me blessed; for he who is might has done great things for me, and holy is his name."

FACT

In reciting the Magnificat, which is based on the prayer of Hannah from the Book of Samuel, Mary shows that she is learned in Scriptures and is heavily influenced by the Jewish concepts of God.

The Rest of Luke's Narrative

The Gospel of Luke shows Mary as pious and obedient to God as it describes the birth of Jesus, the homage of the shepherds, and the presentation in the Temple. For the most part, Mary seems to understand her role in the divine plan. When Jesus has been lost for three days and Mary finds him with the scholars in the Temple, she rebukes him and he replies, "Did you not know I must be about my Father's business?"

ESSENTIAL

Just as Christ ascended into heaven after the Resurrection, the Church asserts that Mary overcame death and was assumed body and soul into Heaven by means of divine power. The Assumption does not appear in the Scriptures but was proclaimed as a doctrine by the pope in 1950.

In the Gospels of Mark and John

Mark and John sometimes portray Mary in a less positive light. Take the passage of Mark 3:20–35 as an example. In this passage, Jesus and his apostles are in a house near the Sea of Galilee, and a huge crowd has gathered outside. Jesus' family comes to take him, for they fear for his sanity. They say: "He is beside himself." When someone tells Jesus, "Your mother and your brothers are outside, asking for you," he replies, "Here are my mother and my brothers. Whoever does the will of God is my brother, and sister, and mother." This passage may lead to the assumption that Mary was not one of the original disciples, and Mark never says that she ever became one.

The Gospel of John initially seems to show that Mary does not have full knowledge of the divine plan. When she tells her son at the wedding feast at Cana to do something since the couple has run out of wine, Jesus replies, "Woman, why turn to me? My hour has not yet come." Yet he does as she asks, even though he seems to think that she does not realize the importance of his work for the Father, and how it should take precedence over family interests.

At the end of the Gospel of John, we see the Virgin Mary at the foot of the cross with one of Jesus' disciples. Jesus says to his mother, "Woman, behold your son," and to the disciple, "Son, behold your mother." The Church interprets this as Jesus giving his mother a spiritual role as mother of the disciples. This role of discipleship is viewed as giving rise to the great doctrines and devotions to Mary that later developed in the Church.

ALERT!

The Immaculate Conception of Mary should not be confused with the Virgin Conception of Jesus. Through the doctrine of the Immaculate Conception, the Church asserts that Mary was conceived and born free from original sin, the lack of grace, and the tendency to sinfulness that marks ordinary mortals.

The Development of Marian Dogmas

Devotions to Mary have waxed and waned over the history of the Church, depending on the mood of the times, the doctrinal approaches of theologians, and the viewpoints of the popes.

The Early Church

Devotions to Mary were very strong in the East. Marian legends and hymns in honor of her were popular. New churches were dedicated to Mary. Christians celebrated Marian feast days and sang hymns to the Virgin.

In the West, devotion to Mary did not take off until the time of St. Ambrose (340–397), who believed that Mary could not have been the

Mother of God without physical and moral purity and affirmed her close relationship with the Church.

The Middle Ages

By the time of the Middle Ages, Byzantine Mariology began to have a great influence on the Church in Europe. Hymns like "Ave Maris Stella," in which Mary is likened to the Star of the Sea, were added to the Catholic devotional practices. The Catholic Church began to see Mary as radiant, pure, and above the angels, a woman who redeemed mankind from the curse of the original sin of another woman, Eve. Mary was venerated as the Ark of Salvation, the ladder by which sinners climb to Heaven.

In 1124, Eadmer, Precentor of Canterbury and a disciple of St. Anselm, produced the first manifesto on the doctrine of the Immaculate Conception, which held that Mary is free from original sin because she is the Mother of the Redeemer and Empress of the Universe.

The doctrine was slow to be accepted. St. Thomas Aquinas held that since Mary was conceived, she must have been born with original sin. Over a century later, John Duns Scotus convincingly argued that Mary was preserved from original sin in anticipation of the divine goodness of Christ. In 1476, Pope Sixtus IV approved the feast of the Immaculate Conception. The doctrine of the Assumption also began to grow in strength during the Middle Ages

The Reformation and Counter-Reformation

Toward the end of the Middle Ages, Marian devotions had become excessive and even superstitious. One popular theologian of the time, Bernardino of Siena (1380–1444), declared that Mary was more powerful than God, that she seduced and enraptured him, and that she did more for God than God did for man.

With the Reformation, the Protestants rejected excessive devotion to Mary, though they did not abandon the Marian doctrines altogether. Luther and Calvin believed in her perpetual virginity and the respect due to her as the mother of Christ. However, Calvin rejected Mary's vital role as an intercessor for all sinners, and Protestants gradually dropped devotions to Mary, whereas Catholics carried on as they had during the Middle Ages.

In the Catholic Church, devotions to Mary did not dwindle but rather gained strength. Saying the Rosary, a practice that started in 1100, gained popularity. (Later in this chapter, the Rosary and its associated prayers are described in more detail.) Common beliefs regarding Mary's role in relation to Jesus and the believers included the idea, proposed by Louis-Marie Grignon de Montford, that the devil feared Mary more than God himself, and that a true devotee would only approach Christ through Mary, being totally consecrated to her. Another theologian, Alphonsus Liguori, contended that all graces given by God pass through Mary and that she intercedes for sinners and softens the anger of her Son.

The Enlightenment

The Enlightenment, an era of rational thought and scientific reasoning, saw the popularity of Marian devotions on the decline because they were seen as emotional excesses left over from a bygone era. The popularity of the Hail Mary and the Rosary waned drastically. Few visited Marian shrines, and feast days in her honor were reduced in number.

The Romantic Era

The interest in emotional and mystical states that characterized the Romantic era was felt keenly in the Church. Devotions to Mary surged back into mainstream Catholicism with the strong approval of the popes. Pius IX (1846–1878) championed the cause of devotion to Mary as an antidote to liberal rationalism. He proclaimed the dogma of the Immaculate Conception in 1854.

Marian Devotions in the Modern Church

Understanding of Mary and her role in the Church continued to change and develop throughout the twentieth century. Pope Pius XII, who led the Church from 1939 to 1958, was a devotee of Our Lady of Fatima; he consecrated the world to the Immaculate Heart of Mary and defined the doctrine of the Assumption—that Mary, like her son, was assumed to Heaven, body and soul. Pius XII also proclaimed 1954 a Marian year, dedicated to celebrating the hundredth anniversary of the dogma of the Immaculate Conception.

Decisions Made at Vatican II

Just twelve years after the dogma of Assumption had been passed, the Second Vatican Council convened in Rome to discuss matters of Catholic doctrines and faith. In particular, some discussions examined Marian devotion.

Although Vatican II devoted a whole chapter to Mary in its *Dogmatic Constitution on the Church,* where it reaffirmed her important position in Catholic dogma, it stopped short of creating a separate document on Marian doctrine, a move that somewhat downgrades the traditionally bountiful veneration of Mary.

The conclusion of the council regarding Mary was to view her as a fellow member of the Church, not as a semidivine being, and to go back to the Scriptures to understand Mary and her role in the Church. The Church fathers warned Catholics not to place belief in Mary's power of intercession over their belief in Jesus Christ as the one mediator between God and humans. All of Mary's ability to mediate rests on the power of Christ, and veneration of Mary must foster our relationship with Jesus. Christ is the one who gave himself for our redemption. Mary, giving herself to God's will throughout her life, is the model of a Christian, but she does not have any special powers. It is unwise for the clergy to exaggerate Mary's role and for the faithful to practice "credulity."

However, Vatican II adhered to the most benign interpretations of Mary's role in Christ's ministry. In addition to being the Mother of God and Mother of the Redeemer, Mary also "belongs to the offspring of Adam and is one with all human beings in their need for salvation"; this is a position that relies most on the Gospels and the early teachings of the Church.

Furthermore, at the closing of the third session of Vatican II (of the four sessions held in total), Pope Paul VI declared Mary the Mother of the Church, the Church's model in faith, charity, and perfect union with

Christ. The Church, like a mother, brings forth her children for Baptism. While Mary has reached perfection, Catholics should see the Church as working toward the example that Mary sets.

Marian Devotions in Light of Feminism

While the Church reassessed Mary's position in its teachings, feminist theologians redefined their understanding of women's roles in the Church in light of Mary's example. They argued that if Mary is mother and minister to the apostles, a larger role in the ministry of the Church must belong to women. Many feminists rejected the view of Mary as submissive to God's will and argued that her love forms a cornerstone of the Church.

Striving for Unity

When Pope John Paul II made advances toward rebuilding the schism between Roman Catholicism and the Eastern Church, he emphasized the beliefs the two Churches share in regard to Mary—in particular, Mary's title as Mother of God and "knowledge that the mystery of Christ leads us to bless his mother." John Paul also mentioned the common history the Catholics and the Eastern Church have in venerating images of the Virgin.

Marian Apparitions

A remarkable number of appearances of Mary have happened in the last few hundred years. One such apparition took place just before the pronouncement of the doctrine of the Immaculate Conception, in 1830. Catherine Laboure, who entered the convent of the Daughters of Charity, had a vision of what was termed the Immaculate Conception. Laboure saw Mary standing on a globe, rays of light streaming toward it from her hands. She is framed by the words, "O Mary conceived without sin, pray for us who have recourse to thee." A medal was struck of that image; it became known as the Miraculous Medal, because of miracles associated with it.

Shortly after the pronouncement of the doctrine of the Immaculate Conception, a fourteen-year-old peasant girl named Bernadette Soubirous, who lived near Lourdes, in France, had a series of visions. Mary ordered her to drink from a spring, which appeared when Soubirous dug the ground. When the girl asked the name of the woman in her vision, the vision replied, "I am the Immaculate Conception." Many cures have been associated with the waters of the spring at Lourdes. St. Bernadette was canonized in 1933.

FACT

The waters at Lourdes were later linked to numerous healings and miracles. Today, Lourdes continues to attract both the sick and the devout as one of the world's foremost shrines to Mary.

In 1917, Mary also appeared at Cova da Iria in Portugal. Three children—Lucia dos Santos and her cousins, Francisco and Jacinta Martos—saw a woman hovering over a tree. The woman promised to return on the thirteenth of every month for six months, when she would tell them the purpose of her appearances. On October 13, the day of the final vision, the woman announced that she was the Lady of the Rosary and that war in Europe would end that day. Then the pouring rain stopped, and those present saw the sun dance around the sky, emitting multicolored rays.

In the Last Fifty Years

These miraculous apparitions continued well into the twentieth century. In 1979, Mary revealed herself to an Anglican man in Australia; in 1980, she was seen by a church sacristan in Nicaragua; in the years 1981–1988, she appeared to children in the poor village of Medjugorje, Yugoslavia. Throughout the 1980s, appearances were documented in Ireland, Egypt, and Italy. Witnesses of these appearances often say that when they saw Mary, she had a message—to seek peace, to build a community of faith, or to return to more spiritual life.

Prayers to Mary

At Mass, Mary and the saints are commemorated during the Eucharistic prayers. Their intercession is requested on behalf of all people, that we may model our lives on theirs and be admitted into their number. Mary is first among the saints, and therefore the first choice for the faithful who ask the saints to intercede on their behalf. Many prayers of the medieval Church that address Mary directly still survive today.

Mary as Intercessor

Catholics commonly ask Mary to intercede for them in prayers for friends and family who are ill and in trouble. This practice dates from the medieval conception that both God and Jesus are stern judges of sinners while Mary embodies compassion and mercy. It was believed that her influence alone could convince Jesus to hear the prayer of a poor sinner. The practice survives despite the modern belief that Jesus is the true mediator between God and mankind.

Like the Church, which is seen as feminine, Mary is referred to as the enemy of the serpent, the New Eve, and even the Bride of Christ (in a spiritual sense), all symbols of the New Covenant between people and God created by the work of Jesus.

Mary's role as a symbol of the Church also reinforces her role as intercessor on behalf of sinners. Like the Church, Mary helps bring us closer to Jesus. In her submission to God's will and her faith during the final days of Jesus' life, she presents a model of how to worship and how to live a faithful life. Contemplating the mystery of Mary's life is a correct attitude for a Catholic approaching God in prayer.

Hail Mary

The Hail Mary is one of the most ancient prayers of the Church. It begins with the words of the angel to Mary, telling her of Jesus' coming birth, as drawn from Luke's Gospel. The second part is an ancient petition. The prayer dates from the time when worship of Mary was growing and touches on many of the themes of Marian theology. It elevates Mary as Mother of God, it implies the belief that Mary was conceived free of sin, and it asks her to intercede for the sinner, now and throughout our lives:

Hail, Mary, full of Grace, the Lord is with thee; blessed art thou among women, and blessed is the fruit of thy womb, Jesus. Holy Mary, Mother of God, pray for us sinners, now and at the hour of our death. Amen.

The Hail Mary is a versatile prayer used during the Rosary, as a penance and as prelude or conclusion to other prayers. The repetition of a prayer aids in meditation as it encourages the penitent to put daily concerns out of mind and concentrate on his or her relations with God. The Hail Mary reminds humans of their sinfulness and that they should be living a life more like Mary's, who is a model of faith and is free of sin.

Hail, Holy Queen

Hail, Holy Queen is part of the Rosary devotion to Mary and entreats her mercy for poor sinners:

Hail, Holy Queen, Mother of Mercy, our life, our sweetness, and our hope. To Thee do we cry poor banished children of Eve. To Thee do we send up our sighs, mourning and weeping in this valley of tears. Turn then, most gracious Advocate, thine eyes of mercy toward us. And after this, our exile, show unto us the blessed fruit of Thy womb, Jesus. O clement, O loving, O sweet Virgin Mary, pray for us, O Holy Mother of God; that we may be made worthy of the promises of Christ. Amen.

The title of Queen is derived from Mary's relationship to Jesus, who is King and Lord. It also refers to a passage in the Book of Revelation, describing the image of a woman clothed with the sun, with the moon at her feet and a crown of twelve stars. Theologians are divided on whether this passage describes Mary.

The Litany of Loreto

The Litany of Loreto, a repetitive prayer that concentrates on the many virtues of Mary, addresses her as Mother, Virgin, Queen, the Mirror of

Justice, Seat of Wisdom, Vessel of Honor, Mystical Rose, Gate of Heaven, and Morning Star—for a total of fifty honorifics. As each epithet is made, the congregation responds with the words "pray for us."

FACT

There are also prayers written from Mary's point of view. The Magnificat, or Canticle of Mary, is a prayer of praise to the traditional God of the Old Testament. In the voice of Mary, the prayerful recall the covenant between Abraham and God and give praise and thanks for his protection through the ages.

The Rosary and Other Devotions

The Rosary is a devotion that encourages the Christian to reflect on the important events, or mysteries, of Christ's life as experienced by Mary. Although it is less emphasized in the modern Church than in the past, it is still an important and meaningful devotion for many Catholics. The Rosary is essentially a series of prayers, spoken while fingering the beads of a rosary, which aids in meditation and the contemplation of the mysteries. There are fifteen decades, or groups of ten beads, the decades separated by a bead in between each group.

The Rosary forms a circle. Hanging down from it is a strand with a single bead, a group of three beads, and another single bead, followed by a crucifix. On the two single beads, the devotee says the Our Father and Glory Be. On the three beads, the devotee prays a Hail Mary. On the crucifix, the devotee repeats the Creed. This sequence is something like an introduction to the Rosary. On each of the ten beads, the devotee says a Hail Mary, on the in-between beads, the Our Father and Glory Be. Each decade is dedicated to a mystery from the life of Mary. (See Chapter 10 for more information on the prayers of the Rosary.)

In addition to saying the Rosary, Catholics may recite one of the novenas, prayers offered nine times or a multiple of nine times. Novenas may be offered in the course of a day or over several weeks and are often associated with a special request for Mary's intercession, perhaps with a severe illness or a particular problem. The Immaculate Heart of

Mary, a devotion that concentrates on the love she bore her son and the piercing of her heart at the Crucifixion, includes a popular novena prayer.

The Angelus is a short series of prayers offered three times a day at the sound of a bell. This prayer, said in honor of the Incarnation of Jesus, recounts the story of the appearance of the angel to Mary, and is interspersed with three Hail Marys. At the end, the Angelus calls for grace and redemption for the penitent. (Another prayer, Regina Cæli Lætare, is substituted in the period before Easter.) The Angelus was traditionally used for indulgences; that is, the prayer was said on earth to reduce the amount of time one would spend in Purgatory.

Chapter 8

The Seven Sacraments

The seven sacraments form an important part of Catholic liturgy and observance. They are meant to give grace at all of life's stages—during the most important moments in each Catholic person's life—and to strengthen the faithful in continuing Jesus' mission of drawing everyone closer to God. The seven sacraments are Baptism, Confirmation, the Eucharist, Penance, the Anointing of the Sick, Matrimony, and Holy Orders.

God's Presence in the World

Christ instituted the sacraments as powers that come forth from him through his ministers and that are performed by the Holy Spirit. Through the sacraments of Baptism and Confirmation, Catholics are entitled to take part in the Church's liturgy (or worship). Ordination is a sacramental bond that ties the priest and the liturgical action to the ministry of the apostles and to Christ. Priests, who are ordained ministers, are there to serve the baptized by administering the sacraments and through celebrating other parts of the liturgy, such as Mass.

FACT

Sacraments are known as instruments of faith because through words and symbols they instruct people in the faith, nourishing, strengthening, and expressing it. Through the sacraments, Catholics profess the ancient faith of the apostles. For this reason, the sacramental rites cannot be changed or modified. Not even the highest level of Church authority can arbitrarily change the liturgy.

Baptism, Confirmation, and the Eucharist are called the Sacraments of Christian Initiation. In the early days of the Church, catechumens (or initiates to the faith) received them all at once. These sacraments are the cornerstones of Catholic life: "The faithful are born anew by Baptism, strengthened by Confirmation and in the Eucharist receive the food of eternal life" (Paul VI, AAS 63 [1971] 657). Penance and the Anointing of the Sick are known as the Sacraments of Healing, and Matrimony and Holy Orders are sometimes called the Sacraments of Commitment.

In addition to grace, the sacraments of Baptism, Confirmation, and Holy Orders confer a sacramental character, or "seal," upon the believers. The indelible sign of each of these sacraments remains as a promise of divine protection and a call or vocation to worship and service, and it helps the believer be permanently disposed to receiving grace.

Through grace, the sacraments are also instruments of salvation. They are efficacious, because Christ and the Holy Spirit are the ones at work through the sacraments, and they stand as reminders and guarantees of eternal life in God.

Sacraments work *ex opere operato,* just by virtue of the action being performed, and irrespective of the righteousness of either the minister or the recipient. However, the disposition of the receiver does affect the fruits or outcomes of the sacrament.

Baptism: A Spiritual Rebirth

The Church teaches that Baptism is the portal to spiritual life and the gateway to other sacraments, a sacrament of purification and rebirth. Through Baptism, Catholics become members of the Church to share in the Church's mission.

Baptism, from the Greek *baptizein,* means to "plunge" or "immerse." The immersion into the water is symbolic of death and rebirth: The baptized person dies in the water and is reborn in Christ, just as Christ himself died on the cross and was resurrected. The waters of Baptism have a cleansing effect, as the soul of the baptized person is washed and renewed by the Holy Spirit. Baptism is also associated with spiritual enlightenment–those who receive Baptism are enlightened in their understanding.

Many stories in the Old Testament seem to prefigure Baptism: the story of the Great Flood, when the water drowned the wicked; the crossing of the Red Sea, which freed the Israelites from bondage; the crossing of the River Jordan into the Promised Land. In the New Testament, Jesus himself is baptized before beginning his mission. After Pentecost, the apostles began to baptize new converts to the faith.

In the early Church, Baptism was part of the Sacraments of Initiation, which also involved Proclamation of the Word, acceptance of the Gospel, profession of faith, the outpouring of the Holy Spirit through Confirmation, and admission to Eucharistic Communion.

The Baptismal Ceremony

Today, the ceremony of Baptism must include the following steps:

1. The sign of the cross
2. The proclamation of the Word of God to enlighten all those gathered

3. Exorcisms pronounced over the candidate, laying on of hands, renunciation of Satan, and confession of faith
4. Consecration of baptismal water (either then or at the Easter Vigil)
5. Baptism proper, including pouring of or immersion in water, and the words, "I baptize you in the name of the Father, and of the Son, and of the Holy Spirit"
6. Anointing with the sacred chrism (special oil)
7. Wearing of a white garment, to symbolize that the person has "put on Christ," and the lighting of a candle from the Easter candle, to symbolize enlightenment
8. Post-baptismal anointing as a forerunner of Confirmation
9. Sacrament of the Eucharist for adult candidates
10. Solemn blessing

Ordinarily, bishops, priests, and deacons are the only ones who have the privilege to baptize. However, the Church considers Baptism so crucial to salvation that anyone, even an unbaptized person, can perform the baptismal ceremony in an emergency—as long as the minister of Baptism follows the ceremony and has the right intentions.

Baptism for Children and Adults

Today, the Church practices both infant and adult Baptism. Adult Baptism hearkens back to the days of the early Church, with the Rite of Christian Initiation for Adults (RCIA). As catechumens, adults prepare to receive the sacraments of Baptism, Confirmation, and Communion. They learn about the mystery of salvation, the virtues, and the life of faith, liturgy, and charity.

Following practices that began in the second century A.D., the Church also conducts Baptism of young children. Because humans are born with the burden of original sin, they need the sacrament of Baptism to be reborn in the light. The Church does not want to deny children this priceless gift, so Baptism is traditionally administered shortly after birth.

Whether child or adult, all the newly baptized need help to grow in the faith. Every baptized person has a godfather and a godmother, who act as the baptized person's sponsors and must therefore be firm believers. The task of the godparents is to help the newly baptized grow in the faith.

ALERT!

The Church extends the saving benefits of Baptism to people who die for the faith without having been baptized and to catechumens who died before being baptized. The Church also teaches that anyone who seeks truth and does God's will insofar as he or she understands it can be saved, despite ignorance of the Gospels and of the Church.

The effects of Baptism include the following:

- The forgiveness of all sins, personal as well as inherited (including the original sin)
- Justification that allows the sinner to believe in, hope in, and love God; to live under the influence of the Holy Spirit; and to grow in the moral virtues
- Inclusion in the Church and a membership in the common priesthood of all believers
- An indelible spiritual mark that demonstrates the baptized person's dedication to Christ

Confirmation: Completion of Baptism

Confirmation is the second Sacrament of Christian Initiation, and it has an important relationship with the sacrament of Baptism. The Church teaches that Confirmation completes Baptism because it tightens the bonds between its recipients and the Church. At Confirmation, the confirmed receive the Holy Spirit more fully, and "they are, as true witnesses of Christ, more strictly obliged to spread and defend the faith by word and deed" (*Lumen Gentium* 11, OC, Introduction 2).

After Pentecost, the apostles were filled with the Holy Spirit and began to proclaim the mighty works of God. Those who accepted the Gospel and were baptized also received the Holy Spirit through what was referred to as the "laying on of hands." The laying on of hands led to the ceremony of Confirmation, which carries the grace of Pentecost through the Church. The confirmed were again anointed with perfumed oil (chrism), in imitation of Christ, who was anointed by God with the Holy Spirit.

Anointing with oil signifies and imprints a spiritual seal; it is a sign of consecration. Those who are anointed take a greater part in the mission of Jesus Christ and the fullness of the Holy Spirit. The seal of the Holy Spirit is on them, symbolizing an affiliation or belonging. The Church teaches that the seal of the Holy Spirit marks the Christian's total belonging to Christ, his enrollment in his service forever, and the promise of divine protection.

The Confirmation Ceremony

In the Catholic Church, the liturgy of Confirmation contains the renewal of baptismal promises and the profession of faith. When adults are baptized, it is usual for them to receive Confirmation and participate in the Eucharist immediately. When confirming adults who have just been baptized, the bishop extends his hands over the whole group and invokes the Holy Spirit: "Send your Holy Spirit upon them to be their helper and guide." Next is the laying on of hands, the anointing of the forehead with chrism, and the words "Be sealed with the Gift of the Holy Spirit." The sign of peace concludes the sacrament.

FACT

Acording to Canon 891 of the 2000 National Conference of Catholic Bishops, Confirmation should be performed before Catholic children are age sixteen. Most Catholic children are confirmed in their early high school years. Although this sacrament is sometimes referred to as the sacrament of Christian maturity, the Church acknowledges that maturity does not have that much to do with age. Many children are spiritually mature and have been martyrs for Christ.

Before Confirmation, most people study the actions, mission, and gifts of the Holy Spirit. They gain an awareness that they belong not just to their parish but also to the universal church. Those who are about to be confirmed receive the sacrament of Penance and seek the spiritual guidance of a sponsor. It is suggested that the sponsor be one of the godparents.

In the Catholic Church, the bishop is the usual minister of Confirmation, though he may also delegate it to priests. If someone is in danger of death without having been confirmed, any priest may confer Confirmation.

The sacrament of Confirmation affects the Catholic in the following ways:

- It increases baptismal grace.
- It unites the recipient more firmly to Christ.
- It increases the gifts of the Holy Spirit.
- It perfects the bond with the Church.
- It brings the strength of the Holy Spirit to spread and defend the faith, to openly admit to and never be ashamed of being a Christian.
- It imprints an indelible spiritual mark, giving the confirmed person the power and the authority to profess faith in Christ to all who would hear.

Eucharist: A Union with Christ

As the third Sacrament of Initiation, the Eucharist is absolutely central to the Church's liturgy, for it is concerned with the Body of Christ, the source of the Church's entire spiritual good.

The Church teaches that the Eucharist is both the outward sign of and the cause of all Catholics' communion in the divine life and with each other. It is the central means by which Christ sanctifies the world, and by which men worship Christ, God the Father, and God the Holy Spirit.

The word *Eucharist* originates from the Greek words *eukharistos* (thankful) and *kharis* (grace or favor). Other names for this sacrament include Lord's Supper, the Breaking of the Bread, Holy Sacrifice, Sacrifice of Praise, Holy and Divine Liturgy, Most Blessed Sacrament, and Holy Communion, because it is the means by which Catholics unite themselves to Christ. The Eucharist is celebrated when the faithful are gathered at Mass, in what is known as the Eucharistic assembly.

Blood and Body of Christ

Bread and wine are the outward signs of the sacrament of the Eucharist; at the Last Supper, these are what Jesus blessed and gave to his disciples in memory of him. As Jesus proclaimed, the wine he offered was his blood;

the bread, his body. The Catholic Church teaches that in a mystical way, the sacramental bread and wine become the Body and Blood of Christ during the ceremony of the Eucharist.

The Church believes that the bread and wine are actually converted into the Body and Blood of Christ, in a process called transubstantiation. Because of the real presence of Christ, the Eucharist is venerated, not only during Mass, but also outside of it. The consecrated hosts are treated with the utmost care. They are stored in a tabernacle, which is kept in a prominent place, usually near the altar.

Bread and wine are symbols that hearken back to the Old Testament. Bread and wine represented the first fruits of the earth and were used as sacrificial offerings in the Temple. Unleavened bread commemorates the bread that the Israelites ate on the eve of their flight from Egypt and the manna that fell for them in the desert. The wine is reminiscent of the Cup of Blessing at the end of a Passover meal.

By leaving this sacrament of his own Body and Blood, Jesus was able to forever remain with his disciples. The continual practice of this tradition is a memorial to Jesus and his life, death, and resurrection; it will be performed until his final coming. The Book of Acts of the Apostles recounts how the apostles preached and taught their followers and then broke bread with them at their homes. Christians usually met to break bread on Sunday, the first day of the week, the day of Jesus' Resurrection. That tradition came down as Sunday Mass, which is the center of the Church's liturgical and community life.

Mass and Communion

The entire liturgy of the Mass, which consists of two parts, is structured around the Eucharist. The first part consists of the gathering or coming together of the faithful; the Liturgy of the Word, with readings from the Old and New Testament (commonly, a passage from the Gospels); the exhortation of the priest to the people, which is known as the homily; and general prayers of intercession for the needs of the faithful.

The second part, the Liturgy of the Eucharist, includes the presentation of the bread and wine, or the Offertory, in which the bread and wine are brought to the altar; the consecration, which includes the Eucharistic prayer of thanksgiving and consecration, in which the priest asks the Father for the power of the Holy Spirit to turn the bread and wine into the Body and Blood of Christ; and finally, the communion. The Our Father and the Breaking of Bread precede the communion proper, whereby all the faithful partake of the Body and Blood of Christ.

Because they are about to receive the sacred body of Christ, Catholics are expected to prepare themselves before communion, to examine their consciences, to confess their unworthiness, and to pray for the healing of their souls. The Church recommends that anyone who may do so should receive communion at Mass, because of the powers of Holy Communion, which include the following:

- It increases the Catholic's connection with Christ.
- It separates the faithful from sin by wiping away venial sins and protecting the Christian from future mortal sins.
- It draws the faithful closer to the Church, the mystical body of Christ.
- It commits the faithful to the poor.
- It promotes unity with all Christians.
- It is a celebration of the glory that is to come.

QUESTION?

What is the difference between venial and mortal sins?
Mortal sins (including murder, adultery, theft, false witness, fraud, and disrespect of parents) are grave and must be committed with full knowledge and deliberate consent. Mortal sins are sins against God, and they result in the loss of charity and the deprivation of sanctifying grace. Venial sins are less serious; they are committed unwittingly or without full consent.

Penance: A Sacrament of Healing

Penance, along with the sacrament of Anointing of the Sick, is the sacrament of Healing that was present from the earliest times of the Church.

Paul wrote, "Those who approach the sacrament of Penance obtain pardon from God's mercy for the offense committed against him and are, at the same time, reconciled with the Church, which they have wounded" (from the Catechism).

Penance is also known by the following names:

- The sacrament of conversion, because it is a turning point for one who has strayed from God through sin
- The sacrament of confession, since it involves disclosing one's sins to a priest
- The sacrament of forgiveness, since the priest's absolution, which is part of the sacrament, confers pardon and peace
- The sacrament of reconciliation, because through God's love the sinner is brought back to union with the Father

Cleansing Away Sins

When Christians are baptized, they are cleansed of all sins. However, the Church recognizes that the Kingdom of God on earth is a work in progress, and Christians cannot always avoid temptation or know how to make the right choices. The sacrament of Penance allows the faithful to turn away from their sins and toward God in a constant cycle of penance and renewal. Penance allows the faithful to experience another conversion, which is interior rather than exterior. Sinners feel sorrowful and repentant, and they respond to grace, which turns them back toward God.

In its tradition, the Church recognizes many ways in which the faithful can obtain forgiveness of sins:

- Fasting, prayer, and almsgiving, which relate to repentance in terms of yourself, God, and others
- Making a change in your ways
- Praying for the intercession of the saints
- Showing concern for the spiritual welfare of others
- Making peace with those around you
- Practicing and defending justice
- Shedding tears of repentance

- Examining your conscience
- Taking spiritual direction
- Accepting suffering
- Enduring persecution for the sake of righteousness
- Following Jesus Christ
- Receiving the Eucharist
- Performing acts of devotion, such as reading Sacred Scriptures, praying the Liturgy of the Hours, and saying the Our Father
- Observing the seasons and days of Penance in the liturgical year, including Lent and Fridays

The Church teaches that only God can forgive sin. However, it also believes that God gave to the apostles and their successors the power to forgive sins in his name, in what the Church refers to as the Ministry of Reconciliation. Forgiveness and reconciliation remain important themes of the Church. Jesus taught us to forgive when he shared his meals with sinners.

The Power in Confession

Penance requires the sinner to feel contrition or sorrow for the sin committed and to make a firm resolution not to sin again. Penance also requires confession, which helps the sinner take full responsibility for the sin. The last component of the sacrament of Penance is satisfaction: The sinner must do something to make amends for his or her sins.

ALERT!

Motives for contrition may vary from person to person. Perfect contrition is inspired by the love of God, whereas imperfect contrition is inspired by a loathing of sin and a fear of the consequences, which might include a punishment like eternal damnation.

Because they have received Holy Orders, bishops and priests have the power to forgive all sins. The Church teaches that confessors should know what is to be expected in Christian behavior, have an understanding of human affairs, and treat the sinner with the respect deserved by each human being.

Because confession is a sensitive matter, the priest is bound to keep secret anything that he is told in confession, and he cannot make use of any knowledge he gains of the penitents' lives.

The Anointing of the Sick

The second sacrament of Healing is the Anointing of the Sick. The Church recognizes that sickness and suffering are serious problems for humanity. While illness does lead some people to turn against God, it can also help the faithful realize what is important in life and turn them toward God.

Jesus showed great compassion for the sick and performed many healings. In curing sufferers, he often asked them to believe; in healing, he used outward signs such as the laying on of hands and getting people to bathe themselves. The sick often tried to simply touch him, realizing they could be healed that way. Through his sufferings, Jesus joined in the sufferings of the sick.

Healing and the laying on of hands were also part of the mission of the apostles. "In my name . . . they will lay hands on the sick, and they will recover" (Mark 16:17–18). Today, the Church strives to care for the sick and make sure they are remembered in prayers. In addition, the Church offers them a special sacrament, the Anointing of the Sick. The purpose of this sacrament is to strengthen those who are tried by illness.

There is testimony that this sacrament has existed since the earliest days of the Church, when the sick were anointed with blessed oil. As time went on, that anointing with oil was reserved for people who were close to death, and the sacrament came to be called Extreme Unction. However, this rite has always contained an intercession and prayer that the sick person recovers, as long as it would be helpful to his or her salvation.

Performing the Sacrament

The Church teaches that anyone who seems to be in danger of death from sickness or old age is eligible for and should receive the sacrament of the Anointing of the Sick. If someone who has been gravely ill receives the sacrament, then recovers, he or she can receive it again in case of another grave illness. If the illness worsens, the sacrament may be received again. People may also receive the sacrament before a serious operation. An elderly person who becomes much more frail may also receive this sacrament.

FACT

For a while, the Anointing of the Sick was called the last sacrament because it was often administered when the sick person was close to death. However, the Church teaches that the Eucharist as viaticum (a word that means, literally, "I go with you,") should always be the last sacrament received on earth, to strengthen the Catholic during the passage to eternal life.

Only priests are allowed to administer the sacrament of the Anointing of the Sick. The Church treats the performance of this sacrament as a communal liturgy no matter where it is celebrated, even in a home or a hospital room. It can be administered to a particular patient or to a group of sick people. The Church celebrates the Anointing of the Sick as part of the Eucharist, preceding it by the sacrament of Penance, if circumstances allow.

The anointing with oil and prayers of the priest confer the following upon the ailing believer.

- Strength provided through the grace of the Holy Spirit
- Closer union with the suffering of Christ
- A contribution to the holiness of the Church
- A preparation for the journey to everlasting life

Matrimony: A Partnership in Christ

Through the Catholic sacrament of Matrimony, a man and woman commit themselves to a lifelong partnership, established for the good of the spouses and the procreation and education of their children.

The Old Testament states that man was made in the image and likeness of God, and that man and woman were made for each other; through marriage, they become one. Furthermore, the Church teaches that since God created man out of love, and calls him to love, it is fitting that the union of man and woman should be a sacrament. The spouses' mutual love mirrors love of God; their children, who are their own creations, are also part of God's creation.

Whereas most of the sacraments are conferred by an ordained minister, priest, or bishop, marriage is different. The spouses actually confer the sacrament of Matrimony upon each other when they express their consent to marry before the Church.

The Church understands that the evil in the world makes marriage difficult. Jealousy, power struggles, and conflicts can lead to bitterness and separation. Hard work and the pain of childbirth are added burdens. However, Jesus taught that marriage is indissoluble: "Therefore, what God has joined together, no human being must separate" (Matthew 19:6). Through the sacrament of Matrimony, the Church teaches that Jesus gives the strength and grace to live the real meaning of marriage. As Paul wrote in exhortation, "Husbands, love your wives, even as Christ loved the church and handed himself over for her to sanctify her" (Ephesians 5:25–26).

The Marriage Ceremony

The marriage ceremony of two Catholics normally takes place at Mass, in memory of the paschal mystery and the way Christ bound himself permanently to the Church, his beloved bride. Numerous prayers ask God's grace and blessing on the couple, and the Holy Spirit infuses the couple with unending love and strength for fidelity.

The exchange of consent between the spouses is an indispensable element of the marriage ceremony. Marriage without consent, performed with coercion or threats, is invalid. The presence of the priest or bishop and of other witnesses testifies to the fact that marriage is part of the Church. As a sacrament, Matrimony is part of the Church's liturgy, and therefore it needs to be celebrated publicly.

Catholic marriage is a vocation (a calling), and it requires the married couple to accept certain obligations toward each other, the children, and the community. Married couples receive grace to perfect their love and to strengthen their unity, to help each other attain holiness, and to welcome and educate their children. The Church teaches that the marriage bond is established by God himself and is sealed with a special sacrament, one that can never be dissolved. It requires total fidelity from the spouses and the openness to bearing children and educating them in the faith.

Interfaith Marriage

If a Catholic person wishes to marry outside the faith, he or she is required to obtain permission of an ecclesiastical authority for the marriage to be valid in the eyes of the Church. The dispensation is based on the couple's acknowledgment of two things: the goals and behaviors of marriage, and the Catholic person's requirement of preserving his or her own faith and ensuring that the children are baptized and raised in the Church.

Some dioceses have programs that help interfaith couples fulfill their obligations, encourage what they hold in common, and increase respect for their differences. The Church believes that Catholic partner's love, practice of family virtues, and prayer can help the other partner to convert.

Holy Orders: In the Apostolic Tradition

Holy Orders is a sacrament conferred on men and by which they carry on the apostolic tradition as ministers of the Gospel and the sacraments. The term *order* comes from the Latin *ordinatio,* which means incorporation into an *ordo,* an established civil or governing body. The Church is made up of three orders: episcopate (bishops), presbyterate (priests), and deaconate (deacons). To join one of these orders, the initiates participate in a sacramental liturgy of induction, which varies depending upon the order.

A Priesthood of Mankind

The Church teaches that two kinds of priesthood share in the high priesthood of Christ. One is the priesthood of the faithful, made up of ordinary people who participate in the priestly character of the Church through Baptism and their own vocations. The Church teaches that everyone shares in the priestly character of Christ, as they share in his life, suffering, and death.

FACT

The Levite tribe of Israel was the priestly order of the Old Covenant. God charged the Levites to look after sacred items and liturgical services, which included sacrifices made to God in the Temple as well as other religious rites. Under the New Covenant, Jesus became the Chief Priest and the one mediator between God and men; he made the sacrifice of himself, the last sacrifice that would have to be performed for God.

The second priesthood is the ministerial, or hierarchical, priesthood of bishops and priests. Christ develops and leads his Church through the ministerial priesthood. Through the sacrament of Holy Orders, members of the ministerial priesthood may act in place of Christ and in the name of the Church.

The Hierarchy of the Orders

Of the three orders—bishops, priests, and deacons—the episcopal order, composed of bishops, holds the highest place in the Church. Bishops are each a link in the apostolic line, an unbroken succession going back to the earliest days of the Church. At the apex of the sacred ministry, they receive the full powers of the sacrament of Holy Orders: to sanctify, teach, and rule. Bishops are also the ones who become pontiffs and pastors. The episcopal order is collegial. Bishops work together in the consecration of a new bishop, and each bishop is responsible for the apostolic mission of the whole Church.

Priests are consecrated to help bishops in the work of the Church. They preach the Gospel, take care of the faithful, and celebrate the holy liturgies. They carry out their ministries in commu-nication with and in service to their bishops, whom they promise to love and obey. All priests are members of a priestly college, or presbyterium.

Deacons are at the lowest end of the clerical hierarchy. They assume Holy Orders through a special imprint or seal that marks them as ministers, deacons, or servants. Deacons are generally attached to the bishop who ordained them. They assist him in celebrating the

Eucharist, distributing Holy Communion, assisting at and blessing marriages, proclaiming the Gospel and preaching, conducting funerals, and working in charitable ministries.

Ordination Practices

The sacrament of Holy Orders is performed by the bishop, who lays hands on candidate and recites a specific consecratory prayer. In the Catholic Church there are accompanying rituals, such as the presentation, instruction, and examination of the candidate.

ALERT!

Only validly ordained bishops can administer Holy Orders, and only a baptized man can receive it. Celibacy is one of the conditions for receiving Holy Orders for all but permanent deacons.

If initiates are to be ordained as bishops or priests, they are anointed with holy chrism, a sign of the special anointing of the Holy Spirit. New bishops also receive the books of the Gospels along with the ring, miter, and crosier as symbols of apostolic mission. The priests receive the paten and chalice, through which they make offerings for the Church to God. The deacons receive the books of the Gospels, to proclaim the Gospel of Christ.

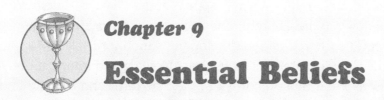

Chapter 9
Essential Beliefs

Catholics begin their profession of faith by saying: "I believe" or "We believe." In addition to being a faith, Catholicism is also a system of beliefs, handed down by God, that have been interpreted and shaped by generations of holy men and theologians over the Church's 2,000-year history.

The Catholic Canon of Creeds

The canon (from the Greek *kanon,* "rule") of the Catholic Church comprises a system of laws and regulations used in governing the vast organization of the Catholic Church and its followers as well as the beliefs (or creeds) of the Church.

The canon did not magically appear at the dawn of Christianity, handed down to the Church to be accepted and practiced without question. The Church had to develop the canon for itself. In fact, it has taken the Church just about 2,000 years to study and interpret the Word of Christ as it has been recorded in the Scriptures and to build up the canon through deep religious and philosophical inquiry, debate, and even controversy. Throughout its struggles to understand, the Church has been infused by the guidance of the Holy Spirit and piloted by the pope.

It's important to understand that the changes in canon law do not constitute any rejection of previously held beliefs. Although canon law has endured debate and subsequent shifts in emphasis to better explain the Lord's Word, the Church teaches that these changes occur because of the vitality and organic nature of the faith.

The Development of Canon Law

It took many centuries for the system of the canon law to be developed and organized in a harmonious way. The Church recognizes three eras of development: the ancient law, the law of the Middle Ages, and the modern law.

- The era of ancient law lasted from the dawn of Christianity to the twelfth century, ending with Johannes Gratian's publication of the *Decretum.*
- The era of the law of the Middle Ages lasted until the Council of Trent (1545–1563).
- The era of modern law began with the Council of Trent, lasting until now.

Gratian is considered the founder of the "science" of canon law in the Church. Gratian was a monk and a scholar who was born in Tuscany in the twelfth century; by the time he had undertaken the project of compiling the Church canon law, he was teaching at a convent in Bologna.

In his exhaustive canonical work, known as the *Decretum,* Gratian included not only Church laws that were already in force but also the principles from the great group of canons collected from the earliest days. Covering jurisdiction, historical information, and liturgical practices, Gratian's impressive treatise remained the principal text of the Church canon until the Council of Trent, in the 1500s.

The Council of Trent, which convened to tackle the controversies of its era—namely the Reformation—established new laws and principles where confusion had reigned. Rulings passed and recorded by the Council included the following:

- Catholic faith is based on scripture and *also* on tradition (this ruling affirmed the Catholic belief in Divine Tradition).
- The importance of *both* good works and faith in the struggle for salvation.
- The actual presence of Christ in the Eucharist.

The Council of Trent also standardized the prayers and rituals of the Mass, which would remain the same until Vatican II, which convened in the 1960s.

FACT

In 1917, Pope Benedict XV issued his comprehensive Code of Canon Law. This was regarded as the canonical authority in the Catholic Church until 1983, when Pope John Paul II issued a new Code of Canon Law, the one Catholics are ruled by today.

Modern Additions to the Canon

Many changes in the Catholic canon took place through the work of a specially convened council, like the Nicaean Council or the Council of Trent. However, the pope also has the power and the authority to issue pontifical laws through apostolic letters (also known as papal bulls). Finally, laws may be passed on a local level, through local ecclesiastical councils, as long as the decisions are made in conformity with Church law.

Bound by Church Law

All Catholics must adhere to Church law. Once they have been baptized and have accepted the authority of the Church, they become full members and must submit to the government by these laws.

But what happens if a Catholic is lax in his or her duty, or rejects some of the beliefs outright? The Church is not hard on those who are negligent, but it also recognizes three formal types of sin against Church law. These are heresy, apostasy, and schism, which draw the severe penalty of excommunication.

Heresy

Heresy is the rejection of a belief at the core of Roman Catholicism. In the early days of the Church, all non-Catholics were considered to be heretics. Although this is still logically true, the Church has in recent years taken a greater interest in charity toward its neighbors and no longer bandies the word *heretic* around.

Apostasy

Apostasy is a much more serious transgression. It is the total repudiation of everything that has to do with Catholicism. It is a lonely route to go, and one that usually only occurs if a Catholic has profound doubts or undergoes a traumatic experience that leads him or her to reject the Catholic faith. Those who abandon their faith are automatically considered to be outside the Church, but they are not formally charged unless they call public attention to their repudiation.

Interestingly, the Church recognizes three distinct forms of apostasy: when a Catholic layperson abandons his or her faith, when a cleric sheds the ecclesiastical state, and when a member of a religious order abandons the religious state he or she once embraced.

Schism

The word *schism* refers to a failure within the faith to submit to the authority of the Roman Pontiff and to recognize the primacy of the pope. Orthodox Churches that broke with Rome in 1054 were referred to as schismatic.

While it might seem an old-fashioned notion, there are actually a number of marginal groups within the Church that challenge the papal authority on issues that bother them or that they disagree with. One such group of ultra-orthodox Catholics is pushing for a return to the Tridentine Mass, spoken completely in Latin.

The Church tolerates the ultra-orthodox, but there are other groups that challenge it in more inappropriate ways. One of those challenges happened in Austria in the summer of 2002, when a bishop who had broken with the Church ordained a group of ex-nuns as priests. Such groups are excommunicated for flouting Church law.

Excommunication

According to Church law, once a person accepts a heresy or apostasy, or joins a schismatic group, he or she is automatically in a state of excommunication and can no longer partake of the sacraments. Excommunication means exclusion from the Church and prohibition from receiving the sacraments. It is really a type of shunning, and it bears severe social stigma. Excommunication doesn't necessarily require a public notice. In serious cases, however, the Vatican issues a formal decree.

The Church does offer means of reconciliation. Lifting an excommunication requires approval from a bishop, although he will often delegate the commission to a priest or confessor at his cathedral. In matters of a truly serious nature, though, reconciliation is not that easy to get.

The Nicene Creed

The Catholic canon is based on the beliefs of the Church. The creed formulated at the Nicaean Council, which is called the Nicene Creed, is composed of twelve articles of faith and incorporates the most basic beliefs found at the heart of Catholicism. The authoritative wording of the Nicene Creed has guided the Church for 1,600 years and forms the expression of faith that Catholics say during Baptism as well as during the liturgy of the Mass.

The formulation of the Creed was a defining moment for the Church, and it came about through a reaction to the rising tide of a heresy called Arianism, which threatened the unity of the Christians in the fourth century by denying the divinity of Jesus Christ. To deal with the growing controversy, Emperor Constantine, the first Roman emperor to convert to Christianity, called a council of bishops to Nicaea.

The Nicaean Council, which met in 325, developed the Nicene Creed from the Apostles' Creed, which is still recognized by the Catholic Church as an important corollary to the Nicene. Until the 1500s, the Apostles' Creed was believed to be a summary of the apostles' faith, since it was neatly comprised of twelve articles of faith, the same number as God's chosen disciples. During the 1400s, though, historians discovered its true origin, an adapted version of the old Roman Creed. (The Apostles' Creed remains the most important creed of most Protestant religions.)

The Nicaean Council refined the wording of the Apostles' Creed so that Jesus' divinity—in addition to his humanity—was plainly expressed and proclaimed. A second ecumenical council that convened in Constantinople in 381 approved and finalized the work of the first council, giving us what we now know as the Nicene Creed.

There is another, lesser-known summary of Catholic faith, called the Athanasian Creed, which also dates back to the fourth century. Most lay Catholics are probably not even aware of it, since it is not in "daily" use, but it is approved by the Church and is part of the liturgy. The Athanasian Creed gives a clear exposition of the Trinity.

Here is the full text of the Nicene Creed. The text in brackets is the original wording—small emendations have been made in the modern text that Catholics now use:

We believe [I believe] in one God, the Father Almighty, maker of heaven and earth, and of all things visible and invisible. And in one Lord Jesus Christ, the only begotten Son of God, and born of the Father before all ages. [God of God] light of light, true God of true God. Begotten not made, consubstantial to the Father, by whom all things were made. Who for us men and for our salvation came down from heaven. And was incarnate of the Holy Ghost and of the Virgin Mary and was made man; was crucified also for us under Pontius Pilate, suffered and was buried; and the third day rose again according to the Scriptures. And ascended into heaven, sits at the right hand of the Father, and shall come again with glory to judge the living and the dead, of whose Kingdom there shall be no end. And [I believe] in the Holy Ghost, the Lord and Giver of life, who proceeds from the Father [and the Son], who together with the Father and the Son is to be adored and glorified, who spoke by the Prophets. And one holy, catholic, and apostolic Church. We confess [I confess] one baptism for the remission of sins. And we look for [I look for] the resurrection of the dead and the life of the world to come. Amen.

Catechism of the Catholic Church

Technically speaking, a catechism is a manual of doctrine, written out in the form of questions and answers, that is used for a fixed and stable scheme of instruction. And certainly, at the level of the dioceses or parishes, when used for the education of children or converts, it is just that. But the Catechisms meant for popular use are local versions of an official Catechism written with the genuine authority of the Holy See in Rome. This Catechism is intended for the particular edification of bishops.

In 1997, Pope John Paul II explained his revised Catholic Catechism this way: "A totally reliable way to present, with renewed fervor, each and every part of the Christian message to the people of our time" (from Catechism of the Catholic Church, United States Conference of Catholic Bishops).

Historical Background

Catechism literally means "instruction by word of mouth." Its system of instruction through question and answer is a long and well-established tradition that dates back to Socrates. The Gospels show how Jesus Christ frequently used questions and answers as part of his method of teaching.

The first official Catechism is known as the *Roman Catechism*. It was formulated in 1566 at the Council of Trent, the council that convened in response to the Protestant Reformation crisis, and was issued by St. Pius V. The Roman Catechism was intended for the use of priests.

A new work was issued after Vatican I in 1870. Later still, in 1962, the Vatican II Council led by Pope John XXIII called for a spirit of renewal and opened a long-scale project that took a new approach to the Catechism. That work was completed in 1977 and was issued under the aegis of Pope John Paul II.

The Catechism Today

The prologue of the new Catechism of the Catholic Church opens with a note of joy: "God, infinitely perfect and blessed in himself, in a plan of sheer goodness freely created man to make him share in his own blessed life." It is from this basic tenet that the Catholic belief system and its instruction follow.

FACT

A number of Catechisms intended for the laity have been published in many countries over the intervening years. Significant are the three versions by Peter Canisius in the 1550s, translated and published all over Europe. Pope St. Pius X produced a simple, brief Catechism for the layman in the early 1900s.

As the Catholic Church is built on tradition, the material is structured in four sections, similar to the Catechism of Pius V, as follows:

1. The profession of faith (including the Nicene Creed)
2. The celebration of the Christian mystery (including the liturgy and sacraments)
3. Life in Christ (the Catholic way to live, including the Ten Commandments)
4. Christian prayer (the importance, relevance, and holiness of prayer)

Within these sections, the material is presented in a way that responds to the questions of the time. Every element of Catholic life and beliefs, from apostolic succession to points of moral ambiguity, is addressed in a perfect, elegant system of the Catechism.

Beliefs That Infuse Daily Catholic Life

The Catholic Church teaches that "the dignity of the human person is rooted in his creation in the image and likeness of God" (from the Catechism of the Catholic Church, 1997). Catholics therefore wish to live a life that is worthy of this honor—a moral life, a life of dignity. God gave us the Ten Commandments through Moses, and they remain a sound basis for a good Catholic life. They are incorporated into the Catholic Catechism, which expounds on their virtue. Moreover, Christ gave us through his followers both moral examples and commandments to achieve that ideal life.

The Practice of Charity

Charity is that virtue that disposes us to love God above all else and to include our neighbors as part of that love. It knits us into our community and is meritorious of eternal life. The Church teaches that if a parishioner helps a person in need, the act actually achieves a supernatural state (according to Jesus' pronouncement that each good deed done for the benefit of another person is also done for Christ). That is because the friend or neighbor or homeless person you helped is considered a child of God.

Another way of saying this is what the Church calls the "vocation to beatitude," which is a duty of each Catholic person. (Vocation is a "call" and Catholics are called to help others.) The Catechism explains that the beatitudes portray Christ's charity (see Chapter 2). Beautiful and paradoxical, the beatitudes are precepts meant to comfort believers and inspire them to practice the charity for the meek, the poor, the hungry, and disenfranchised, that Christ spoke for so eloquently in his Sermon on the Mount.

The word *beatitude* actually means "supreme happiness." It is not easy to be happy, especially in these modern, materialist times that place such great stress on our family lives. But Christ wanted his followers to achieve happiness. He insisted on it. The beatitudes are his guidelines to help us achieve it.

The Catholic Catechism teaches that "the love of our Lord must always be made accessible, so that anyone can see that all the works of perfect Christian virtue spring from love and have no other objective than to arrive at love." To that end, the monastic orders have been instrumental since the Middle Ages in helping to educate the poor, feed the hungry, comfort the sick, and aid those suffering from injustice.

The modern Catholic Church has hundreds of agencies and associations, founded by activist priests or the Christian laity, that address specific needs or minister to particular groups, either at home or elsewhere in the world. And, of course, Catholics are encouraged to behave with charitable feelings toward those around them.

The Ten Commandments

The Ten Commandments, also known as the Decalogue, have great significance in the Catholic Church. The first three commandments are those God gave for appropriate worship of him. The next seven attest to the behavior of a good Catholic toward his or her neighbors. The basic obligations of religion and morality are as follows.

1. I am the Lord your God. You shall not have strange gods before me.
2. You shall not take the name of the Lord in vain. [Oaths, perjury, and blasphemy are forbidden.]
3. Keep the Sabbath holy. [The Church interprets this commandment to mean that attendance at Mass on Sunday is expected, and that on this day a good Catholic should not turn his or her mind to other distractions, like work. The Sabbath is a day of worship.]
4. Honor your father and your mother.
5. You shall not kill.
6. You shall not commit adultery.
7. You shall not steal.
8. You shall not bear false witness against your neighbor.
9. You shall not covet your neighbor's wife.
10. You shall not covet your neighbor's goods.

The Catholic Church teaches that sinful humanity needed the revelation of these commandments to help them acquire a moral life and, by proper observance, to achieve a state of grace. The Catechism of the Catholic Church states that the commandments "express man's fundamental duties."

Proclaiming the Scriptures

The Scriptures—including both the Old and the New Testament—should be an integral component of each Catholic's daily life. Although in the past the Catholic laity was discouraged from reading the Bible, the importance of studying the Holy Book both in church and at home has been emphasized ever since Vatican II.

In the past, the Church worried that evil might come from the laity studying the Scriptures because they would be in danger of misinterpreting biblical passages, and they decreed that scripture may be interpreted by those ordained in the Church. Today, however, reading and understanding the Bible does not seem the daunting task it may once have been. In fact, the Church has recently noted growing enthusiasm and interest in the Bible among the Catholic laity, who form study groups and gather informally to read and discuss the Scriptures.

FACT

Vatican II pronounced: "Through the reading and study of the sacred books 'the word of the Lord may speed forward and be glorified' (2 Thessalonians 3:1), and the treasure of revelation, entrusted to the Church, may more and more fill the hearts of men."

The Power of Prayer

The Catholic Church deeply believes in the power of prayer to establish and uphold a very powerful spiritual relationship between God and man in Christ. Some Catholics call it "keeping company with God." The Catholic Catechism refers to it as a covenant relationship. As with everything else in the Church, the wellspring for this prayer is Christ made man, which is the Creator's ultimate act of love.

The revelation, or call to prayer, occurs first in the Old Testament and then is fortified in the New Testament. What's more, the style and mood of prayer changes from the Old Testament to the New Testament. The Old Testament is full of prayers of lamentation. In the New Testament, there are many prayers of petition and hope in the risen Christ.

Catholics try to achieve a perfect state of prayer. Some of the elements of a perfect state of prayer are devotion (or deep belief), concentration, acknowledgment of dependence on God, a sense of gratitude to the Almighty, and attitudes of worship and praise. The example set before them is what the Church calls Jesus' "filial prayer"—his state of prayer when addressing his Father as well as the example of his life and sacrifice. The Church says that filial prayer, which is characterized by solitude, is the perfect model of prayer in the New Testament.

At the core, the prayers of the Catholic Church include the following:

- Our Father
- Hail Mary
- Glory Be
- Apostles' Creed
- Stations of the Cross
- The Rosary (a cycle of seven prayers)

Our Father

The Our Father is the fundamental prayer of the Catholic Church. It is considered a summary of the Gospels and was taught to the apostles by Jesus. It is said during every Mass. This prayer, along with the Hail Mary, is the most common prayer said by Catholics, among the thousands of other prayers available to them.

Our Father

Our Father who art in Heaven,
hallowed be thy name.
Thy kingdom come.
Thy will be done on earth, as it is in Heaven.
Give us this day our daily bread,
and forgive us our trespasses,
as we forgive those who trespass against us,
and lead us not into temptation,
but deliver us from evil.
For the kingdom, the power, and the glory are yours,
    now and forever.

The Church teaches that besides vocal prayer, there is contemplative prayer. Contemplative prayer is silence. In this type of prayer, the Catholic opens his or her mind to God. The Catechism of the Catholic Church says this: "The Father speaks to us his incarnate Word, who suffered, died, and rose; in this silence the Spirit of adoption enables us to share in the prayer of Jesus."

Practices Left by the Wayside

While the basic core of beliefs has not changed since Revelation (the Word of God delivered by Jesus Christ), some Catholic practices have. Within the tradition of the Church, some customs have been left behind, such as the practice of weekly confession. This is only natural, as the Catholic Church has adapted to the needs of its membership at different times.

Practicing Abstinence from Food

Traditionally, Catholics practiced various types of abstinence from food as a penance for sins, and therefore a kind of cleansing, particularly before holy days, but these customs have changed over the years.

One form of abstinence involved having only one full meal per day. Another prescribed the avoidance of meat or meat-based products and flavorings. This practice was reserved for Fridays, in recognition of Good Friday, when Jesus died on the cross, and explains why Catholics always ate fish on Fridays. However, it is no longer necessary to abstain from meat on Fridays, although believers may do other forms of penance to commemorate Christ's suffering. In the United States, Catholics still avoid meat on the Fridays during Lent as well as on Ash Wednesday.

At one time, Catholics were required to fast prior to partaking of the Holy Communion (usually from midnight to the following morning, until the Sunday Mass). These fasts are no longer required. Catholics usually abstain from eating one hour prior to communion.

A Place Called Limbo

Limbo is a place and a concept that served to allay the fears of parents whose children died before they could be baptized. In the past, Catholics believed that the souls of those who were not baptized could not get access into Heaven and that they therefore ended up in Hell. Catholic parents rushed their babies to the church for Baptism shortly after birth, but some babies still died without receiving Baptism.

Catholics could not accept the idea that God would let innocent babies go to the fires of Hell only because they did not have an opportunity to receive Baptism, and so, they reasoned, babies must go to another place—Limbo (from the Latin for "border").

No one is really sure where the concept of Limbo came from, but for a long time Catholics were taught about this place—not quite Heaven or Hell, but a third possible eternal location. For a while, theologians discussed whether the infants experienced any kind of pain, but this idea only lasted until the thirteenth century. Catholics then settled on the idea that Limbo is a place where the infant souls dwell in natural bliss, if not exactly the true joy of being in the presence of the Lord. However, Church canon law does not include any mention of Limbo, and so eventually this idea was rejected. The new Catechism of the Catholic Church does not mention it, and the Church has no official position on the concept of any such place or state.

FACT

A heretical group named Jansenists once pronounced that unbaptized infants were condemned to burn in Hell. Pope Pius VI condemned this idea with horror in 1794. He taught that a Catholic should think of Limbo as a "middle state."

Changes in the Mass

One of the most sweeping changes in the Catholic Church, and therefore one not without controversy, has to do with the rituals around the Mass. The changes in conducting Mass were promulgated by Pope Paul VI after Vatican II. The most significant change was that vernacular (that is, the native language of the congregation) was allowed to be used in the conductance of the Mass. When reciting the Nicene Creed and other prayers, the congregation's native tongue ensures their full understanding and that they are able to relate to what they are saying. Although Latin was dropped from most parts of the service, it has not been discarded completely. It remains one of the unifying features of the Church.

Other changes included moving the altar so that it now faces the congregation; decreasing the number of prayers said during Mass; and encouraging parishioners to join in the singing (rather than listening to a choir).

Veneration of the Saints

Veneration of the saints has long been an issue both within and outside the Catholic Church. In the days of the early Church, holy men and women who were martyred for their faith gained the respect and veneration of the other Christians. Gradually, this practice threatened to become idolatry, and many ecclesiasts warned that excessive veneration of saints detracted from worship of the Lord.

By the time of the Council of Trent, the Church decided that prayer to saints is acceptable as long as the faithful ask the saints to intercede with God on their behalf and understand that saints do not have divine powers. Furthermore, the Church saw the saints as shining examples of sanctity for the faithful to observe and emulate.

There are thousands of saints, and little is known about many of them. It wasn't until 1171 that the Catholic Church made official the process of canonization of saints and decreed that only the Holy See had the right to determine this sainthood.

In the 1960s, Pope Paul VI undertook a reassessment of saints as part of Vatican II. This reassessment has been broadly misunderstood. It is incorrectly believed by many laypersons that he decanonized saints, including the popular St. Christopher.

What Paul did was to review the saints' feast days, which he felt were crowding the ecclesiastical calendar at the expense of feast days devoted to worship of the Lord. He wanted Catholics to properly refocus their attention and decided that since the Church is universal, the Church should celebrate only universally important saints with official feast days. In 1969, the pope reordered the ecclesiastical calendar, in which fifty-eight obligatory and ninety-two optional saint's days were included, in addition to the more significant figures of Christ and his contemporaries. St. Christopher's feast day was one of the days dropped from the calendar.

Chapter 10

Devotional Practices

Catholicism is a sacramental religion that is enriched by many rites and practices: visits to sanctuaries, participation in religious processions, immersion in holy water, various postures such as genuflection, special prayers, and veneration of statues. Understanding the outward signs of devotion that Catholics perform is crucial to understanding the internal devotion and piety of the people who practice the Catholic faith.

Outward Signs of Devotion

In the Catholic worldview, God is revealed in all things, even in words, objects, and places. These are known as sacramentals, which are not to be confused with sacraments. Sacramentals are instituted by the Church; the sacraments are instituted by Christ.

The sacramentals provide grace that encourages Catholics to do good works, help diminish any venial sins they may have committed, and generally protect the soul. When Catholics practice "popular devotions," they are expressing ardor for God. These external practices of piety are often devised by the faithful, but in accordance with Church thinking. According to the ruling of Vatican II, "Devotions should be so drawn up that they harmonize with the liturgical seasons, accord with the sacred liturgy, are in some fashion derived from it and lead the people to it, since the liturgy by its very nature far surpasses any of them" (from *Sacrosanctum Concilium*—Constitution on the Sacred Liturgy—Article 13).

The Holy See (that is, the high Church office in Rome) does not allow devotional extravagances to get out of hand. Every once in a while, it issues a ruling that prohibits a practice it finds objectionable.

The Power of Blessings

Catholics believe in the power of a blessing, which may be in a form of a prayer that celebrates God, a request for spiritual guidance, or a wish that only goodness follow the person or thing being blessed. The Old Testament is full of examples of God blessing people and objects, from Noah and his sons to the children of Israel.

The Church gives priests the authority to confer blessings on children, parents, and religious objects, and they may also give general blessings during Mass. Bishops are given the privilege of blessing churches and cemeteries as well as blessing the men who receive the sacrament of Holy Orders in preparation for priesthood. Blessings made by laypeople carry a personal wish and do not have a liturgical component.

There are private blessings as well, and they are made in Catholic homes. For example, children say prayers before bed, and parents bless them and pray with them. Private prayers include requests for God's blessings for his continued presence in our lives. Catholics also ask for blessings from God in the form of grace before meals, so that they may eat and enjoy their food.

FACT

The Blessing of Throats is done once a year on the feast of St. Blaise (February 3). St. Blaise was a physician before he was martyred. According to popular belief, he is the patron saint for the sick and, in particular, healer of throat illnesses. The Blessing of Throats is performed by blessing the throat with two crossed candles.

Ceremonies and Practices

There are dozens of individual prayers for every occasion and for every detailed expression of faith and belief. But a few special types of prayers are highly devotional and symbolic in nature. These prayers are so elaborate that you may think of them as religious ceremonies or rites.

Stations of the Cross

The Stations of the Cross is a veneration that originates from the story of the Crucifixion. The Gospels recount how Jesus Christ was sentenced by Pontius Pilate and taken to Golgotha, where he was put on the cross, and how he died. His journey, also known as Via Dolorosa, is broken down into fourteen stations, and each one has a symbolic role that helps the faithful contemplate the Crucifixion and, in a way, experience it so that they may be forgiven for their sins. The stations commemorate the following events:

1. Jesus receives his sentence—death by crucifixion.
2. The soldiers hand him the wooden cross, which he must carry.
3. Jesus falls (for the first time) while carrying his cross.

4. On his way, Jesus encounters the Virgin Mary.
5. Simon of Cyrene carries the cross for Jesus.
6. Veronica gives Jesus her veil so that he may wipe his face.
7. Jesus falls again.
8. Jesus encounters the women of Jerusalem, who weep for him.
9. Jesus falls for the third time.
10. The soldiers strip Jesus' garments.
11. Jesus is nailed to the cross.
12. Jesus dies on the cross.
13. The soldiers take Jesus' body off the cross.
14. Jesus' body is laid in the tomb.

It has become customary for Catholic churches to set up the Stations of the Cross, each one represented by a picture or plaque placed around the inside walls, so that if you go up through the outside aisle and down the other, you can visit all of the stations while saying the attendant prayers.

The practice of following the Stations of the Cross started during the Crusades, when pilgrims to the Holy Land visited Jerusalem and followed the Via Dolorosa to the Church of the Holy Sepulcher (the site of the tomb where Jesus was buried and where he rose from the dead). It wasn't until the eighteenth century that Stations of the Cross were introduced inside churches.

Novenas

Novenas are prayers, either private or public, that may have a sense of urgency because of the specific intention of the prayer—to pray for someone who is very sick or in trouble of some kind. In a novena, prayers are said for nine consecutive days to obtain special favors or to make a special petition. The nine-day cycle of the novena symbolizes the time between Christ's Ascension into Heaven and the coming of the Holy Spirit. During those nine days, Mary and the apostles devoted their time to prayer, waiting for divine guidance and inspiration.

Though novenas don't have an official place in the liturgy of the Church, they are very popular. The faithful can use any prayer—the Rosary or particular prayers to one of the saints. The choice of saint usually depends on the specific request. For example, you might pray to St. Peregrine, the patron of cancer patients, for special intervention for a loved one suffering from that illness or to St. Jude for desperate situations and hopeless cases, which could be anything from a runaway teenager to an out-of-work husband to a family member suffering from a mental disease.

One popular novena is the Divine Mercy Novena, handed on to us from a Polish saint, Faustina Kowalska, who died in 1938. She was canonized in 2000 because, during her life, she helped convey new forms of devotion to divine mercy.

The Rosary

The Rosary is a set of prayers and meditations that Catholics recite to express their devotion to Mary, mother of Jesus. The word *Rosary* itself means "crown of roses" because according to tradition, each Hail Mary prayer is a rose and each Rosary is like a crown of roses that the person reciting the Rosary presents to Mary.

The Rosary consists of two main sections. The first is made up of a crucifix followed by one large bead, three small beads, and another large bead. These are attached to the chaplet, a loop made up of five decades (groups of ten small beads), where each decade is separated by a large bead. Each small bead represents a Hail Mary, and each large bead represents one of several other prayers: an Our Father, Apostles' Creed, Salve Regina (Hail Holy Queen), or Fatima.

Catholics usually recite five decades while reflecting on one set of mysteries, then go around for the next set of mysteries, and then a third. The three sets of mysteries cover key moments in the New Testament, as follows:

1. The Joyful Mysteries are the Annunciation, the Visitation, the Nativity, the Presentation of Jesus in the Temple, and Jesus found in the Temple.
2. The Sorrowful Mysteries are the Agony in the Garden of Gethsemane, Scourging, Crowning with Thorns, Carrying of the Cross, and the Crucifixion.

3. The Glorious Mysteries are the Resurrection, Ascension, the Holy Spirit revealing itself, Mary taken into Heaven, and Mary crowned Queen of Heaven.
4. The Light Mysteries, which have been added by John Paul II, are Baptism of Jesus, Wedding Feast at Cana, Proclamation of the Coming of the Kingdom of God, the Transfiguration, and the Institution of the Eucharist.

It is said that St. Dominic, who lived in the thirteenth century, preached the importance of saying the Rosary daily because he believed it would protect Catholics from evil and sin. Originally, the faithful recounted 150 psalms, but because many of the faithful were illiterate and could not memorize all of them, they said 150 Our Fathers instead. Still later, the sequence of Our Fathers was replaced with Hail Marys.

Sacramentals Inside the Church

Many devotional practices center on the Mass services, which are held inside the church, and several of the objects that enhance these services are considered sacramentals. Understanding the role these objects play in the Church helps bring a greater understanding of the services themselves and what they mean to those who practice them.

The Altar

The altar is the centerpiece of Catholic worship. It consists of a raised, tabular surface, on which the celebration of the Eucharist is performed during a Catholic Mass. Catholic laity may have small private altars at home to be used for prayer, but the sacrifice of the Mass cannot be performed there. Church altars must be consecrated.

The altar has a number of physical attributes, but the essential one is the tabernacle (from the Latin word for "tent"). Simply put, this is where the consecrated communion bread is kept. Because of the holiness of what they contain—the Body of Christ—tabernacles are kept locked. Larger basilicas and cathedrals also have high altars, which are additional altars that are placed higher in the sanctuary.

Holy Water

Holy water is an important sacramental that dates back to A.D. 400. Priests bless water to make it holy; in turn, the holy water may be used for blessings, to remove venial sins, and to purify worshipers in the presence of the Lord. That is why it is always found in a fount at the entrance to churches, (except during Lent in some places). When parishioners enter the church, they dip a finger in the water and make the sign of the cross over their person.

The most important use of holy water is in the sacrament of Baptism. When a baby is baptized, a little holy water is sprinkled over its forehead to symbolize the washing away of original sin; the same applies during the Baptism of adult converts.

FACT

If you have ever been inside a Catholic church, you may have noticed the initials IHS inscribed on the priest's vestments or on prayer books. The monogram IHS is made up of the first three Greek letters in Jesus' name—anglicized—and it was adopted as a code during the Roman persecution. Later, it was adopted into Latin usage in the Church.

Candles and Incense

Candles and incense are both used in Catholic churches to set the somber, mystical mood appropriate for prayer and spirituality. Christian churches have burned incense since ancient times. The deep pungent smell lends an aura of solemnity to church services. The smoke drifting toward Heaven is a symbol of the direction of prayer toward God. Incense is most often used at grave occasions such as funerals and processions.

The Church also relies on candles, an important and comforting part of the Catholic's surroundings while at prayer, meditation, listening to the priest, or lost in the splendor and beauty of the building. Candles were commonly used in pagan rituals, but from very early in the history of the Catholic Church, candles have also been a part of the ceremony and celebration of Christ. The candle is an outward and visible sign that reading the Gospel brings joy to the church.

Many Catholic ceremonies involve the use of candles—indeed, the rites of all but one sacrament (Penance) require them. It is forbidden to say the Mass without the presence of burning candles. The "tabernacle light" kept lit before the presence of Christ is in honor of his being among us at Mass. It is a tradition that began in the 1200s and was made Church law in the 1600s.

Churches make use of many different candles. There are altar candles, which must be made of beeswax and should be white (in the ancient world, it was believed that bees were virginal, and using their wax would reflect the attributes of the Blessed Virgin Mary). The color of the candles changes to yellow during Holy Week.

Small votive candles are placed in front of statues of saints. These small candles provide powerful symbols of prayer. To pray for a favor or to be remembered to Mary or Jesus, parishioners pay a small token to light one of these candles and place it before the saint being petitioned.

Church Bells

The tolling of bells has long been associated with churches and church service—think of the great bell towers the world over. On Sunday mornings, you can hear church bells ringing in churches, inviting people to join the congregation for Sunday Mass.

It seems that the Catholic Church adopted bells as an essential part of church services sometime during the eighth century. Churches use bells in a number of ways. The great bells in the tower are used to announce the hour of church services. In addition, a smaller bell placed on the epistle side of the altar is rung at the Sanctus, during a High Mass, to signal the adoration of the consecration of the bread and wine.

Confessionals

Although confessionals are now an integral part of church furnishings, they weren't introduced until 1565. In the early days of the Church, the sacrament of Penance—asking for absolution for sins committed—was a public ritual reserved for very serious sins, such as murder, where the sinner made a public apology and received a heavy penance.

Because these confessions were public, not many people stepped forward to confess voluntarily. In the Middle Ages, Irish monks instituted the idea of private confession, between a priest and the confessor, which usually took place before the altar. Later, this idea spread through the rest of the Church. In 1565, St. Carlo Borromeo, a powerful cardinal, designed a box that held a chair to provide anonymity for the confessor. By the 1600s, the Church had mandated that all confessions be heard this way.

Today, the private confession always takes place in a confessional box. This is usually a wooden structure with a compartment for the priest and two additional compartments on either side for the confessors (so the priest can listen to one confession while the other confessor is getting ready). The compartment opening is covered with a heavy curtain, which makes it fairly dark inside. The confessor kneels, facing the priest. There is a sliding partition with latticework—called a grille—so the confessor can glimpse the priest, if not see him wholly.

Physical Acts of Devotion

Physical actions or changes in posture can become sacramental as well. In prayer, Catholics have incorporated several such postures in order to display their devotion and respect. These actions or postures include the following:

- **Genuflection.** The bending of the knee before sitting in the church pew is known as genuflecting, a sign of acknowledgment and grace to God.
- **Kneeling.** A common position while praying, it is seen as an expression of penance, esteem, and humility in relation to God. Kneeling is the traditional position of prayer, confession, and receiving communion.
- **Prostration.** Only intense forms of prayer require this position, which expresses adoration as well as penance.

In the fifth century, a priest and his confessors would prostrate themselves before the altar as part of the ritual of confession. According to the Gospels, Jesus himself prayed this way on the night before he was crucified.

Sign of the Cross

By far the most well known gesture of Catholic devotion is the sign of the cross. This personal sign of respect and devotion began in the Middle Ages. To make the sign of the cross, you begin by touching your forehead, moving your hand down to the breast, and then across to the left and then right shoulder. While making the sign of the cross, you recite the names of the persons of the Trinity: "In the name of the Father, the Son, and the Holy Ghost."

Catholics begin prayers with the sign of the cross; priests who officiate at Mass make the sign of the cross before and during the ceremony. Other occasions for using the sign of the cross include the following:

- Bishops and priests make the sign of the cross in the air when they make blessings.
- The bread and wine of the Eucharist are blessed by the sign of the cross, an act that is part of the Liturgy of the Sacrament.
- The sign of the cross is used during baptism of children. The priest makes a cross with his thumb on the child's forehead, then the mouth, and then the breast.

Religious Objects and Artifacts

Symbols of Christ's suffering, representations of the Blessed Virgin, and other religiously significant medals, pictures, and statues comprise another type of sacramental, which has a special place in both the church and the home. It's important to understand that Catholics do not worship these items but rather use them as a reminder of Christ, Mary, and the saints.

The Crucifix

The crucifix, one of the universal symbols of Catholicism, venerates Jesus' suffering on the cross. The plain cross—two pieces of wood, a smaller length set about the third of the way down on a longer length at right angles—did not appear until the fourth century, at the end of the persecutions.

The crucifix, which is a cross with the body of Christ figured on it, did not appear until the fifth century. It was frequently decorated with jewels during the fifth and sixth centuries, a highly glorified symbol. Nowadays it is usually much plainer and simpler, and it can be fashioned from any type of wood or metal. The crucifix is a symbol of hope and power. It is worn by many as a symbol of belief in their religion and a sign of rejoicing in their spirituality. You can also find crucifixes in Catholic homes and—of course—at any Catholic church.

Other Images and Statues

Catholics show their devotion not only through the crucifix. Images and statues honor Mary, the Mother of Jesus, as well as many saints. Usually, each saint is represented by a specific characteristic or symbol. Statues of St. Peter show him holding keys, to represent his authority as the first Bishop of Rome. Mary is frequently pictured as the Madonna, given her religious significance as the Mother of Christ.

Saintly Relics

Another way of venerating the saints is through relics. The word *relic* comes from the Latin *reliquiae,* "remains." Relics are material objects left behind after a holy person has passed away. They include personal possessions, such as clothing, or even actual human body parts of a departed saint. These objects have a purpose similar to that of other religious symbols, to help the faithful recall their union with the saints and to inspire them to lead lives of prayer and service.

ALERT!

In earlier times, a relic of a patron saint might actually be embedded in the altar of a particular parish. Now they are usually kept in holy places or in very special churches in the Holy Land, in Rome, and in other centers of early Christianity.

Scapulars: In Veneration of Mary

Catholics wear scapulars to show how devoted the wearer is to Mary, the Mother of God. The scapular is made of two pieces of brown cord made from woolen cloth and has pictures of Mary at either end of the cord. The bands rest on the shoulder and the pictures are laid on the breast and the back at an equal distance from the shoulder.

Here is where the practice of wearing scapulars came from. In the thirteenth century, St. Simon Stock saw an apparition of Mary, who told him that all who wore the scapular would be saved from Hell, for on the Saturday after their deaths she would take them to Heaven.

Holy Cards

Holy cards are not intrinsically holy objects, but once a priest blesses a holy card, it becomes efficacious. Holy cards are meant to be inspirational. They are often given out to commemorate someone who has died, participation in an event, or a pilgrimage. They may also be handed round as small gifts to mark religious occasions, for instance, during Baptism, First Communion, or Confirmation. A holy card may feature a picture of a saint on one side and a prayer on another; some holy cards include inspirational quotes or the Ten Commandments. Ⓔ

Chapter 11

The Catholic Liturgy

Liturgy incorporates the formalized expressions, or rites, of public worship in many religions, and Catholicism has certainly developed its own liturgical ensemble. The Catholic Church teaches that those who participate in the liturgy are sanctified through it. The word *liturgy* descends from a Greek word that means "public duty," because liturgies are always conducted in a public setting.

The Development of the Liturgy

The liturgy arrives to us in its present form after development over 2,000 years. During the early days of the Church, the rites were not harmonized in any standard format. They were a fluid group of elements, often practiced with different customs according to local preference. It wasn't until the Council of Nicaea in 325 that the liturgy of worship started taking on a formalized order and shape.

Since then, the rites and customs of public worship have been fine-tuned, adapting to the changes of history and the modifications in Church canon law. The two councils that were especially significant in implementing official shifts in emphasis were the Council of Trent and the Second Vatican Council, commonly known at Vatican II.

The Council of Trent ruled that Christ is *actually* present in the sacrifice and celebration of the Eucharist. Furthermore, the council's decisions led to the publication of a missal that standardized the prayers and rites of the Mass.

FACT

The great blossoming of musical liturgy in the Catholic Church is attributed to Pope Gregory I (540–604). Under his leadership, monks developed the printing and use of sheet music and began a tradition known as Gregorian chants. Another of Pope Gregory's achievements was the implementation of a system of music covering the liturgies of the feast days.

Notable changes to the liturgy made by the Vatican II included introduction of the vernacular during the service of the Mass (although Latin still plays a major role in the liturgy). The Holy See also redirected emphasis to interior worship, reminding Catholics that they must celebrate Mass in a "right form of mind." This ruling was made in reaction to a misconception that observing the rituals is enough to get salvation. The Church wanted to impress on the faithful that they needed to pair observance of the rituals with interior prayer to achieve a state of grace.

Within Catholicism, the Mass, or Eucharistic celebration, is the central liturgical service. But because of the sacramental nature of Catholicism, Catholics can worship through all things. So, for instance, the administration of the sacraments is also considered a great part of the liturgy of Catholicism, as are other formalized rituals, such as the Liturgy of Hours.

In addition, the liturgy of the Church is attuned to the year, or seasons, as they pertain to Christ's life. Indeed, each day holds a special significance in the Church, although there are certain high points that take place in the course of a year. The most important is the Easter cycle, but a number of solemnities, feasts, and memorials also have special significance.

Structure of the Catholic Mass

The Mass incorporates the profession of faith (through the recitation of the Creed), reading of Scripture, and the sacrament of the Eucharist. The liturgy of Mass begins with the Last Supper; the Passion, Death, and Resurrection of Christ form its nucleus. The Mass is both a banquet and a memoriam of the Crucifixion.

The liturgy of Mass includes High Mass and Low Mass. The High Mass, which is much more intricate, is reserved for special feast days and is usually performed by a bishop or another venerated ecclesiast. It also requires the assistance of a deacon and the presence of a choir. A priest, attended by an altar server, generally performs the Low Mass, which is held daily. Sunday Mass, of course, has special significance, and the Church requires attendance of its members on this day.

Introductory Rites

The Mass begins with greeting rites that prepare the assembly—as a community—to hear the Word of God and celebrate the Eucharistic sacrifice. First, the congregation does the entrance antiphon by singing (or chanting) a few lines from a psalm. There is a greeting period, which is followed by a penitential rite (a rite of blessing and sprinkling). Then, the congregation recites Gloria (Glory to God) and the opening prayer.

Liturgy of the Word

The introductory rites are followed by the Liturgy of the Word, which is the first major part of the Mass. The purpose of this section of the Mass is to proclaim God's Word to the assembly, as it is understood from Scripture. Here the Word of God is spoken, responded to, explained, embraced, and appealed to.

The First Reading is almost always taken from the Old Testament. The congregation follows the reading with a Responsorial Psalm. (In a way, the congregation is "speaking" in response to God.) The Second Reading is an encouragement, taken from one of the epistles of the New Testament. At the Gospel Acclamation, the Alleluia, all members rise. The Gospel is the central reading of this part of the Mass.

When going to Mass, it is important to note that the liturgical calendar, in Sunday worship, follows a cycle that changes over a three-year period: Matthew is the primary Gospel in the first year, followed by Mark the following year and Luke the third year.

The priest then gives his homily, a short speech drawing relevance from the Gospel to daily life. There is a moment of silence, then the recitation of the Nicene or Apostles' Creed. The congregation recites the Prayer of the Faithful, a common prayer in which calls for special intercessions may be made, as appropriate.

Liturgy of the Eucharist

The second major part of the Mass reflects Christ's actions at the Last Supper and fulfills his request to eat bread and drink wine as his body and blood in memory of his life, death, and resurrection.

At this point, the priest will spend a few minutes going about the Preparation and Offering of the Gifts. There is an Offertory song, a kind of brief anthem, and Preparation of the Altar, the bread, and the wine. This includes folding of special cloths to catch any fragments or drops of the bread and wine once it is consecrated, mixing a little water with the wine, and getting the communion wafers, or "hosts," ready for the assembly.

The priest washes his hands in a ritual suggesting purification and invites the assembly to prayer. As he turns back to the Gifts, the faithful say one brief prayer, and then what Catholics consider the awe-inspiring moment takes place. The Eucharistic Prayer, a prayer of thanksgiving, is spoken.

The Eucharistic Prayer consists of these elements: an introductory "Dialogue," Preface (Lord Be With You), Sanctus, Thanksgiving, Acclamation, "Epiclesis" (when the priest asks God to consecrate the host and wine), the Narrative Institution (the actual formal moment of consecration), the Anamnesis (that Christ comes to us through the Apostles), the Offering (Jesus offered to his Father), Petitions or Intercessions for the people, Doxology (or the Gloria in Excelsis: the angels' song at the birth of Our Lord), Memorial Acclamation, and Great Amen. This is the high point of the Mass. The gifts of bread and wine become the Body and Blood of Christ in what is known as transubstantiation.

The Mass now turns to the Communion Rite itself, which begins with the Our Father, also known as the Lord's Prayer. The members of the assembly turn to each other to give the Rite of Peace, a sign they are one with each other and that the Holy Spirit unites them.

FACT

The Kiss of Peace descended from the apostles, but at one time it was dropped from the liturgy. Vatican II reinstated it in the 1960s. Now called the Rite or even the Sign of Peace, it is not literally a kiss anymore. Parishioners usually shake hands with those next to them, saying "Peace be with you."

In the Fraction Rite, the priest "breaks" the bread (no longer an actual loaf of bread). The assembly says a prayer called the Agnus Dei (Lamb of God). The priest says a private prayer to prepare himself, and then he shows the host to the assembled and they humble themselves with a small prayer that begins, "Lord, I am not worthy . . . ." Everyone moves in procession to the sanctuary at the front of the church to receive communion. The Liturgy of the Eucharist ends with a prayer after communion. Once the Mass is concluded, the priest blesses the congregation before they are dismissed.

Objects Used to Celebrate Mass

All solemn occasions are given more drama through the use of beautiful objects in ritual. This is true for the Mass as well. The wellspring of Catholic religion is the celebration of Christ's sacrifice on the cross; therefore, the sacred objects are of special value.

First among sacred vessels, the chalice is the large cup that holds the wine that becomes the blood of Christ during the Eucharistic ceremony. The chalice must be made of either gold or silver. If it is silver, the bowl is gilded on the inside. A bishop must consecrate a chalice before it is used; only priests and deacons are permitted to hold it.

The chalice has a long, rich history in the Church. Beautiful artifacts from the Middle Ages still exist, so that we can see the development of this wide-based, sometimes double-handled vessel, sumptuously decorated, to its present-day form. The chalice has adjuncts (additional components) that are called the pall, the purificator, the corporal, the burse, and the chalice veil. The adjuncts perform the following functions:

- **Pall:** A stiff, square piece of white linen that is placed over the chalice. The pall also requires a special blessing.
- **Purificator:** A white linen cloth resembling a napkin, used to wipe and dry the chalice, or the priest's lips, after the ablutions.
- **Corporal:** A white linen cloth, smaller than the breadth of the altar, where the priest places the Sacred Host and the chalice during Mass.
- **Burse:** A cover to keep the corporal from getting dirty; it has only been used since the sixteenth century.
- **Veil:** The veil issued to cover the chalice and paten when they are brought to the altar.

ALERT!

The use of linen is symbolic. It represents cloth "sprung from the earth, as the Body of our Lord Jesus Christ was buried in a clean linen shroud" (attributed to Pope Sylvester).

Other objects used during Mass are the paten, ciborium, decanter, and communion cups, as follows:

- The paten is a shallow, saucer-shaped disk used to hold the bread that becomes the body of Christ. Just as the chalice, the paten must be made of precious metal. In the earliest days of the Church, patens weighed as much as twenty-five pounds; today, they tend to be smaller, weighing only about a pound.
- The ciborium is a sacred cup-like vessel that holds the hosts once they have been consecrated. The ciborium is used to distribute Holy Communion to the faithful and is also used to keep the consecrated particles of the Blessed Sacrament in the tabernacle. Like the chalice and paten, it must be made of a precious metal and consecrated by a bishop. Its distinguishing feature from the chalice is that it is raised in the middle, so that the remaining blessed particles may be removed easily.
- The decanter, or flagon, is a vessel brought forth with the gifts at the early part of the Mass. It holds the wine that will be consecrated for the communion of the people.
- Communion cups are used infrequently, when the people receive wine at communion. These are kept nearby and brought to the altar at communion time.

Liturgy of the Hours

The Liturgy of the Hours is a liturgy of prayers for every day of the year, when prayers are assigned for particular times of each day. Priests, laypeople, and those belonging to Holy Orders are all encouraged to follow the Hours. All the prayers, hymns, psalms, and readings that comprise the Liturgy of the Hours can be found in the Breviary, which is a voluminous compendium of prayers used by the clergy.

The tradition of the Hours goes all the way back to the early days of the Church when monks and priests prayed every morning at sunrise and every evening at sundown, relying on a psalter, or Book of Psalms. The Book of Psalms forms the basis of the Liturgy of Hours. Over the years, prayers, songs, psalms, and meditations were added to the original contents of the psalter.

At first, bishops and choirs chose the psalm that seemed suitable for the occasion. Different psalms might be better suited to morning or evening prayer, or to particular feast days. At one time, monks tried to recite the whole 150 psalms in one day. When this turned out to be too time-consuming, the recitation was spread over a week, each day divided into hours.

Vatican II Council established that "By offering praise to God in the Hours, the Church joins in singing that canticle of praise which is sung throughout all ages in the halls of heaven."

Divine Office

In the 1960s, Vatican II revised and formalized the system of prayers, and the Liturgy of the Hours became known as "Divine Office." Now, once a year, Catholics can get a published work with the prayer structure formalized and laid out—with special psalms for particular feast and saints' days—so that all Catholics can worship in the same way.

In a single day, the Divine Office consists of Lauds and Vespers for morning; Matins, a prayer that may be recited at any point during the day; Terce, Sext, and None, prayers for midmorning, noon, and midafternoon; and Compline, which is the night prayer. In cathedrals and monasteries, Mass is celebrated after the Terce (which is said at the "third hour," or 9 A.M.).

The Liturgical Calendar

The liturgical calendar (see Appendix A) is a way of making time, an essential part of creation, sacred. This highly developed structure that encompasses the entire year did not exist in the early Church. Sunday, the day for celebration of the Eucharist, contained the essential elements of the entire year—the Passion, Death, and Resurrection—so the "paschal festival" was renewed every Sunday. On the annual anniversary, though, the day would be celebrated with great solemnity, and eventually Easter became the focal point of the liturgical year. The feast of Easter was clearly linked to that of the Pentecost, the festival celebrating the Descent of the Holy Spirit on the apostles, fifty days after Easter.

Today, some feast days are fixed while others are based on seasonal changes and moon phases. For instance, the date for Easter is linked to the spring equinox. Every year, the date changes—Easter Sunday always occurs on the Sunday after the full moon following the equinox. Christmas, however, is fixed on December 25. This means that the liturgical calendar fluctuates from year to year.

Furthermore, the Church year consists of two distinct cycles, the temporal cycle and the sanctoral cycle. The temporal cycle is a series of solemn events celebrating the mystery of Christ—Advent, Christmas, Lent, Holy Week, Easter—divided into two cycles (the Christmas cycle and the Easter cycle), plus what the Church calls ordinary time, or the remainder of the year. The sanctoral cycle includes all the saints' feast days and many of the Marian feast days.

The Christmas Cycle

The Church year begins with the Christmas cycle, which encompasses the events surrounding Jesus' birth. The Christmas cycle begins with Advent (which starts in late November) and with the baptism of the Lord (third Sunday after Christmas), which celebrates the beginning of Christ's public ministry.

Advent: A Time of Expectation

Advent is a four-week season that anticipates the upcoming birth of Christ; *advent* literally means "arrival." Advent is a season of preparation, which begins on the Sunday closest to November 30, the feast day of St. Andrew the Apostle. Advent is a season of mixed themes—of both penance and joy. The Advent wreath, with its four candles, symbolizes the end of darkness and the turning toward light in the coming of the Lord.

Christmas: A Birthday Celebration

The word *Christmas* is derived from the phrase "Mass of Christ" because the Church holds special Masses on Christmas Eve and Christmas morning. Catholics celebrate Christmas, or the Nativity of Jesus, on December 25. However, the actual date of Jesus' birthday is not known. One of the explanations for why the Church chose this particular day is that in the early days of the Church, some of the feast days were appropriated from earlier pagan celebrations. In the case of Christmas, this particular date was also chosen because it is also the time of the winter solstice.

FACT

Some theologians attribute the formation of the Nativity festival to an attempt by the Catholic Church to foster Catholic belief in the humanity of Jesus Christ and as a way to counter an early heresy called *Docetism*, which denied Jesus' human nature.

Christmas is followed by Epiphany, which is celebrated on January 6. Epiphany commemorates the arrival of the three wise men who came bearing gifts to honor the Christ Child in the manger. The Christmas cycle ends on the third Sunday after Christmas. A period of ordinary time ensues that lasts until the day after Mardi Gras, the beginning of the Easter Cycle.

The Easter Cycle

The Easter cycle comprises two periods: Lent and Easter. Lent begins on Ash Wednesday, the day after a popular Catholic festival known as the Mardi Gras (French for "fat Tuesday"), a day of carnivals and celebrations. In contrast, Ash Wednesday is a somber day. One popular custom is for parishioners to mark their foreheads with a thumbprint of ash from burned palms, reminding them of their sins. After Ash Wednesday, Lent continues for a forty-day period of fasting, abstinence, and prayer; the last day of Lent is the Thursday before Easter.

The Catholic Church used to shroud statues and other icons as a way of showing mourning during the whole somber season of Lent and to hide the glory of the triumphant Christ. Today, this practice is generally limited to the fifth Sunday of Lent.

Holy Week

The greatest of all Catholic feasts takes place during Holy Week, the center of the Church year. Holy Week begins with Palm Sunday, the day of Jesus' arrival in Jerusalem, when he rode in on a donkey and was welcomed by people waving palm branches. Despite the joy of this reception, the purpose of this day is to remember the suffering Jesus was about to endure.

In the following week, Holy Thursday, the last day of Lent, celebrates the Last Supper; it is followed by Good Friday, the anniversary of Jesus' crucifixion. On Saturday, churches hold a special Mass, and during the night Catholics hold the Easter Vigil, which anticipates Jesus' Resurrection on the following day—the glorious day of Easter Sunday.

Following Easter

Fifty days after Easter Sunday, the Church celebrates Pentecost, the day when the Holy Spirit descended to the disciples—often considered the birthday of the Church. Originally, the Feast of Ascension of Christ was also celebrated during Pentecost. By the late fourth century, its date had been moved back ten days, and it is now celebrated forty days after Easter. Pentecost completes the Easter cycle, and another period of ordinary time follows until the next Advent.

Each liturgical season has its own symbolic color: violet for Advent, white for the Christmas season, green for Epiphany, violet (again) for Lent, white and gold for Easter, and red for Pentecost. These colors appear in the vestments of the clergy and in church decorations.

Solemnities, Feasts, and Memorials

The liturgical calendar includes Sunday celebrations and holy days of obligation, which commemorate special events or persons of high reverence. The days of chief importance in this group are called solemnities. They begin with the Vespers, an evening rite of prayer, on the night before the holiday. Some of these solemnities may be part of a larger cycle, such as the Epiphany.

The solemnities for the full liturgical year include the following:

- **January 1**: Mary, Mother of God
- **January 6**: Epiphany
- **March 25**: Annunciation
- **May or June (Sunday after Pentecost)**: Holy Trinity
- **Sunday after Holy Trinity Sunday**: Corpus Christi
- **Thursday forty days after Easter (or the Sunday after it)**: Ascension
- **Friday following second Sunday after Pentecost**: Sacred Heart
- **June 24**: Birth of John the Baptist
- **June 30**: First Martyrs of the Church of Rome
- **August 15**: Assumption
- **November 1**: All Saints
- **Last Sunday in ordinary time**: Christ the King
- **December 8**: Immaculate Conception

Feast days are saints' days or days celebrating the Virgin Mary; generally, they are days of lesser significance that originally sprang from the people, not the Church itself. They are commemorated within the natural day. (We should note that some of the Marian devotions have been elevated in importance.) Memorials are less significant, and they are not obligatory. For instance, Mark the Evangelist has a feast day on April 25, while Catherine of Siena is honored with a mere memorial day on April 29.

Marian Devotions

Veneration of Mary, the Mother of God, holds a special place in the Catholic Church. Known as "hyperdulia" because of the difference in degree from other forms of veneration, it is higher than veneration of saints but lower than veneration accorded to God. Several feast days are celebrated in Mary's honor:

- **January 1**: Solemnity of Mary, Mother of God
- **May 31**: The Visitation of the Blessed Virgin Mary
- **July 1**: Immaculate Heart of Mary
- **August 15**: The Feast of the Assumption
- **August 22**: Queenship of the Blessed Virgin Mary
- **September 8**: Birth of the Blessed Virgin Mary
- **November 21**: Presentation of the Blessed Virgin Mary
- **December 8**: The Solemnity of the Immaculate Conception

Chapter 12

The Catholic Approach to Scriptures

atholics believe that one of the ways God communicates with his people is through the Bible, which is divided into the Old Testament (revealed to the Hebrews) and the New Testament (the Gospels and other Christian works). This chapter describes how the Church interprets the Scriptures and the importance of tradition and papal authority in scriptural studies.

How the Bible Was Created

The Old Testament, drawn from the Jewish tradition, is a collection of Hebrew and Aramaic writings that Jews of Jesus' day used to guide their devotional life. The version the early Christians used was the Septuagint, the Hebrew Bible translated into Greek by scholars of the Jewish community in Alexandria, Egypt, around A.D. 250. By the end of the fourth century, St. Jerome made another translation from Hebrew into Latin. This version is known as the Latin Vulgate. Later editions of the Vulgate continued to be used for the next thousand years.

The writings compiled into the New Testament were composed in the first and second centuries, as the new Church was growing and expanding through the Mediterranean region. These writings included the Gospels—Matthew, Mark, Luke, and John—as well as epistles and other writings in Greek. At the Council of Trent (1545–1563), the gathered bishops re-affirmed which of these devotional writings would be accepted as sacred.

FACT

The Catholic Bible is a collection of poems, history, literature, and letters. The Church believes the Holy Spirit guided the bishops at the Council of Trent as they chose the writings that would be deemed sacred. The complete list is called the Canon of Scripture.

The Old Testament

Jesus was a Jew, and many of his earliest followers, including Paul, were also Jewish. They saw their belief in Christ's death and resurrection as a continuation of the Jewish tradition. Through their forefathers Abraham and Noah, the Jews had established a covenant with God. Part of this covenant was the promise of a Messiah who would save mankind. Jesus' birth and death fulfilled the message of the prophets and established a New Covenant between God and man. The ancient writings that foretold a Messiah and gave the history of the people are thus part of the Christian tradition.

At the time the Bible was compiled, letters were laboriously copied by hand onto parchment scrolls. Many sacred writings may have been lost, and other works may have been considered too incomplete to include. At the Council of Trent, the Church named forty-six Old Testament books that must be considered "as sacred and canonical," seven more than are included in most Protestant Bibles. In addition, the Catholic Bible contains portions of the books of Esther and Daniel that do not appear in the Hebrew Bible.

The first five books of the Old Testament, known as the Pentateuch (Greek for "five books"), recount the stories of Creation, the covenant between God and Noah, and the law delivered by God to Moses. Following the Pentateuch are the historical books. These end with the books of Tobias, Judith, and Esther, which occupy the last places because they relate personal history. Following the historical books are the books on law, arranged by the Council of Trent to reflect their order of writing. Then come the books of the Prophets: The first four are known as the Major Prophets, and the last twelve are Minor Prophets, arranged in chronological order.

ALERT!

Christians read the Old Testament in the light of Christ crucified and risen. But the Old Testament retains its own intrinsic value as revelation reaffirmed by the Lord himself. Jesus quoted frequently from books of the Old Testament.

The New Testament

Early Church fathers divided the New Testament into the Gospel and the Acts—works that occurred in the lifetime of Jesus and the apostles and the later didactic writings. The New Testament begins with the four Gospels written by Jesus' followers in the years after his death. The Gospels hold a unique place in the Church, as they are the heart of all the Scriptures and the center of the liturgy. The didactic writings are a series of letters from Paul to scattered Christian groups struggling against a hostile world; the later Catholic epistles are additional letters on Church life. All of the writings were completed around the year 100.

Catholics believe the New Testament has to be read in the light of the Old. Early Christian catechesis made constant use of the Old Testament. As an old saying put it, "The New Testament lies hidden in the Old and the Old Testament is unveiled in the New." When Church scholars seek biblical interpretation, they may consult additional Hebrew, Aramaic, and Greek writings of the period, including earlier versions of the Bible and works such as the Dead Sea Scrolls.

Divinely Inspired Infallibility

The Church was able to establish the books that truly belonged in the Bible because of its tradition that some of the laws issued by the pope are infallible. Another tradition holds that the Church cannot have erred in its past rulings, though it can err in its actions. This is actually a modified definition of papal infallibility, devised by the 1965 Vatican II Council. (From the time of Vatican I, all popes were seen as infallible in both their teachings and their actions.)

Catholics are expected to accept the Church's interpretation of God's Word as inspired by the Holy Spirit. The Bible, being God's Truth, is seen as equally infallible.

Papal Infallibility

The pope, who is the visible head of the Church, is infallible in his teachings on matters of religion in morality. However, the Church does recognize the fact that popes can and do make mistakes in their actions. Teaching must now be "received" by the whole Church to be seen as truly infallible.

"In order that the full and living Gospel might always be preserved in the Church the apostles left bishops as their successors. They gave them 'their own position of teaching authority.'" Indeed, "the apostolic preaching, which is expressed in a special way in the inspired books, was to be preserved in a continuous line of succession until the end of time" (from the Catechism of the Catholic Church).

This evolving concept of infallibility has eased ecumenical discussions with other religions. Pope John Paul II, in his overtures to the Eastern Orthodox Church, acknowledged that the Church erred in its actions and contributed to the Great Schism that split the Catholic Church.

Scriptural Infallibility

Scripture is a Sacred Deposit entrusted to the care of the Church. The Catholic Church considers all of the Scriptures to be sacred and infallible; because they are God's Word dictated through the Holy Spirit, they are entirely true and correct. The Church acknowledges that the Bible sometimes contains contradictory verses and advice. However, Church fathers believe that each passage must be studied in the context in which it was originally written and in light of the overall message of God's love.

How Catholics Interpret the Scriptures

Catholics do not interpret the Scriptures as the full message of God but as a component—the written message that must be interpreted together with the oral traditions passed down to us by the apostles. Through the example of their lives and work, their preaching after Jesus' death, and the institutions they established, the apostles continued to pass on the Gospel. Today's Church leaders are direct successors to the apostles, passing down through the ages the wisdom learned in earlier times.

Church tradition and acquired belief is just as important as words written in the Bible. Alone, the Bible is not sufficient for understanding the full Christian message. Catholics must also listen to the teaching of the Church to make sense of the Scriptures. The Catholic Church does not insist on the literal meaning of the Bible, but it looks behind the words for the intent of the Great Author.

Church tradition includes a long and rich heritage of biblical interpretation. Catholics believe the interpretation provided by the Church in any era is the best received wisdom of the time. Thus the Holy Spirit speaks to Church fathers to help them interpret the Bible, but they can only understand within the bounds of current human knowledge.

Who Says What It Means

The task of giving an authentic interpretation of the Word of God, whether in its written form or as tradition, is entrusted to the Church, a living, teaching office instituted by Jesus Christ. In the Church, the authority of interpretation rests with the bishops and the pope. The role of ordinary Catholics is to accept and understand these teachings and submit to their authority.

According to the Catholic Church, the Bible does not contain all of God's truth. The role of the Church is to reveal God's truth throughout the ages, and so the Church itself is an instrument to proclaim the Word of God. It is a witness and guardian of revelation and thus more qualified than individuals to determine the meaning of the Divine Word.

Apostolic Tradition

In its insistence on balancing Scripture and tradition, the Catholic Church continued a Jewish tradition of oral interpretation, or elaboration, of the law. In making Peter the rock on which he built his Church, Jesus set in motion a hierarchy. The pope or Bishop of Rome is the successor to Peter. Each of these Church leaders is seen as having power and access to the Holy Spirit. The Catholic Church continues this tradition of apostolic succession up to the present day.

How Significant Is the Bible

Catholics share the conviction that the Bible is the Word of God. The Holy Spirit inspired and spoke through the writers of Scripture. Although they were ordinary men who acquired knowledge through ordinary channels, they speak with divine authority. The Word of God is transmitted through their pens. The Bible is a constant source of revelation as Church fathers return to it to reinterpret God's Word for the modern age. It is also a constant mystery, as human understanding does not extend to the full power of God's message.

Individual Bible Study

Catholics put great value in catechesis, or an education in the faith, of children, young people, and adults. This includes especially the teaching of

Christian doctrine and Bible study, plus an awareness of Church interpretation and Church history. Catholic schools begin the education process with religion and family life classes. But Christian catechesis continues with adult Bible study, programs of individual devotions and study, and the messages Catholics receive during Mass from their priests. Catholics believe that study increases their sense of spiritual reality and that the Scriptures can grow with the one who reads them.

ALERT!

The Church publishes an exhaustive catechesis that helps explain the mysteries of the faith for Catholics. American Catholics can view a full authorized catechesis online at the Web site of the U.S. Conference of Catholic Bishops (✑ *www.nccbuscc.org/catechism*).

The Church exhorts all the Christian faithful to learn "the surpassing knowledge of Jesus Christ" by frequent reading of the Bible. It is a wellspring to which Catholics return for support, comfort, guidance, and food for the soul. The Church believes strongly that access to the Sacred Scriptures ought to be freely available to the faithful, wherever they live.

Still, Catholicism is not a "religion of the book." It is the religion of the Word of God, a living word that requires a vibrant tradition of interpretation by bishops and priests who instruct believers. At the same time, the Holy Spirit must be at work to open our minds with understanding.

Approaches to Understanding the Scriptures

In the Scriptures, God spoke to humankind in a way we could under-stand. To interpret Scriptures correctly, the reader must be aware of what the human authors truly wanted to affirm and what God wanted to reveal in their words. Bishops, priests, and laypeople educated in theology have spent untold hours puzzling over the meaning of the words and stories of the Bible.

The Bible is a work of history and literature, switching from genealogy and historical accounts to poetry and parables. It is an ancient text that has been copied by scribes over and over again. Furthermore, it is a work in translation from ancient Hebrew, Aramaic, and Greek, languages spoken thousands of years ago.

FACT

In 1947, Bedouin shepherds in the Judean Desert found a cave with jars that contained ancient scrolls. Over the next decade, archeologists searching the area discovered thousands of scroll fragments from eleven caves. We know these writings as the Dead Sea Scrolls. Carbon dating established that the scrolls dated from the third century B.C. to A.D. 68, making them older than any other surviving manuscript of the Hebrew Scriptures.

Keeping all this in mind is important. Readers must remember that while there may be a literal meaning to many Bible stories and passages, there is nearly always a spiritual meaning as well. In fact, a rich reading of Scriptures should encompass four senses:

1. **The literal sense**: The literal meaning of the passage as a story or instruction.
2. **The allegorical sense**: A more profound understanding of events in the Old Testament can be achieved by understanding their parallels in the New Testament.
3. **The moral sense**: The Scripture is written for our instruction and ought to lead us to act justly.
4. **The anagogical sense**: We can view today's events in terms of their eternal significance. (*Anagogical* comes from the Greek *anagoge*, "leading.")

Bible as History

Catholics believe the Bible is a historical work. It reflects a history of a certain people, the tribes of Israel in the Old Testament, followed by a history of the early Christian Church in the New Testament. Catholic scholars and historians agree on the historicity of the Gospel tradition, but they may differ about the extent to which each Gospel story can be affirmed as historical. The Church accepts that many writings were influenced by the historical context of the time, and they might have much less relevance for succeeding generations.

The stories of the history of the Israelites and Abraham's descendants are one of the ways that God shows us his presence in the world. God communicates himself to man gradually, with his deeds as well as his words. These include the great flood, the choice of Abraham to lead God's people, and the Exodus from slavery in Egypt. The divine plan of revelation begins in the Old Testament, but the plan is not clear or fully revealed until the New Testament. In the Hebrew stories, God is preparing man to the person and mission of the incarnate Word, Jesus Christ.

Symbols and Metaphors

Catholic interpretations accept that the Bible is full of symbols and metaphors that are not meant to be taken literally. As science and human knowledge progress, the Church has been able to reconcile the stories of the Bible with current knowledge. By contrast, some Protestant faiths take the Bible literally and believe, for example, that human history began 6,000 years ago with Creation.

Catholic scholars point out the myth and legend involved in some biblical stories, which may have been written down after being passed on orally for generations. The Creation myth is one example of using symbols to show God's plan for the world. The Church does not insist that it is pure history. Instead, it is willing to accept the theory of evolution and scientific theories that attempt to explain the origin of the earth. The Creation myth is seen as a metaphor for God's master plan for the world. God made everything that exists and everything he made is good. Throughout evolution, he allows higher forms of beings to emerge from lower, less complex forms. His pinnacle of creation is man.

The rainbow is a powerful symbol of God's covenant with Noah and his successors. The crossing of the Red Sea is a sign of Christ's victory and also of Christian baptism. A journey in the wilderness is a powerful metaphor for a spiritual search—Jesus performed such a journey, following the example of his forefather Moses and of the prophets. Water is a recurring symbol throughout the Bible—it washes away sin and symbolizes new life.

Bible as Literature

Catholics see the Bible as a literary work that was written by people who were speaking to their contemporaries. As a piece of literature, it contains imagery and storytelling that best illustrates the points the writer wanted to emphasize.

Like all literature, some books of the Bible are stronger than others. The Church regards some pieces as better written, some as more filled with the power of the Holy Spirit than others. The Book of Job is often held up by both theologians and writers as a work of great literature. Some books, such as the Psalms and the Song of Songs, were written as poetry.

The Gospel writers took great pains to tie Jesus' birth and the events of his life to the messianic predictions of the Old Testament. There are mystical parallels running through biblical stories: the forty days of Noah's journey and Jesus' forty days in the wilderness; Jonah's three days in the whale and Christ's three days in Hell. Jesus' new commandment, to love one another, is an extension of the ten given to the Jewish people by Moses.

Stories emphasize the way Jesus lived his message. For example, he is frequently shown working with the poor, the sick, and the social outcasts. Symbols such as the tree and the cross, the vine and the vineyard, the bread and the wine appear repeatedly in the texts to illustrate Jesus' covenant with the world. The parables—Jesus' anecdotes that illustrate man's relationship with God—are powerful stories within the Gospels.

Bible as a Translation

It has been the practice of the Church to provide newly converted nations with vernacular versions of the Scriptures. In the first five hundred years of the Church's history, translations of the sacred writings were common. In its second millennium, the Church began to fear heresies and misinterpretation of the book and the spiritual welfare of untutored people who might read the translations.

In 1564, however, Pope Pius IV began to allow vernacular editions of the Bible to be studied among learned men. Many later clergy had doubts about the laity having access to translations of the Bible, but in the evangelical age, when the Church was sending missions to all corners of the globe, the Bible was widely translated.

The Catholic Church understands that any vernacular Bible is an imperfect translation of God's original message. Words and phrases in both Greek and Hebrew can have several meanings. A scholar educated in these languages must go back to the earliest versions available to make a fuller interpretation.

Chapter 13

Heaven and Hell: The Afterlife

Eschatology is the study of final things, and this chapter covers the Church's views on eschatological concepts like death and the afterlife, as well as the final coming of Christ and Judgment Day. According to Catholic dogma, every human being is judged at death and is sent either to unite with God in Heaven, to be purified in Purgatory, or to eternal punishment in Hell.

The Soul's Journey Through Life and Death

The Church advises Catholics to avoid sin, receive the sacraments, pray, and do good works because how they live their lives here on earth will influence what happens to them in the afterlife. Death brings a separation of the soul from the body, but it is not an end of existence. Immediately after death, the soul of the departed is subject to a particular judgment.

Depending on how a man has lived his life, he will go to Heaven, where he will have the vision of God; to Purgatory, where he will go through a purification process before being allowed the vision of God; or to Hell, where he will be denied the vision of God. At the final judgment (the end of the world), the Parousia or Second Coming of Christ, all the just will be reunited with their glorified bodies, to live forever in glory with God.

The Church does not believe in predestination. Man has free will to choose to live a life of virtue or to turn away from God and live a life of sin. God is merciful and will forgive even the most grievous of sins up to the last minute of a person's life—provided the person is truly repentant. However, hardened sinners who do not seek repentance cannot take advantage of God's mercy.

QUESTION?

Does the Church believe in reincarnation?
The Church does not accept the idea of reincarnation of souls: "It is appointed that human beings die once," wrote Paul (Hebrews 9:27). We have only one lifetime during which to get close to God. This creates a sense of urgency, to do good and acquire grace during the one lifetime one has.

Catholic Understanding of Death

Over the course of their lives, men are born, grow up, mature, grow old, and die. The cycle of life is the same for all life on earth—for animals and plants as well as for human beings. What separates humans is our awareness of death and our ability to choose to do good during our limited time on earth. After death, we can no longer make choices regarding our destiny.

Death is one of the evils attendant on man in his fallen state; it entered the world on account of sin, as is described in the Book of Genesis. However, death is also viewed as the gateway to everlasting life. For Christians, death is also positive, for it is through death, shared with us by Christ, that we can also share in his glory. "The saying is trustworthy: if we have died with him we shall also live with him," wrote Paul (2 Timothy 2:11).

Through the sacrament of Baptism, the Christian has already identified with Christ's death. Those who die in Christ's grace share his death more completely—they become totally incorporated in him. Catholics can experience a desire for death, like that expressed by saints and mystics. Paul wrote, "I long to depart this life and be with Christ" (Philippians 1:23). "I want to see God, and, in order to see him, I must die," wrote St. Teresa of Ávila in her *Life of Teresa of Ávila*.

ALERT!

The Church teaches that the suffering and the dying should be treated with respect and care because they are members of Christ's body, and as such, that they participate in the suffering and death of Christ. The sacrament of Anointing of the Sick and the Holy Eucharist are rites the Church uses to help the faithful prepare for death.

The Church encourages people to prepare themselves for the hour of their death. The ancient Litany of the Saints contains the petition, "From a sudden and unforeseen death, deliver us, O Lord." St. Joseph is the patron saint of the happy death, and in the Hail Mary, one of the most popular Catholic prayers, Catholics beseech Mary to "pray for us now and at the hour of our death."

Particular and Final Judgment

Each man will be judged according to the merits of his life to determine where and how he will spend eternity. The Church teaches that there are two kinds of judgments—particular and final.

God makes a particular judgment of each individual immediately after death, when there is a reckoning of his deeds and intentions. The parable of Lazarus and the rich man, which appears in the Gospel of Luke, is all about particular judgment. When he was alive, Lazarus would sit outside the rich man's gate and beg for scraps of food that fell from his table. But after both men died, Lazarus went to Heaven as a reward for his humility. The rich man went to Hell, where he begged Lazarus to dip his finger in water and give him a cooling drop. Each man got what he deserved.

Each soul's destination is determined at the moment of the person's death. Those who are in a state of grace and not in need of purification go to Heaven; those souls who have faith but who are in need of purification go to Purgatory. Unrepentant sinners who have committed grave acts of moral evil go to Hell.

On Judgment Day

On the day of Final (or Last) Judgment, all souls, "both the just and the unjust," will rise from the dead, reunited with their bodies. When Christ "comes in his glory . . . he will separate them one from another." The evil will "go off to eternal punishment, but the righteous to eternal life" (Matthew 25:31–32, 46).

St. Augustine wrote in one of his sermons that at the Last Judgment, each person's relationship with God would become transparent. The consequences of what they did in their earthly lives would be revealed, down to the smallest detail. "Would that you had known that my little ones were in need when I placed them on earth for you, and appointed them your stewards to bring your good works into my treasury. But you have placed nothing in their hands; therefore you have found nothing in my presence."

When will the Last Judgment occur?
The Church teaches that only God knows when the Last Judgment will be, when Christ will return in glory. At that time, Christ will pronounce the final word on all history.

QUESTION?

The Last Judgment will bring revelation and understanding to the minds of men. They will comprehend the meaning of Creation and the work of salvation and will understand the wonderful mystery of God's providence. The Last Judgment is also a vindication of faith in God. It will show how God's justice triumphs over any earthly injustice and that God's love is stronger than death.

The concept of the Last Judgment is meant to inspire a healthy respect for God and his justice and to bring men to conversion while they still have time. It is also meant to inspire the hope of God's coming.

The Glory of Heaven

Those who die in God's grace and are purified get to live with Christ forever. They see God as he is, face-to-face. This communion of life and love with the Trinity, the Virgin Mary, the angels, and all the blessed is heavenly—the ultimate object of the deepest human desire and the state of supreme happiness. In Heaven, men live with and in Christ, but they still retain their true identity.

By his death and Resurrection, Jesus Christ opened Heaven to all who choose to accept it. Good people benefit fully from Christ's redemption. Those who have believed in him and have remained faithful become partners in his glory. Heaven is a community of all who have lived in Christ.

How Heaven functions is a mystery. It is far beyond what man can comprehend, so the Scriptures describe it in images that man can relate to: life, light, peace, wedding feast, wine of the kingdom, the Father's house, the heavenly Jerusalem, paradise.

Beatific Vision

God is the primary object of man's mind and will in Heaven. Once there, men receive "beatific vision," the ability to see God in all his glory. The secondary object of the beatific vision is the knowledge and love of those people whom Christians have known on earth.

Church theologians teach that because it is not a bodily activity, beatific vision does not require sense and imagination. Beatific vision and love are activities of man's spiritual faculties.

Man needs an even greater ennoblement and strengthening of his spiritual faculties, greater than the virtues of hope and faith, to enjoy the beatific vision. *Lumen gloriae,* the light of glory, is the name given to the permanent ennoblement of the intellect by which man can unite with the Trinity in the beatific vision.

A State of Bliss

Theologians speak of Heaven as the state of happiness. They explain that we exist to give God glory and to find our happiness, but we find our happiness only in giving glory to God. In Heaven, the members of Christ's Mystical Body glorify God by their participation in the glory of Christ—it is only in Christ that they can do so. Christ is the final Temple where God is perfectly adored, and Heaven is its sanctuary.

FACT

Because Christ and Mary are now glorified in body, and because a body requires a place in which to dwell, Church tradition follows Scripture in teaching that Heaven is a place. However, it will exist in the fullest sense only after the Parousia, when those who are saved regain their original bodies.

The essential element in the state of heavenly glory is the union with the Blessed Trinity in mind and heart, resulting in the beatific joy. All who die in the state of grace possess essential glory as soon as their purification is completed. However, the fullness of glory will come to them when they receive back their bodies after the Second Coming.

Theology teaches that God destined man for happiness. For man to gain his final end, he must gain happiness. Therefore, Heaven must bring man to a state of perfect bliss. The concern here is not physical satisfaction; true contentment is associated with fulfilling the noble aspirations of the soul.

Since he has always been intended for the supernatural union with God, man has no destiny other than the supernatural one. Thus, his ultimate happiness is union with God. God is the primary object of the beatific vision. God alone is able to satisfy the human and angelic intellect made for the possession of truth; God alone is able to satisfy the desires of the human heart or angelic will.

The infinite perfection of the Blessed Trinity and the infinite love of God provide never-ending satisfaction. This happiness does not grow tiresome because it is not mixed with material pleasure, which, by its nature, cannot last. The happiness of Heaven is permanent; there can be no anxiety that it will diminish or go away.

Here is an outline of what the Catholic Church teaches about heavenly bliss:

- It varies from one person to another, in correspondence to the state of the individual's union with God at the time of death.
- Martyrs, virgins, and teachers of the faith receive a special mark or halo that denotes their dedication to Christ or his work during their lifetime.
- Members enjoy the Company of the Elect—that is, each of the blessed takes delight in the others, including Our Lady, the angels, and the saints. How they lived on earth will give them affinities with certain of the blessed, though there will be full accord of spirit with all.
- There will be the Resurrection, or restoration, of the body. The blessed in heaven will have the same bodies, however, those bodies will have special characteristics, including the following:

  - **Splendor:** Gives bodies a supernatural radiance and makes them beautiful to look at
  - **Agility:** Enables the glorified body to move through space in an instant
  - **Subtlety:** The complete subordination of the body to the soul, so that both are perfectly integrated
  - **Impassibility:** The glorified body no longer suffers and does not need to eat or sleep to preserve itself from wear and tear

Renewal of the world, together with the restoration of the body, completes God's plan for salvation. The renewed universe is the ultimate glorification of Christ and contributes to the happiness of the blessed.

An Obstacle to Overcome: Purgatory

Purgatory is where those who die in a state of grace and who have the love of God in their hearts go for purification. In Purgatory, the souls make expiation for unforgiven venial sins or receive punishment due to venial and mortal sins that have already been forgiven in life. These souls are confident that they will have eternal salvation, but they need to be purified from the effects of sin.

The souls in Purgatory can receive help from the living. Because one cannot dictate to God, there is no assurance that one's prayers help an individual soul in purgatory, but the Church believes that the prayers and intentions of the faithful help God to speed the journey of souls through Purgatory. From its earliest history, the Church has commemorated the dead and offered up prayers and Masses for them. The Church also recommends that the living faithful give alms, practice indulgences, and undertake penitential acts on behalf of the dead: "Why would we doubt that our offerings for the dead bring them some consolation? Let us not hesitate to help those who have died and to offer our prayers for them," writes the great orator St. John Chrysostom in his homily on 1 Corinthians 41:5.

Purgatory is not specifically mentioned in the Bible, but belief in its existence has grown due to the doctrines expounded in both the Old and the New Testaments of divine judgment, the forgiveness of sins, the mercy of God, and the temporal punishment due to sin. The Israelites believed that the dead were to be judged according to their works, that their sins made God's judgment a fearsome thing, that people needed God's merciful forgiveness to enter Heaven, and that living brethren needed to pray for God to show the departed his mercy.

The Church formulated its doctrine on Purgatory at the first and second council of Lyons and at the councils of Florence and Trent, where the following authoritative statements on Purgatory were issued:

- It's a state where those dying with unrepented sins may be cleansed before being admitted to Heaven.
- There is basis for Purgatory in Sacred Scripture.
- In Purgatory, punishment due for forgiven sins is carried out.
- Prayers and other good works of the faithful on earth can help souls in Purgatory.

The Nature of Purgatory

The nature of Purgatory has been hard to define. For example, no one knows how much time souls need to spend in Purgatory, because the souls live in Aevum, not in worldly time. During that period, the soul becomes highly aware of its failings and transgressions, and is totally focused on reparation.

The nature of the punishment is not completely known either. Some theologians hold that the temporary deprivation of the beatific vision, the longing for a God so near and yet so far, has to be the primary punishment of Purgatory. Knowledge that the suffering they are enduring could have been prevented if only they had prayed and performed good works during their lifetime probably torments the souls. Some theologians also postulate that there must be a more positive punishment that frees the souls of their sins and brings them closer to God.

While the Catholic Church has always held that the pain of Purgatory is imposed by real fire, that is not an essential belief of Purgatory. And no one has been able to define the intensity of the pain of Purgatory, though many theologians have debated it. Some popular writings and sermons have dwelt on the horrors of Purgatory.

For fear of sullying the dignity of the souls in Purgatory or of scandalizing the faithful, the Church chose to err on the side of caution. The Council of Trent forbade priests from discussing difficult questions around Purgatory in their sermons and banned descriptions that would give rise to curiosity, superstition, terror, or repulsion.

The Positive Purpose of Purgatory

Purgatory purifies the soul. Persistent sinful habits and uncontrolled desires can leave deep scars that penetrate into the personality of the sinner. These must be removed before the soul is ready to go to Heaven and experience the overwhelming presence of God.

This is a more positive view of Purgatory than just a place where souls undergo punishment for sins committed during their lifetime. The point is not the punishment itself (the Church does maintain that punishment is received), but the intent of punishment—to transform the soul to a state of wholeness and purity so that it is fit to behold God.

Key to the positive view of Purgatory is the concept of salvation. The souls of Purgatory are confirmed in grace. They have the assurance that they will see God one day. They do not feel anguish or horror; rather, they voluntarily accept their sufferings as a means to an end: the ability to join God. They do endure pain but do not despair. They are already in contact with the Holy Spirit, because they are part of Christ's Mystical Body. They will not be disengaged from Christ and the Spirit.

The Concept of Hell

Hell is a place or state in the afterlife reserved for unbelievers and Catholics who die unrepentant in a state of mortal sin. Forgoing repentance, the Catholic chooses to exclude himself from God and his grace. If he dies in this state, he is denied for eternity the vision of God and communion with the blessed.

The word *Hell* is derived from the Germanic *hel* ("realm of the dead"). This word was not used in the Old Testament. Rather, the Old Testament counterpart was "Gehenna," an actual place near the territories of the tribes of Judah and Benjamin, where human sacrifices were offered to Canaanite gods Baal and Moloch. Jewish thinking was that the remains of those who turned against Yahweh would lie there. (This idea of Gehenna remained prevalent in Jesus' time.)

In the New Testament, Jesus speaks of Gehenna and of the unquenchable fire, where those who refuse to believe or repent will be sent. Jesus declares that he will "send his angels, and they will collect . . . all who cause others to sin and all evildoers. They will throw them into the fiery furnace" (Matthew 13:41–42), and he then will condemn them by saying, "Depart from me, you accursed, into the eternal fire!" (Matthew 25:41). This vivid apocalyptic imagery is meant to dramatize the urgency of the Kingdom and the serious attitude toward salvation that Christians needed to have.

According to the Apostles' Creed, Jesus' own descent into Hell was to the underworld, Sheol, where he met those who had died before him, to share his victory over death. He died and stayed among the dead for a short time.

QUESTION?

Is hellfire a literal fire?
The Church teaches that immediately after death, those who die in mortal sin descend into Hell, where they suffer eternal fire. There is not necessarily a literal fire. The chief punishment of hell is eternal separation from God, because only by seeing God can man possess the life and happiness for which he was created. Hell is self-annihilation: Rejection of God is the rejection of the state of being and the choosing of a condition of nonbeing.

The Church's teachings on Hell serve as a warning to man to make the best use of his time on earth. No one is predestined to go to Hell. It's an act of free will to choose mortal sin, to turn away from God, and to persist in that stance. The Missal contains prayers whereby the Church prays for the mercy of God, who wants all to repent. "Grant us your peace in this life, and save us from final damnation" (Roman Missal, EPI, Roman Canon, 88).

Chapter 14

The Catholic Ministry

I n Latin, the word *minister* means "service," and in a way, all Catholics participate in the ministry of the Church. However, ordained ministry still has authority over the faithful laity. The pope rules over the hierarchy of the Church. Ordained bishops and priests serve in dioceses and parishes; their responsibilities include administering the sacraments. Members of religious orders who take vows of poverty, chastity, and obedience, also fulfill special aspects of the Church's ministry.

At the Top of the Hierarchy

The hierarchy of the Catholic Church is composed of the pope, bishops, priests, and deacons. They are ordained and dedicated to ministry to the faithful. Through dioceses and parishes, they teach and confer the sacraments.

At the top of the hierarchy, which is essentially a pyramid, is the pope. As supreme pontiff and Bishop of Rome, the pope follows a tradition that dates back to St. Peter and the earliest days of the Church. The pope is believed to be infallible when speaking on matters of faith or morals, although he generally consults his advisory body, the College of Cardinals, before he makes a decision affecting the Church.

FACT

Since Vatican II, there has been a greater emphasis on the collegiality of bishops worldwide, an encouragement for them to have greater autonomy in their own dioceses and to work with the pope in the leadership of the Church.

The hierarchical structure of the Church has existed in more or less the same form since the twelfth century, when Pope Gregory VII instituted many reforms that increased papal control over the Church as a whole. One of these primary reforms did away with lay investiture; that is, public officials and monarchs lost the right to invest a bishop in their diocese. From then on, only the pope had the right to appoint a bishop, and in turn the bishops reported only to the pope. Gregory's aim in passing this reform was to prevent secular control over the Church's properties and activities.

It was at about the same time that the Church began to recognize the power of Canon Law, which codified all the activities of the Church, covering questions ranging from who could administer a sacrament to how the pope was chosen. The Code of Canon Law functioned as a kind of constitution for the Church. It determined procedures that were to be followed in the governance of the Church and thus clearly structured and supported the framework of the hierarchy.

The College of Cardinals usually elects the pontiff from among their membership. Once the pope is chosen, he remains the head of the Catholic Church until his death. As well as being the chief bishop of the Roman Catholic Church, the pope is also a ruler of a city-state, Vatican City, which allows him to have independence from any earthly political jurisdiction.

Cardinals

In the actual governance of the Church, the next step down on the hierarchical pyramid are the cardinals, who have the authority to elect and advise the pope. All cardinals are ordained bishops. They keep their Episcopal sees, whether they are titular or residential (that is, whether they are bishops of an actual place, such as the archdiocese of Chicago, or honorary bishops, by title only), along with their responsibilities as bishops. There are three levels of cardinals:

1. Cardinal bishops, or Episcopal cardinals
2. Cardinal priests, or Presbyter cardinals
3. Cardinal deacons, or diaconal cardinals

The cardinal bishops are the titular bishops of the seven titular suburban sees of Rome. They elect a dean and subdean from among their members. The dean presides over the college, with the subdean acting in his absence, making them the second- and third-highest ranking clerics in the Church.

Cardinal priests are the ordinary bishops of dioceses who have been made cardinals. Cardinal deacons are titular archbishops who work for the Roman Curia and who have been raised to the cardinalate. Together, the cardinals make up the Sacred College of Cardinals, which acts as an advisory body to the pope.

The Roman Curia

The cardinal bishops work full-time in the Roman Curia. The Curia is the central body of the Church, which is subdivided into departments that handle such matters as Canon Law, heresies, the election and governance of bishops and dioceses, administration of the sacraments, matters concerning religious orders, missionary work, rites and liturgies, ceremonies, and religious studies. Certain departments of the Curia also make decisions regarding special petitions to the Curia, such as annulment petitions.

Decisions on cases involving Canon Law that are too serious to be handled at the diocesan level or on matters that apply to the Church as a whole, including questions of morality, observance, and theology, are referred to the offices of the Curia.

Bishops—Community Leaders

The word *bishop* comes from the Greek, and it has the meaning of inspector, overseer, or superintendent. In the writings of the early Church, the terms *bishop* (*episcopes*) and *priest* (*presbyter*) were interchangeable. However, as early as the second century, Christians began to distinguish between these two roles. "Priests of the second grade" became what we know as priests; "priests of the first grade" evolved into bishops.

Bishops fulfilled the high priestly roles exemplified by Christ: They were priests, prophets, and kings. As a priest, each bishop had the power to consecrate, offer the Eucharistic Sacrifice, and forgive sins. As a prophet, he had the authority to teach and to forgive sins. As a king, he had primary pastoral responsibility to guide his flock. At consecration, he received special graces to equip him for his office.

However, the power of bishops waned in the twelfth century as they lost some of their independence to the pope. At that time, the bishop became a kind of papal legate, a representative of the pope in his diocese. He followed strict guidelines and submitted a review of his activities on a regular basis. Power and authority were highly concentrated in the pope and the Curia.

Since Vatican II, the role of bishops in the Church has gained importance through the efforts to empower them in their dioceses, in national gatherings, and in worldwide councils or synods. Bishops share their leadership roles in the service of the faithful with the pope, who is the Bishop of Rome. The bishops' empowerment serves as a counterweight or balancing force to the central control exercised by the Curia.

Today, the pope still decides who will be made a bishop. However, local councils of bishops are encouraged to help the pope make the decision by giving him their recommendations. Church tradition prescribes that candidates for the position of bishop should have integrity, piety, prudence, and a zeal for souls. They should be trained in theology or canon law, and may not marry.

Hierarchy of Bishops

The highest bishops are the archbishops (or metropolitans). They have authority over an ecclesiastical province and over the bishops within that province. The bishops who report to them are known as suffragans. As part of their obligations, metropolitans must convene provincial synods to make laws and decisions for the province.

FACT

There is also a category known as titular archbishops. In a sense, these are honorary archbishops of some extinct archdiocese, or they may be administrative bishops who have no suffragans.

Bishops proper preside over dioceses. Each diocese is broken into districts consisting of a number of parishes and administered by archpriests or deans.

In some cases, bishops report directly to the pope and are known as exempt bishops. Titular bishops are consecrated, and have a title belonging to a diocese, but they have no jurisdiction in that diocese. They may function as auxiliary bishops or coadjutors to diocesan bishops. The *praelati nullius cum territorio separato* heads up a territory that does not belong to a designated diocese. He has episcopal rights over an area that does form part of a diocese.

The bishop also has assistants. Chief among them is the vicar-general. Furthermore, the bishop is advised by a council or chapter composed of canons—priests affiliated with the cathedral, whose approval he needs to proceed in certain matters. The chapter has the power to nominate the *vicar capitular* to run the diocese in case the bishop's seat is vacant.

The Bishop's Role

At its most basic, the role of the bishop is to govern the diocese in spiritual and temporal affairs. Here is an outline of the bishop's powers and responsibilities:

- He can adopt laws for his diocese that the faithful must follow (unless they are given specific exemptions).
- He acts as judge in any ecclesiastical matter.
- He must enforce the observance of ecclesiastical laws, especially where the spiritual welfare of his flock is concerned.
- He is the principal preacher in his diocese and must personally preach the Word of God to his people.
- He is expected to reside within his diocese for most of the year and to be present at his cathedral church during Advent and Lent and at Easter, Pentecost, Christmas, and Corpus Christi.
- He must offer Mass for his diocese on Sundays and major feast days.
- Every five years, the bishop must submit a report on the state of his diocese to the pope. At the same time, he travels to Rome to visit the Holy Father and to worship at the tombs of Peter and Paul.
- He is expected to visit every corner of his diocese and to cover the entire territory over a five-year period (three years in the case of American bishops). The purpose of the visit is to preserve sound doctrine; uphold morality; correct abuses; promote innocence, piety, and discipline among the clergy and faithful; and promote the welfare of the Church.

Priests—Mediators Between Man and God

The role of priests is to serve as mediators between God and man as ministers of divine worship. In the Catholic Church, there are two degrees of priests: The bishop, who is in a sense a high priest, possessing all the powers of the priesthood and in control of divine worship, and the priests of the second degree, who are most often affiliated with a parish. Every priest has the power to offer the Sacrifice of the Mass, forgive sins, bless, preach, and fulfill all liturgical obligations and priestly functions not reserved to the bishop.

In the early days of the Church, all priests (or presbyters) belonged to a council that looked after the affairs of the Church, which included liturgy and worship, and they worked together in cities under the supervision of the bishop. As the Church grew and spread to suburban and rural areas, priests were assigned to reside in parishes and to look after the spiritual needs of the faithful. These priests could no longer work closely with the bishop. However, the bishop had authority over those priests, as their parishes were part of his diocese and subject to his jurisdiction. This arrangement persists in the Church today.

Priests may be diocesan or parish priests, or they may be ordained through a religious order. (The section of this chapter titled "Poverty, Chastity, and Obedience" provides more information on the latter). A pastor or parish priest has the role and duty known as Cure of Souls (*Cura animarum*). His job is to nurture the spiritual welfare of Church members by preaching, bestowing the sacraments, and supervising and counseling the faithful in matters they bring to him. He usually has a certain number of souls to look after (that is, the Catholic population of his parish), and he gets a salary for his work.

QUESTION?

What is a rector?
A rector heads a church not officially designated as a parish and has the same rights and responsibilities as a parish priest. The term may also apply to priests who preside over missions, or to the heads of universities, seminaries, colleges, and religious houses of men.

Some pastors are irremovable. They cannot be transferred unless there is a serious reason, such as violation of a canonical or criminal law. Other pastors or rectors are movable, but a bishop would usually need a good reason to transfer a priest against his will.

Parish priests, or pastors, are supposed to provide religious instruction (especially to the young), administer the sacraments to parishioners, look after the Church and its property, and oversee the needs of their parishioners in matters of faith and morals. Canon Law obliges them to say Mass for their flock on Sundays and designated holy days. If a priest's parish becomes too large or duties too numerous, the bishop may appoint an assistant or auxiliary priest or priests to help him.

Revisions of the Priestly Role

In the early days of the Church, the priest was a local leader who grew up in his community and, in a sense, was chosen by that community to serve it. As Church history and the history and theology of the sacraments evolved, priests developed in relationship to their powers. They had the power to offer the sacrifice of the Mass and to confer sacraments. They received special education, and they developed an environment that kept them apart from the faithful. Many rites and rituals were performed exclusively by the priests and were at times inaccessible to the laity.

Vatican II took it upon itself to diminish the cultlike status of the priests and return them to their original roles in the community. In the Decree on the Ministry and the Life of Priests, Vatican II declared that all the faithful are part of the priesthood, and that the priest is there to serve the faithful just as all the faithful are there to serve each other.

Vatican II recommended that priests be prepared and educated to serve in the community. As well as administering the sacraments and preaching, priests were called upon to act as teachers and examples among the faithful, to lead the faithful in various ministries, and to cultivate the appropriate interpersonal skills.

Deacons—Ordained Ministers of the Church

The word *deacon* is from the Greek *diakonos*, meaning "servant" or "helper." In the early days of the Church in Jerusalem, the apostles appointed seven deacons to help minister to widows and the poor so that the apostles could devote themselves to teaching. From the third to the eighth centuries, both men and women were ordained deacons. Women had a role in assisting at the baptism of other women, admitting new female members to the assembly, caring for items in the sanctuary, distributing Holy Communion to sick or elderly women at their homes, and caring for sick and needy women in the parish. However, they were excluded from altar service, public proclamation, and administering solemn baptism, and they were not involved in teaching or leadership positions in the Church.

ALERT!

By the time of the Middle Ages, the notions of Roman Law, supported by Church fathers and theologians, had contrived to push women out of involvement in the deaconate. However, very solid historical evidence of women's previous involvement is now used as fuel for the current push to ordain women.

Deacons are ordained ministers; their role in the Church appears below that of priests on the hierarchical pyramid. Today, most men who are deacons are on their way to becoming priests. However, the Church once had a permanent deaconate, in which deacons fulfilled specific functions.

Over the centuries, the roles and the duties of the deacon were quite extensive:

- Assisting the priest at Mass and with other liturgies
- Reading the Gospel
- Leading the faithful in gestures and responses during services
- Pronouncing the dismissal after Mass
- Instructing the catechumens in the sacraments of Initiation
- Preparing the altar for Mass and looking after the sacred vessels, the chalice, and ciborium

Deacons oversaw the care of the poor, the sick, and the elderly, reporting to their bishops on the state of things and following the bishop's directives. In some locations, they served as managers of the goods and properties of the Church. They could also act as inspectors for the bishops and as emissaries to political officials, such as kings and local councils.

Vatican II encouraged the re-establishment of a permanent deaconate in the Church. Today, deacons still care for the chalice and can offer the chalice to the faithful when they receive communion under both species.

Poverty, Chastity, and Obedience

Religious orders still play a huge role in the ministry of the Church. Religious orders consist of groups of men or women living together and dedicated to a particular ministry, be it teaching, nursing, or even contemplation. For instance, the Sisters of Charity, founded by St. Vincent de Paul, have dedicated themselves to the care of the poor and founded many hospitals. The Carmelites are a cloistered order devoted to prayer and meditation.

St. Benedict established the first monastic order; the Benedictine monks founded a monastery in Monte Cassino, Italy, around 520. Eventually, monasteries became prevalent throughout the Christian world; they served as centers of religious learning, and they often became financially successful in farming, winemaking, and other endeavors.

All members of religious communities, whether monks, nuns, friars, or brothers, practice the evangelical counsels. That is, they take voluntary vows of poverty, chastity, and obedience. They do not marry, hold no private property, live communally, and practice strict obedience to their superiors.

In addition to monastic orders, the Church also saw the rise of the mendicant orders. Friars belonging to these orders did not live in seclusion but went out into the world in order to exercise the sacred ministry. They were not allowed to earn an income but had to exist on donations. A "brother," such as a Christian Brother, is a type of friar.

Ordained Priests

Ordained members of religious orders are known as clerics; technically, the Jesuits were clerics because most were ordained for the purpose of active missionary work for the Church. Basilian priests, members of the order of St. Basil, are also clerics. Many orders, such as the Dominicans and the Augustinians, have both ordained and unordained members. The priests serve the needs of the community but can also hold posts outside the community under the supervision of a bishop.

Lay Associates

More recently, some Catholics have chosen to become lay associates. A lay associate is a layperson who attaches to a religious community and becomes an associate member. Lay associates take no vows but may practice voluntary poverty, chastity, and obedience. They usually take a training/orientation course lasting between twelve and eighteen months to learn about the purpose and the ministry of the order.

Because many orders have lost as much as half their memberships in the past fifty years, they now welcome lay associates—a step encouraged by the Vatican. By some estimates, there are now 25,000 lay associates, with 2,000 more in training, in the United States.

Renewal of Religious Life

The popularity of religious orders has seen many declines and revivals. The twentieth-century decline in the memberships of religious orders prompted Vatican II to deal with the matter by issuing a decree on the up-to-date renewal of religious life, in which the council made a number of recommendations, including the following:

- Religious orders should return to their roots—get in touch with the original purpose for which the order was established and return to those traditions. They should maintain and faithfully perform their specific apostolates.
- Vows of poverty, chastity, and obedience should be firmly upheld.
- Religious orders should share fully in the life of the Church as they

carry out their ministry.

- Religious orders should understand the contemporary situation and evaluate their ministry in its light.
- Contemplative orders are ensured an important place in the hierarchy.
- The principles of monasticism should be upheld but adapted to the present day.
- Common life, prayer, and sharing should be a constant, and every member should have the same status; they should be distinguished only by the duties they perform.
- Laymen and laywomen can adequately perform ministries and profess the evangelical counsels.

Challenges to the Ministry

Since Vatican II, the winds of change have blown through the Catholic Church. Even as they have sometimes blown away some of the cobwebs, they have caused major upheaval in a number of areas.

Despite an emphasis on the collegiality of bishops, and on greater participation of the faithful, the Catholic Church still has an authoritarian, hierarchical structure that sometimes causes anger and alienation among the faithful in every rank. While there are more Catholics than ever, and even as their numbers continue to grow, there is a decline in vocations to both the priesthood and to religious orders.

In the United States, there are fewer Catholic schools relative to the population of Catholics, putting more of an onus on parents and catechetical programs to educate the young in the faith.

Celibacy is no doubt an issue, but the clergy has also lost its revered status and its special place in the hierarchy. With the acceptance of the idea of the universal priesthood of Christ, the clergy is now merely a subset of the priesthood of the faithful. With fewer young seminarians and priests coming in, an ever-growing number of ailing and elderly priests have to be cared for. This is a drain on the financial and personal resources of the Church. With fewer priests to look after parishes, there are also fewer priests to staff the missionary endeavors of the Church. Islam is a huge threat to the growth of the Church in Africa, for example.

Nuns and Catholic laywomen are still battling for the right to be ordained. However, the Church has ruled that only men can be ordained because priests must imitate Christ, the bridegroom of the Church. The Church points to the fact that Christ chose only men to be his disciples, even though he had a good relationship with women.

Facing the Challenge

The Church has developed a number of strategies to help remedy some of the current problems facing the ministry. It has adopted techniques for determining who is qualified to handle the demanding role of diocesan priests and has improved the education programs in seminaries that prepare men for the priesthood. The Church has also encouraged bishops to provide support for their priests.

The Church is also confronting the Catholic dissatisfaction with its rigid stands on birth control and divorce. The Church does not permit any form of artificial contraception, but many clergymen at high levels within the Church do recommend it. Divorced Catholics are not allowed to remarry while their partners are still alive, and if they do, they are not allowed to receive the sacraments. Regardless, some pastors have gone so far as to bless second marriages, even though they could not marry the couple.

Individually, the clergy recognize the gray areas that exist in marriage and family life. Prominent theologians have concurred that singular moral rules and moral judgments cannot be applied to humanity as a whole. Where there is a human relationship, each case must be judged on its own merits.

Despite the Church's authoritarian structure and tradition, there is more debate and dissension as well as openness to new ways of thinking and approaching issues around morality, tradition, and ecumenism. Theologians are coming to acknowledge that doctrines reflect the tenor of the times in which they were enshrined and must be interpreted as such. And Catholic dialogue with other faiths has made great strides.

FACT

In July 2002, a weeklong event called World Youth Day was held in Toronto to help raise enthusiasm for vocations among the young. Young people came from all over the world to rally, learn, and worship together.

The Church is, despite its problems, vigorous and healthy. It displays the four qualities by which it has come to be defined:

1. It is catholic in its embrace of all humanity.
2. It is one in its common beliefs.
3. It is holy in its union with the Father, Son, and Holy Spirit.
4. It is apostolic in its succession, tradition, and ongoing mission.

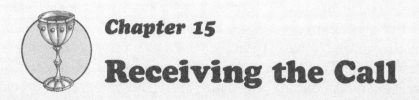

Chapter 15

Receiving the Call

The Catholic faith is a wonderful community that enriches all its members. Catholics are able to participate in this community through assembly and support of each other, through the Church, and through the body of Christ. Catholics practice their ministry through their community as they receive their call as laity, through vocation in the Church, or through membership in some form of religious order.

The Call to Each Individual

First and foremost, Catholic individuals receive their call to ministry by virtue of their being Catholic. Through Baptism and Confirmation, Catholics are joined in Christ with the Church and work the ministry of Christ in their own special ways. Outside of organized lay work, Catholics have ample opportunity to offer services in their own parishes. They can help a sick neighbor, organize a bake sale for their church or parish school, teach a children's class at Sunday School on a weekly basis, drive food baskets around at Christmas, assist the church with tithes or donations, or simply carry the offering plate during Mass. There are literally dozens of small ways to help out. These Catholic heroes may go unsung, but they are the pillars of the church, what Vatican II called "the salt of the earth."

The Call to Holiness: The Priesthood

The Catholic Church teaches that we share in the tasks of Christ, and, as such, we share in the "common priesthood of the faithful" (as the Catechism of the Catholic Church calls it). This means a general call to the laity to share and spread the Word of God. But beyond this general call, there is the special call to the ordained priesthood: the sacrament of Holy Orders.

Priests preach Christ's Gospel in their efforts to bring people to Catholic maturity. Once "signed with a special character"—in other words, once they are ordained—priests are, in a sense, set apart. This helps them dedicate themselves to God's ministry with complete devotion. Laypeople who take on the important work of helping priests assist them in being the leaders of the faithful that they need to be.

Called to the Priesthood

Many men are called, but few are chosen. Until about twenty-five years ago, it was very common among ardent Catholic families for at least one son to choose the priesthood. For one thing, it was a badge of honor. For boys raised in a thickly atmospheric Catholic environment, the call to the priesthood was often glamorous and appealing. These boys were first initiated into some of the rites of the Church by becoming altar boys. They went to Catholic schools and were taught every day about the glory of the Church. Many might have had a charismatic priest as a mentor. The boys who thought they had the gift went to seminary fairly young, midway through their teens.

FACT

Pope John Paul II has established February 2 as the World Day of Prayer for Consecrated Life. This is a time to focus on the women and men who have dedicated themselves to God through the different forms of consecrated life; it is also a time to give thanks for the gifts they offer to us and to pray that consecrated life remains a prophetic and vital part of the pilgrim people of God.

Nowadays, the secular world has greatly encroached on the call to Holy Orders. Catholics live in a culture that trivializes religion and instead seems to exalt consumerism, materialism, and moral relativism. There are more distractions, and hence fewer men are joining the priesthood. It is difficult in such a busy world to heed a call or indeed even to be aware of it.

Still, there are men to whom, for one reason or another, the call gets through. They go through a variety of stages before they are anointed. But one of the most important is doing a lot of thinking—and praying. After these men are accepted into the seminary, they undergo a number of tests—not paper examinations so much as tests of doubt—before they are sure their vocation is true. Along the road, a number drop out.

It isn't easy being a priest in today's world. There are many more complex problems to deal with. Priests have to counsel women about birth control and abortion. Families seem to be under particular stress. Sometimes the priest must take on a role of a social worker, conducting marital therapy sessions or helping children of broken homes.

It takes a man with a particular set of skills to deal with both the ministry and the mission, especially in the dynamic urban centers. Today's Catholics have easy access to almost every temptation there is, and priests need to be sophisticated enough to understand this world and help guide their assembly through it.

Discernment

Knowing whether you have a calling is called "discernment." Certain questions and considerations come up time and again for those considering the priesthood. Those who go into religious orders have to take vows of chastity, poverty, and obedience. Understandably, this may be upsetting to family and friends.

To reach discernment, men often go through a period of doubt. They have many questions that have not been answered, such as the following:

- How do I tell if God is really calling me to become a priest?
- How do I know if he wants me to enter into the vocation of marriage instead?
- My faith is growing and with it my wish to become a priest. I have been praying to God for answers, but I haven't heard anything. Will I really recognize the call from God, when it comes?

These types of questions could easily apply to a woman trying to decide whether to become a nun. It is an agonizing one for young people and not easily answered. To help them, they might turn to a mentor or a vocational adviser. The advice to these young people is to continue in their life of faith, to continue to pray and receive the sacraments, and to read a lot so that their feelings will develop from a vague idea to real conviction.

Once he achieves a certain degree of certainty, the young man must then turn to a priest he trusts. The priest's guidance will help him figure out whether he has really experienced the call to priesthood. The next step is to enroll in a seminary or to join a religious order that most closely corresponds to the young man's religious aims or convictions.

Those considering a vocation can take part in "discernment groups," in which they meet with other potential initiates and talk to diocesan priests and seminarians. Within these groups, they get discussion, prayer, and fellowship.

The Call to Community: Religious Orders

There is a world of opportunity for those who want to heed those words of Jesus, "Follow me." One option is for Catholics to join a religious order and do ministry work as monks or nuns. Plenty of places are in great need of their help: hospitals, missions, parishes, prisons, schools, seminaries, and universities. They can choose to work as a priest associate (to a religious order), a religious brother or sister, or a missionary abroad.

According to a Web site run by Catholic Doors Ministry, about 125 organizations are currently recruiting members. These range from the great male mendicant orders, such as the Augustinians, who are still going strong today, to a large number of Marian groups, such as the Little Group of Mary, a community of vowed women founded in Australia in 1885.

Becoming a member of a religious order is a demanding vocation. Life is completely ordered within the hierarchy of the organization, and each person must be able to fit into that hierarchy and submit to its authority. "Vowed" orders take vows of chastity, obedience, and poverty.

Those who choose to join a religious order must find an organization that appeals to them and to what they would like to do, whether it's work in a faraway mission or a monastic life of seclusion. And, of course, those considering joining an order should examine their doubts. In almost every religious person's life, there comes some event that shakes his or her faith. In some cases, when the shaking is profound, the person might be asked to leave the order. In others, he or she may be offered a type of "time-out" to reconsider the vocation.

The Call to the Laity

The Catholic laity includes all the members of the Church who do not belong to the clergy. Since the reforms pioneered by Vatican II, lay movements, associations, and organizations have experienced growth and expansion. Today's laypeople have a lot to offer the Church, both through their own efforts and by cooperating with the Church.

Catholics outside of the clergy might feel a special call (that is, a call to ministry) to help spread the Word of God or to do good works in a special field, and there are probably hundreds of organizations that a Catholic layperson may either join or support. The Church now recognizes that members of the Catholic community have many special gifts. Perhaps they are good at business, or maybe they have a musical gift or a special gift for teaching. Whatever the gift, the Church recognizes that these talents should be tapped.

Bishops and Laity

All over the world, Catholics have formed lay organizations that work under the authority of the Church to train and to foster ministry and mission work of the laity. In the United States, the Committee on the Laity is subordinate to the U.S. Conference of Catholic Bishops (under its Secretariat for Family, Laity, Women, and Youth). The Committee is overseen by eight bishops or auxiliary bishops, who act as advisers; they hail from all over the United States—from Los Angeles to Indianapolis to Philadelphia.

Every two years, the Committee sponsors a Lay Forum for the leaders of lay organizations. For instance, a Jubilee forum was held in the year 2000 to celebrate the millennium at both the diocesan and national level.

FACT

In 2000, 550 people gathered in Rome for the World Congress of the Catholic Laity, as part of the Jubilee of the Lay Apostolate. The Catholic Laity Congress closed with this message: "The work of the Lord in our life [is] truly ecumenical, which gives value to every sincere attempt, open and attentive, for the dignity of every person, especially the poor who suffer injustice."

In addition, the Committee on the Laity has two subcommittees, which have special concerns. One is the Youth and Young Adult Subcommittee, established for the express purpose of working with Catholics in their late teens, twenties, and thirties. The other is the Lay Ministry Subcommittee, formed in 1994, which focuses on six areas of discussion about lay ministry:

1. Theology of lay ministry
2. The relationship between lay ministers and ordained ministers
3. Education and formation of lay ministers
4. Multicultural issues
5. Financial and human resources issues
6. The term *lay minister* and its definition

Lay formation programs are now operated in about 65 percent of all dioceses in the United States. In 2001, there were about 300 training programs, ranging from diocesan certification classes to graduate programs in seminaries and universities. The enrollment was up to 35,000, and, most interestingly, women's enrollment was double that of men's.

Lay Ministry

Lay ministry is not a new trend. It has been an expected part of Catholic life since Jesus exhorted us, "Do unto others as you would have them do unto you." But there is a special movement in the Church, both in response to Vatican II and in response to the declining number of priests.

Because there are not enough priests to fulfill all the diocesan duties or get to all the street ministries, lay Catholics accept the roles of formation director, parish life coordinator, and pastoral associate. These laypeople take on some of the responsibilities normally carried out by priests in diocesan offices, parishes, and seminaries all over the United States as well as other Catholic countries.

Of the many groups in operation in addition to the Conference of Bishops, the National Association for Lay Ministry is worth noting. Formed in 1981 by laypeople, the vowed religious, and clergy, the goal of this organization is to share their expertise and provide mutual support in the important work of establishing and improving programs of lay ministry formation.

The association has about 1,000 members and now represents 100,000 Catholic adults in the United States. A third of its members hold jobs in various capacities that may be considered full-time in ministries that might specialize in such fields as the liturgy, nursing, teaching, or youth. Two-thirds give up some time every week to help out in hospitals, prisons, schools, and soup kitchens.

ALERT!

Many ad hoc lay groups exist too. For instance, Christians in Commerce is a national network of Roman Catholic business leaders seeking to "transform the marketplace for the glory of God." Bringing a spiritual atmosphere to the workplace is a growing trend in the wealthier nations.

Reverend Cardinal Avery Dulles

Avery Dulles, S.J., is a prominent American and Jesuit. The son of the former U.S. Secretary of State John Foster Dulles, Avery received one of the highest Church honors when he became a cardinal on February 21, 2001, the first U.S. theologian to do so.

Avery Dulles exemplifies a modern call to ministry. Born in 1918, he was raised in a Presbyterian family, but he called himself an agnostic by the time he got to Harvard. He converted to Catholicism in 1940, calling it "the best decision he ever made" (from his own book, *Testimonial to Grace,* 1946). A great thinker, along the lines of Thomas Aquinas, he said that his conversion was a gradual, rational process.

Cardinal Dulles's conversion shows the impact one person's life can make on the world as a whole. Today, his authority and achievements are widely recognized. His family was not particularly happy about his conversion at the time, but they grew to accept it because of the strength and courage of his faith.

Avery Dulles's Models of the Church

Among his many, many accomplishments and contributions to the Catholic Church, one stands out: *Models of the Church* (1988), a book that discusses the community models of the Catholic Church throughout its history. Dulles examined the development of the Church and outlined the five frameworks that the Church has based itself on through certain periods of history. These models are instructive because they show how the Church reinterprets itself over time and in response to the world at large.

Significantly, Dulles calls the Church to attention today. He feels that it has gone off the rails a bit. Why? Cardinal Dulles thinks the Church is developing along a secular line, increasingly taking part in the world outside its domain, and that it is therefore following a flawed path, swaying with passing fads. Not everyone agrees, of course, but if you really want to come to grips with Church history, and therefore form an opinion yourself, it is helpful to see where it has come from.

The five ecclesiological models do not follow a strict chronological order. Rather, a model tends to attract a following within the Church. It is accepted, and then new models develop and overtake it. Some models are from the past; some are from the present. Some of the current models actually exist simultaneously (this is, after all, theological theorizing). Keep in mind that these are not hard-and-fast "structures" but interpretations of how the Church (or factions within the Church) views itself.

The Political Society Model

Dulles begins his book by examining the Church in the period of 1600–1940. During this period, the Church was very much a part of and an influence on the secular world, so it is appropriate to look at its organization in terms of a political society or state. Indeed, in a

catechism published during this period, the Church referred to
Catholicism as "the Perfect Society."

FACT

The political society model is derived from Robert Bellarmine, one
of the major influences in Dulles's personal development of
ecclesiology. Bellarmine described the Church in a 1588 document
with the following words: "The one true Church is as visible and
palpable as the Kingdom of France or the republic of Venice."

The political society approach can be seen most clearly in how the
Church operated during the Counter-Reformation. During that time, the
Church stressed the visible and structural elements of Catholicism. It saw
itself as a community of sacraments and of government, based on bonds
of publicly professed faith.

Although a great deal of heroic missionary work was accomplished
during this period, the Church's expressed aim was earthbound: to construct
a Catholic society. The weakness in this model is that it stresses the visible
at the expense of the invisible—a life of grace. The great central mysteries
were underrepresented. Dulles concluded that the political society approach
resulted in "clericalism, juridicism, and triumphalism."

The Body-of-Christ Model

The body-of-Christ model is based on the approach of the early
Christians. It was eventually dropped in favor of other models, but it was
again resurrected in the nineteenth century. Much more democratic, this
model put the focus back on the Catholic virtues of faith, hope, and
charity. It also attempted to fix the imbalance of the political structure
model, re-emphasizing the spiritual/mystical side of things.

Interestingly, this model raised two new heads of the Hydra. Stressing
mysticism turned out to lead to anti-institutionalism. And by organizing
and discussing the church assembly as the body of Christ, the
community (taking its leadership from the top, of course) began to think
of this as a literal application of what is essentially a metaphor.

Vatican II tried to balance this seesaw between the supernatural community of grace in Christ and the visible community, saying that neither one nor the other is correct in itself. Vatican II stated that the society furnished with hierarchical agencies and the Mystical Body of Christ are not to be considered as two realities but as "one interlocked reality."

The Sacramental Model

The sacramental model, while not dominant in the Church today, still carries a lot of weight and its influence is strongly felt. In every Catechism or book on Catholicism that you read, you hear over and over again about the importance of the sacraments and sacramentals in Catholic life and teaching.

This model, which was also adapted from what we know of the early Church, re-emerged in late 1940s. Vatican II wrote about it in its constitution: "The Church is in Christ as a sacrament or sign and instrument of intimate union with God and of the unity of all mankind."

As discussed in earlier chapters, the sacramental life of the Church is very important to Catholics because it is a means to express the inexpressible: Spirituality made reality. In the sacramental model, a sacrament is described as both a sign (of God) and an instrument (to worship God).

In fact, acceptance of this model resulted in a very famous and subtle change of wording in the Dogmatic Constitution of the Church (made at Vatican II): "The unique Church of Christ is the Catholic Church" was changed to "The Unique Church of Christ subsists in the Catholic Church."

The Pilgrim People Model

The pilgrim people model also sprung out of Vatican II. In a way, this model is the most exciting one, and it certainly demonstrates a radical change in Church thinking. This model acknowledges that the Church is not static, that it is unfolding through history, and it embraces the idea that new insights and new methods will be met along the way.

Basically, this model is metaphorical. It sees the Church as traveling with God on a pilgrimage to the future. Vatican II states that the Church is "specially graced in order to lead the rest of mankind on a pilgrimage to its ultimate destiny."

The problem with the pilgrim people model is that it underemphasizes the relationship between the people and Jesus Christ. Apparently, this model never really caught on outside the Curia and the Vatican II documents.

Human Community Model

This kinder, gentler model of the Church addresses basic human needs and what the Church calls its "pastoral strategy": breaking the Church down from its formidable overpowering size and hierarchy into more approachable components, fostering prayer groups, house churches, and even Pentecostal gatherings. However, the danger to this model—and one that the Church would never tolerate—is that it can (and has) led to individual collectives breaking away from the Church and forming underground "Churches" that then run the risk of becoming sects.

The Church-as-Servant Model

The final model introduced by Avery Dulles is a theological one, really an astonishing volte-face from such an authoritarian structure. It is based on the simple idea that Christ came to serve, and therefore the Church must serve the whole world. It is a call for the "servant" Church to share in the problems of human life, rather than dominating it.

This low-key, humble model introduces a fresh attitude of listening to the world. This leads to the social call to action and justice, now promoted throughout many Church documents. The Church's task is to work for peace, liberation, and justice in the secular world, just as much as it is to try to save souls. Church thinkers call this an exciting model, but they prefer to wait and see how it plays out because "further clarifications are required."

Chapter 16

Salvation in Community

The Catholic Church teaches that we seek salvation in community and solidarity and that we work in communion with our brothers and sisters to reach perfect communion with the Lord. To reach an understanding with God, we must also be at peace with our coworkers, family, neighbors, and people all over the world—people of all ethnic groups and all cultures. This is not an easy task, but it is part and parcel of Catholic faith and belief, the basic dogma of a "one, holy, catholic, and apostolic Church."

The Everyday Catholic

Each Catholic strives to achieve spirituality in his or her daily life so that he or she may reach salvation. However, this is not a process that is undergone alone. Salvation of each Catholic can only be achieved through community, whether they worship the Lord in church every Sunday or reach out to others in need through a Catholic organization. In a way, each Catholic is like a member of a sports team, and if some members do not hold up their end of the bargain, the whole team suffers.

Encounters with the Divine

To have the right state of mind is essential to a good moral compass. That is one reason prayer is central to the life of a Catholic. You might have an image of someone kneeling by their bed or altar with hands folded. That is a beatific vision, but it is rarely the norm.

Prayer has a meditative quality. It is therefore a peaceful, calming way of counting your blessings as well as of saying thanks. It can help you sort out your decision-making and reset your moral compass. It is a private act.

Prayer can involve having a conversation with God, going over some thoughts in communion with him, or reciting a Rosary and reflecting on the mysteries. It can be the Our Father at the end of the day before bed, or it might be a line thrown out to the Almighty on the way to work. Through prayer, Catholics keep returning to the teachings of Christ (and of the Church), and it gives them strength to deal with others.

At the heart of prayer is the act of celebrating the Eucharist. It both adheres Catholics into the divine and draws them out of themselves. It is a public act. Trying to be a good Catholic can be humbling, but God's mercy shines through, especially at Mass. Partaking of the Body of Christ is healing and inspiring. It helps return Catholics to the path, inspirited to go about their daily lives in a healthful way—and, of course, as part of a community.

The Power of God's Forgiveness

Catholicism is a demanding religion. Its principles—or, really, the Word of God—require that Catholics always strive to be the best. This isn't easy, of course; in fact, it is virtually impossible. But the wonderful thing about Catholicism is that it teaches that no matter how often you fail, God is all-forgiving.

This forgiveness is a tremendous gift to daily life. It means that when you are distracted or troubled or harassed, or when you fail to live up to the highest principles, you can still pick yourself up and go on. What's more, with your Father's loving mercy, you can go on feeling emboldened to try to behave better. This forgiveness gives courage, strength, and support in a way nothing else ever could. It helps make Catholics better citizens in the world as well as better citizens in Christ.

Doing Good Deeds

Hand in glove with the constant effort to be good is the impulse to *do* good. You may have heard of the phrase *random acts of kindness*. This is a secular idea that has long been fostered by the Church. Helping out and spending time with the less fortunate, the sick, and those struggling with alcoholism are all useful efforts in the scheme of the mission, which is service to others.

Dozens of organizations in the United States offer opportunities for work within the Catholic community. One is called the Catholic Network of Volunteer Service (on the Web as ✑ *www.cnvs.org/a-con-n.htm*). Its purpose is to connect full-time volunteers with Christian programs.

This is the true meaning of the word *charity*: kindness and thoughtfulness toward others. Again, this is what it means to be part of a community. Catholics want to foster in themselves a generosity of spirit (whether that means teaching, giving money, or helping others) and to try to see that life can be made easier for others. Charity is unbelievably rewarding, but, more important, it knits Catholics into the community of the world.

In addition to individual initiatives such as foundations to help get asbestos out of housing developments or to lobby for arms control, there are at least 1,400 Catholic charitable organizations operating in the United States. They serve 18 million people and include such agencies as the Catholic Health Association with its 600 hospitals and 300 long-term care facilities, or the Campaign for Human Development that works to help the poor. This organization collaborates with 200 smaller chapters of antipoverty groups, whose efforts aim to improve laws affecting low-income people.

Devotional Habits of the Catholic Family

The family is the lifeblood and central unit of any Catholic parish. Indeed, the metaphor of family informs the entire structure of the Catholic Church. The family is an inviolable unit, one that—lived well—gives great strength, comfort, and support in faith and that leads to a happy, healthy life. It is no coincidence that the beginning of a family, matrimony, is one of the seven sacraments of Catholicism.

The Bonds of Prayer

Tying a Catholic family together are the bonds of prayer. Prayer brings holiness into the family and creates a ritualistic setting where the family can unite in their common wishes and their faith. Parents introduce their children to prayers at a young age, and children grow up with a deep connection to prayer as a form of communication with their family and with God.

A simple grace before every meal is one fine way to gently bring the Lord into daily life. Food means comfort and sustenance. It is important to remember that it doesn't get on the table by itself. The parents provided and cooked it. And God made the world from which the food springs. Thanking God is a good way to remind children not to take life for granted.

Also, many children are taught to say a simple prayer before going to bed. This simple ritual of saying a bedtime prayer helps them calm down, forms a lovely bond with their parents, and becomes a long-lasting tradition. Most important, it sets the stage for the development of faith as children grow older. Here is a sample bedtime prayer that many Catholic parents teach their young ones:

> Matthew, Mark, Luke, and John,
> Bless the bed that I lie on.
> Four angels round my bed,
> Two at the foot, and two at the head.

Regular Sunday Worship

A family is also strengthened by its weekly adherence to Sunday worship. Attending Mass as a family unit is enriching. Praying and worshiping together during the liturgy spreads warmth that can't be denied. It raises everyone up and helps them feel a little better about themselves. When children are older, partaking in the Eucharistic celebration is ennobling. The children are now soldiers of Christ and well on their way to becoming full-fledged members of the congregation.

FACT

Catholic children usually attend Confraternity of Christian Doctrine (CCD) classes, where they receive an age-appropriate introduction to Bible stories. This gives them a taste of the great mysteries at the heart of Catholicism as well as instruction in catechism to help them begin their journey to becoming Catholic adults with a firm grasp on Catholic beliefs.

Once introduced to simple devotional habits, a Catholic child will probably go to a Catholic school to learn their catechism properly and receive more disciplined Catholic teachings. But it is the parents who set the educational stage. By teaching children about prayer and making it part of daily life, parents give their children an exemplary model for personal help and meditation for their whole lives.

A Community Support Network

There is "one body and one Spirit," just as "you were also called to the one hope of your call" (Ephesians 4:4). Catholics are communal people. They feel a need to be part of a bigger community and to receive challenging feedback from others with similar ideals. In a spiritual sense, they want support and company on their journey to God. Many Catholics enjoy the enriching experience of belonging to a faith community because of the interaction and the relationships they form there among people with common interests and beliefs.

The parish is obviously the epicenter of each Catholic community. Here you have people seeking God together in prayer and the Catholic devotions. But there is also a growing movement toward more casual "faith communities": small gatherings at church socials or even at specially built centers (usually attached to a chapel or church) where people come together for discussion and prayer. These are more informal groups that, in a way, represent a beautiful tradition that dates back to the early Christian gatherings, when people met in private homes to practice their faith in secret.

Spiritual Centers

For some, a faith community might be at a monastery; for others, it might be a casual prayer group. For example, college students can find a spiritual home at a Newman Center on their college campus. In a broader sense, a Catholic high school is a faith community because each student is surrounded by others who share a Catholic upbringing.

FACT

A Newman Center is a center on campus for the spiritual life of Catholic students. It is named after the inspiring Cardinal John Henry Newman. Now a worldwide movement, the Newman Apostolate originated in 1893 at the University of Pennsylvania, when a few students decided to organize in order to take action spiritually, intellectually, and socially.

Spiritual centers allow individuals a greater degree of participation in and understanding of their faith while reinforcing their sense of community. In a group setting, prayers become much more meaningful and also more natural, as people share their devotion with their friends.

A Community of Saints

Saints are the spiritual leaders and role models of the Catholic community, those who have lived a life of great piety and sacrifice and set a shining example of pure and immaculate spirits. The first saints were martyrs—those who died for their faith. These martyrs were inspiring and the faithful lavished devotion on them. In the days of the early Church, Christians would gather on the anniversaries of their deaths to honor them. When persecution ended, there was an outpouring of love and honor, complete with immense tombs and special liturgies. The liturgical calendar was deluged with feast days for each saint.

Devotion to the saints, long a cherished Catholic tradition, seems to have waned in recent years. The Scripture does not really dwell on the mystical bond with the saints in any depth. Today, it may be harder to believe in the existence of such "supernatural" beings who can intercede for Catholics with Christ. Or it may be hard to think about martyrs of 2,000 years ago in any meaningful way, when there may not be much more than a myth and a few shreds of cloth or a shrine to remember them by. But many in the Church ask if this is only a temporary state.

Why We Need Saints Now

Devotion to the saints can be a powerful aid to living a Catholic life in a troubled world, and Catholics are certainly expected to believe in the "communion of saints," who are with God in Heaven but still in communion with the followers on earth through a common faith.

This belief is upheld in the Apostles' Creed, which states, "I believe in the Holy Spirit; the holy Catholic Church; the communion of saints." It is a resource and a community worth tapping. The saints can be called on to intercede with God on behalf of the faithful. (At Vatican II, the

Church confirmed its teaching that Catholics should pray to the saints for intercession.) Catholics can also receive saintly guidance from these heroes and heroines of faith for their virtues of compassion, forgiveness, honesty, justice, patience, and wisdom.

The saints are wonderful guides to helping explain the mystery of "indwelling." According to this mystery, God is present in a special manner in the "justified." This is something the true saints have experienced and that they can help us glimpse.

Many of the saints were inspired writers. Today, Catholics seek out the words and works of such saints as St. Ignatius Loyola, St. Teresa of Ávila, St. Thérèse of Lisieux, and St. Clare, who—among others—help enrich understanding of God.

In Frances de Sales's book *Introduction to a Devout Life,* he wrote that saints stressed frequent short prayers, such as this: "Admire his beauty, invoke his aid, cast yourself in spirit at the foot of his cross, adore his goodness, a thousand times in the day."

The Social Vision of Catholicism

The saints did not gain their status through faith alone. Most of them also exemplify the good works they did for mankind in the name of God. Part of the spirit of the Catholic Church is helping others, particularly those who are less fortunate. It is each Catholic's most honorable duty to take part in the world and minister to others.

First Calls to Action

Time and again, Jesus Christ stressed compassion for the poor, meek, oppressed, and humble. Think of the Beatitudes. Jesus certainly identified with those who were downtrodden by the powerful or corrupt. By following his example, Catholics also wish to help the poor and hungry. They support peaceful action for freedom in countries where people are not free to worship as they wish or to live in peace and harmony.

According to the teachings of Paul, social isolation is a sin because those who are isolated are morally out of sync with their communities. Paul felt that Catholics could not achieve the important work of transforming the world (to Christ's vision) if they were working out of harmony with one another.

Luke's social vision was more radical. Seeing the injustices between the rich and the poor, he attacked the improper amassing of personal wealth and preached a new vision of a community that would share what it had and help those in need.

Changes in Attitude

As the Church established itself over Europe, and as it continued to wrestle for political power through the Middle Ages, its social vision shifted. The Church and its officers were intent on making (and then keeping) Catholicism the preeminent religion, taking the Word of God as far as possible, initiating as many new peoples as possible into the Church, and, you might say, dominating the landscape in a physical (churches, cathedrals, universities) and in a spiritual and social way (working hand in glove with the civil authorities).

The "triumphalist" bent of the Church did not abate until the 1960s, when the charismatic Pope John XXIII called all Catholics to reconsider where they came from and get back on a solid footing with Christ's original teaching. The pope reminded the Church that it should strive to be humble and accept its role as a servant of the world. With that pronouncement, issued from Vatican II, he ushered in a whole new era of social justice in the Church.

New Social Concerns

Pope John recognized the abundance and prosperity in the Northern Hemisphere, and he did not disapprove of it. But the gap between the wealthy industrialized nations and Third-World countries distressed him. In his encyclical *Mater et Magistra: Pacem in Terris* (1963), the pope discussed a wide variety of social concerns: capitalism and labor, agricultural practices in underdeveloped nations, and socialization (the forming of volunteer societies to help the dispossessed). Strikingly, the pope denounced the idea that all people are entitled to own private property. (This idea had been long held by the Church, but, theologically speaking, it really does go against the grain of Christ's teachings.) He leaned toward a welfare state model, which horrified a lot of conservative Catholics.

FACT

Social reconstruction became a major force in the United States, with the formation of the Social Action Department of the National Catholic Welfare Conference after World War I.

In a remarkable stand on world issues, the pope also condemned the nuclear arms race—truly a courageous and worldly pope. This engagement with the world was a marked departure from the policies of the popes preceding him. For his leadership, he could be compared to Pope Leo the Great and Gregory the Great, two popes who had the personal will to establish reforms in the structure of the Catholic Church.

Pope John recognized that the Church could not provide concrete solutions to world problems. According to him, it was the individual Catholic's duty to work toward a more humane world.

Leadership of John Paul II

In 1981, Pope John Paul II took up the thread of thought espoused by Pope John XXIII regarding a social model suspiciously close to communism. He agreed that workers should have control of their work, but he also recognized the flaws in any system that did not allow for self-criticism.

In his encyclical, he stressed that it was the responsibility of the laity, more than the Church, to get involved in secular affairs—such as aiding a nation in a state of oppression—because they are of the secular world and therefore more competent to find solutions within it. He also stressed the importance of the poor trying to help themselves. This was a departure from all previous thinking (except that of Pope John XXIII). Rather than being helped by a powerful body, John Paul made a radical suggestion that the poor should take responsibility for bettering their own lots in life.

Salvation Through Faith and Good Works

The Church has seesawed between an emphasis on faith—that you achieve salvation through private worship of the Lord—and stress on good works. Clearly, it takes a combination of both things to be a good Catholic and to live life as Christ wished us to do. But how can we achieve this balance?

What Is Salvation?

Salvation means overcoming sin and the basic flaws of the human condition and returning to the ultimate, longed-for state of spirituality. The example we have of salvation is Christ's Resurrection, in which he was transformed into a new mode of existence. That transformation is what we are all striving to achieve.

While there is a strong judgmental quality to this idea—that the wicked will be punished—we must also remember that it is tempered by Jesus' compassion. So we trip and fall, ask forgiveness, and soldier on again.

It is every Catholic's individual responsibility to work out his or her salvation, and the framework of the Church provides plenty of help for every Catholic to reach that goal. As the bishops proclaimed at Vatican II, the values that we cherish on earth, "human dignity, brotherly communion, and freedom," are of "vital concern to the kingdom of God."

A Full Catholic Life

To be a Catholic, it is not enough to observe the outward signs of worship, such as going to Mass and confession and having sacramentals around your house. That falls short of achieving the state of inner worship that is critical to becoming one with the Lord. It is not enough to only do good works. No matter how generous you are with your time, you must still observe the obligations of worship that membership in the Church requires.

It is the Catholic's responsibility to permeate society, strengthened in purpose by faith, and to try to be a force for good. As the Catholic Catechism attests, "If a bad apple affects the good ones, cannot we as Christians and Catholics reverse the procedure and be the good ones that affect the bad?" We want to help those systems of justice whose aim is to save humanity from its sometimes misguided cultural and temporal interests. Ⓔ

Chapter 17

Milestones of a Catholic Life

In the United States, the vast majority of Catholics are born into Catholic families and raised in the Church. For them, the six sacraments of Baptism, Penance (or reconciliation), Communion, Confirmation, Marriage, and the Anointing of the Sick are important milestones in their lives and faith communities. Public liturgies and milestone rituals affect individuals and those who are around them. They can be opportunities for reflection, meaningful change, and celebration.

Entering the Church Through Baptism

There are special liturgies and preparations for adults who convert and are baptized in the Catholic faith (see Chapter 18). However, the majority of Catholics are baptized as infants, a tradition that dates back to the early days of the Church. Since Baptism washes away sin, and the Church taught that it was necessary for salvation, both parents and Church ministers were reluctant to wait for children to grow up. On the positive side, there seemed no reason to wait to give the baby the gift of purity and grace. Thus the practice of infant baptism took hold.

Catholic parents today make the decision to have the baby baptized a few days after birth. They choose a name or names for the child. It's customary to give the child a first or middle name that belongs to a saint, with the hope that the child will be under the saint's protection and will grow up to emulate the saint's virtues.

ALERT!

Godparents have an important role. For every infant who is baptized, the parents choose godparents, who must be Catholic. The understanding is that godparents are there to help the parents in acting as spiritual guides and as role models. They are also expected to make sure the child gets a Christian education if the parents are lax about it.

Babies are too young to have faith because they lack perception. However, the Church teaches that they can receive grace because the sacrament works *ex opere operato*—by virtue of its own action.

Baptismal Ceremony

Baptism is usually a day of celebration for the infant's family. Extended family and friends gather for the ceremony, which is usually held in conjunction with Mass. First the priest pronounces prayers of exorcism over the baby. Then he anoints the child with the oil of the catechumens. Next, on the baby's behalf, the parents and godparents renounce Satan and all his pomp and works (the sins and vanities of the world). Then, the adults say the Creed, pronouncing their own faith and faith on behalf of the infant, whom they promise to raise in the Church.

Next, the priest carries out the actual baptism by pouring water over the head of the infant and saying, "I baptize thee in the name of the Father, and of the Son, and of the Holy Spirit." Through the pouring of the water the infant is reborn again with and in Christ.

The final actions include the anointing with chrism (the sign of Christianity, in which the anointed shares in the essential powers of Christ) and adornment in a snowy white garment (a symbol of purity of the infant's soul, full of grace and free from sin). Finally, the priest passes a lit candle to the godparent and says a prayer that the newly baptized may be faithful to Christ unto his last day.

FACT

Initiates into religious groups typically wear white clothing; the baptized child is being initiated into the Catholic faith. Also, the white garment identifies each baptized infant with the shining garment in which Christ appeared during the Transfiguration.

First Communion

First Holy Communion is a major and significant milestone in the life of a young Catholic. Church writings have said that it is appropriate for Catholics to make their First Communion once they have "reached the use of reason," that is, once they are around seven years old. By that point, they know, or can figure out, the difference between right and wrong. Cognitively, they are able to learn quite a bit through stories and examples; developmentally, they can be cooperative and attentive during the course of a school day.

At the Right Time

James Fowler, a graduate of Harvard Divinity School, wrote a book called *Stages of Faith*. He talks about faith development through the various life stages of man. At age seven, about the time they make their First Communion, children are on the cusp of two stages of faith that are called the intuitive projective and the mythic literal.

As is appropriate for children between the ages of three and seven, they still feel the influences of intuitive projective faith. This means that they may not always be able to distinguish between fact and fantasy. Through images and stories, they are able to grasp the concerns of the primary adults in their lives. They think with their perception and imagination, rather than through logical processes. Age seven is the ideal age to learn about the Eucharist and to understand lessons from the life of Christ. Children of this age are usually eager to please and cooperate. If they have been raised with love and attention, they can naturally show care and concern for others.

Children between the ages of seven and eleven, about the age when First Communion is taken, begin moving into the stage of mythic literal faith. In this stage, they begin to think logically about life's actual experiences. They are interested in learning beliefs, myths, and moral rules; however, they tend to take their lessons quite literally.

Many Catechism studies for the early grades appeal to both the imagination of the intuitive projective stage and the thirst for rational knowledge of the mythic literal stage by focusing on stories and parables from the life of Christ. Teachers also use stories and examples to teach the Beatitudes along with the importance of getting along with others, caring for others, having a pure and joyful attitude, and helping the less fortunate.

ALERT!

Usually, the Church requires that children have two years of religious instruction before receiving their First Holy Communion. They learn prayers such as the Our Father, Hail Mary, and Glory Be.

Rather than focusing on sin, catechetical teaching before First Communion wisely focuses on the positives. It uses stories and examples to teach children how to be holier and more Christlike, in preparation for receiving the body of Christ. With their increased attention span and growing cognitive skills, seven-year-olds can take in this information. By this age most children are socialized enough to engage in a comfortable give-and-take with peers and to hang in for the course of a school day.

These developmental signs, as well as their preparation, make them ready to receive the Eucharist in the fullest sense of the word. As they trust and love their parents, they can trust and love Jesus. They can accept that God is their Father in Heaven and that Jesus is present in the Eucharist, though they may not grasp the full implications of it all. They can understand how to live like Christ in the world, which means treating others with love, apologizing when wrong, helping the less fortunate, and so on.

As members of their families and of their school communities, they are also ready to partake of communion, and to be full-fledged members of the faith community. Like other Catholics, the Church realizes that as children struggle to grow up and live in the world, they need the grace and benefits of the sacrament of the Eucharist.

The First Communion Ceremony

A child's First Holy Communion is usually a joyful occasion. Often, the children don new suits or new white dresses for this special day. Usually, the First Communion is a public, communal ceremony that includes all the boys and girls in their Catechism or second-grade class. Family members and good friends are present to share in the liturgy and the celebration afterward.

These public groupings are very important and symbolic, for the Eucharist is a meal shared by the entire body of the Church. It is a sacrament that not only draws each person closer to Christ, it draws them closer to the other members of the Church, so that the Church becomes as one body.

First Reconciliation

Reconciliation offers grace and the remission of sin to whoever receives it, and at whatever age. However, each person's approach to reconciliation is very different, depending on age, stage of life, and development as a person. In fact, people adapt reconciliation to a particular milestone or stage of life rather than adapting themselves to reconciliation.

Penance, also called reconciliation, or confession, was introduced as a formal sacrament at a later stage in Church history. In the first centuries of the Church, the main concern was with really major offenses such as adultery and debauchery. Known sinners were not allowed to attend the celebration of the Eucharist; they were excluded from the liturgy by the faith community. Paul wrote that unrepentant sinners should be excluded and avoided, as there was no way of getting through to them anyway.

As time went on, the Church developed formal penances for grave sins. If someone fasted, prayed, wore sackcloth and ashes, and generally atoned for a specific period of time, and if they then found a sponsor who could vouch for their true contrition, they could be admitted back to the fullness of the sacraments.

FACT

Confession as it is known today began in late medieval times, as the outgrowth of a custom in Irish monasteries. There, monks had regular talks with a mentor, counselor, or friend who helped them with their spiritual development. That practice spread to monks and priests in Europe, then began to be adopted by the faithful.

Today, Catholic children normally have their first reconciliation around the age of seven or eight. First confession was once a prerequisite for First Communion; today, that is no longer the case. Most theologians acknowledge that most children do not have serious sins to take care of before receiving the Eucharist. So children normally make their confession in second or third grade. Some parishes let the parents decide whether or not the children are ready. The criterion is that the child knows the difference between more serious and less serious sins.

Confession Is Good for the Soul

The benefit of confession at a young age is that it establishes the habit of using the sacrament of Penance. After all, the Church requires regular confession. It is mandatory for all Catholics to confess once a year as part of the Easter season.

Sins may vary by age. A child may be more concerned with obedience; a teenager, with stealing and impure thoughts; an adult, with any one of the seven deadly sins (pride, greed, lust, anger, gluttony, envy, and sloth). Whatever the age, the sacrament of Penance demands a full examination of conscience preceding confession, a willingness to be completely open and honest during confession, true contrition, and an agreement to do penance and to amend one's ways.

Penance can be therapeutic in the truest sense for children just as well as for teens and adults. This sacrament can truly bring healing to a person's life by helping him or her regain a clear conscience, make amends, get some guidance, and start again.

A first reconciliation can be a memorable experience in a child's life. Cognitively, children are able to learn the commandments and what is expected of them. They are also concerned with what is just and fair. However, it is in later years that, alongside the markers and milestones of adolescence and adulthood, reconciliation can be significant both in helping with problems and pressures and as an instrument of personal growth.

Confirmation of Baptism

In the earliest days of the Church, the sacraments of initiation—Confirmation, Baptism, and the Eucharist—were all administered together to converts. Today, the same practice is applied to adult converts. However, while communion may be administered by a priest, only bishops can carry out the final anointing of Confirmation (literally, a confirmation that the person has been baptized). As the practice of infant baptism grew and contact with the bishop became more limited, Confirmation of young children came to be postponed to a later stage in their lives.

Appropriate Age for Confirmation

Today, a Catholic child is usually confirmed around about the age of fifteen, during early high school. Fowler explains that as young people move beyond their families, they begin to experience new cultures, behaviors, and beliefs, along with different lifestyles and loyalties. At this time, as adolescents learn to drive, face new groups, feel their sexuality more intensely, and begin some employment, they need a strong inner core and philosophy that will help them make sense of their changing lives.

> At about thirteen, the child is leaving the second stage of faith development, mythic literal faith, and entering stage three, synthetic-conventional faith. Adolescents in stage three are looking for a faith center in the form of a philosophy that will ground them and give them a sturdy inner platform from which to deal with life.

While teens may explore, discuss, and question various issues around faith, they often choose as their center the faith they have been raised in. The faith will be very deeply felt, and it gives a real sense of meaning and purpose to their life.

During the catechetical studies leading up to Confirmation, the adolescent can review important articles of faith and can raise questions and discuss issues with a supportive teacher and a group of interested peers. It's a good time for concepts to be solidified and for the students to ask questions, determine how they feel, and define their point of view. It's a time of synthesis before jumping off into full-fledged adolescence.

The Benefits and Gifts of Confirmation

From the point of view of the Church, adolescence is also a good time for Confirmation. Confirmation is a reaffirmation of Baptism and baptismal grace. There is an outpouring of the Holy Spirit, as there is in Baptism. Confirmation completes initiation into the Church community. It is a sacrament of maturity, in that it strengthens the recipient to grow into his faith, to live it more fully and actively, and to never be ashamed to tell the world that he believes in the Gospel of Christ.

The lessons leading up to Confirmation teach that the grace of Confirmation can strengthen recipients to resist any peer pressure that might lead them into sin. On the other hand, Confirmation catechesis teaches that a devout Catholic should never bully or pressure another into accepting his beliefs. As a sacrament of maturity, Confirmation requires and supports good judgment in the Catholic.

Gifts of the Holy Spirit at Confirmation help strengthen the Catholic's faith. They include the following:

* Knowledge, wisdom, and understanding, which help Catholics to set their store by God, virtue, and prayer, to gain an insight into the mysteries of faith, and to be able to explain their faith to others
* Counsel in helping Catholics follow God's plan for their lives by making correct decisions
* Fortitude to be faithful Christians even when it's difficult to do so
* Piety, which inspires Catholics to love God and to worship him through prayer, liturgy, good works, and ministries
* Fear of the Lord, which means an awareness of the evil of sin and a sense of awe and wonder at God's greatness

ALERT!

As a milestone or marker in the life of a Catholic, Confirmation dovetails nicely with the coming of age of a child. It supports and reaffirms the maturation process and the development of faith.

The confirmed also receive the fruits of the Holy Spirit manifest in relationships with God and with others. These include the following:

* **Charity.** Love for God and fellowmen
* **Joy.** Happiness that comes from living a Christian life
* **Peace.** Inner calm despite life's difficulties and trials
* **Kindness.** Concern and empathy for others
* **Goodness.** Living justly as an example for all
* **Continence.** Restraint and moderation in the pursuit of pleasure
* **Mildness.** Gentleness in words and demeanor
* **Fidelity.** Loyalty to God, spouse, family, and friends
* **Long-suffering.** Patience in enduring suffering of any nature
* **Modesty.** Respect for one's own body and the bodies of others in dress, conversation, and behavior
* **Chastity.** Control over sexual impulses and a respectful attitude toward others

The Marriage Vows

Matrimony is unique among the sacraments of the Church for a number of reasons. First, it was the last of the sacraments to be established, around the year 1200, which is quite late in the history of the Church. Second, the husband and wife, rather than a member of the clergy, administer the sacrament to each other. Third, the purposes of marriage within the Church have changed and have been challenged since earliest times.

In the early days of the Church, married couples who converted to Christianity did not have to be remarried in the Church; their marriage was considered valid. The Church also recognized civil ceremonies between two Christians as valid for creating a Christian marriage. The Church did not require the blessing of a priest or any other liturgical trappings.

During the Middle Ages, when European tribes overtook the Roman Empire, a conflict arose between Roman civil law and European law and custom regarding marriage. European law held that marriage was a contract; that the couple owed each other sexual rights to procreate; and that witnesses and a formal ceremony were required. Parents who arranged marriages for their children to increase their power and property wanted marriages to be public contracts. Roman law held that only the couple's vows to each other were important and that they could be taken in private. A whole series of popes declared on the side of Roman law, ruling that marriage was the result of a couple's mutual consent and nothing else. No witnesses were required, and no contract needed to be signed.

However, such privacy led to problems. Parents who arranged marriages in what they held to be the best interest of themselves and their children were still being thwarted. There were abuses as well. Jealous or greedy people could prevent someone's marrying by claiming they had already wed someone else in private, and no one could dispute these false charges.

In the twelfth century, at the Second Lateran Council, theologians declared Matrimony to be a sacrament; it was later upheld by the Councils of Lyons and Florence. The Church decided upon three essential statements on matrimony:

1. The grace of the sacrament is to assist the couple to grow in holiness and perform their married duties.
2. To reflect Christ's fidelity to his Church, marriage must be indissoluble.
3. The real ministers of the sacrament of Matrimony are the marriage partners themselves; they confer the sacrament on each other.

QUESTION?

Given the indissoluble nature of the marriage bond, have there ever been any grounds for dissolving a marriage?
Yes. Spouses seeking to get out of a difficult marriage have been able to do so through the process of annulment. If one party forced or tricked the other into marriage, did not want to or was unable to consummate the marriage, or never intended to have children, the other partner can have the marriage declared invalid. More recently, some marriages have been annulled on the grounds that a "community of love" could not be entered into or sustained.

Toward Modern Marriage

The more public form of marriage did not receive a formal introduction until the Council of Trent decided in 1563 to consider valid only those marriages that had been celebrated before a priest and two witnesses. Later, in 1917, the Code of Canon Law went further. Marriage gained status as a contracted, legal proceeding that was understood to be the exchange of rights to sexual intercourse with the purpose of begetting children (the primary purpose of marriage).

Vatican II softened this strict view of marriage by redefining it as a sharing of life between two human beings who love each other. The begetting of children is seen as a natural development from this sharing.

Modern Catholics face many social issues: high divorce rates, changing social patterns that see couples living together outside of marriage, the use of fertility technologies to allow single women to have children, and other stresses on the traditional family unit. The Church sees these practices as problematic and has come to appreciate even more the love and faithfulness in an authentic marriage. Today, the Church places less emphasis on marriage as a contract, on whether each member of the couple is a baptized Catholic, and on how children fit into the picture.

The Question of Divorce

The Church understands that valid marriages sometimes become untenable for one or both partners. However, given the indissoluble nature of the bond of marriage, a Catholic cannot remarry while the former spouse is still living. Otherwise, the person commits a grave sin and cannot receive the Eucharist or enter fully into the life of the Church. If, while the former spouse remains alive, the person lives a chaste life, he or she remains a member of the Church in good standing.

Marriage is a celebration of the transcendent mystery of the couple's love and faithfulness. The Church supports those virtues through pre- and postmarital counseling and education, helping the couple grow, develop, and sustain their affection and fidelity over the years of their married lives.

When Health Is Failing

People who have been religious or spiritual throughout their lives tend to become more observant as they age. As Catholics age, their thoughts turn to the afterlife. Death, an important transition, looms before them. The sacrament of Anointing of the Sick, or Extreme Unction, as it used to be called, is the final anointing, which is given to the Catholic on his or her deathbed. As such, it is a fitting and useful milestone in the life of a Catholic.

Of late, however, the Church has emphasized the sacrament's healing role. Not just the dying, but also the elderly who have suddenly grown frailer, the very ill (no matter what their age), and people about to undergo surgery are all urged to take advantage of the sacrament of Anointing of the Sick. The elderly are entitled to receive this sacrament any number of times, whenever there is a worsening of their condition.

Spiritual Growth

The Church teaches that the sacrament of Anointing of the Sick has actual properties for healing the body because there is a connection between body and soul. Elderly people often suffer from depression and weariness, and they may be more focused on what is to come than their present existence. Sick people fall into despair, become very self-absorbed, and may give up all hope. They are focused only on their own suffering. The sacrament of Anointing of the Sick can help them rise above their illness and find a hopeful spiritual focus.

Testimony of priests and other witnesses suggests that after the elderly and the sick receive the sacrament of Anointing of the Sick, their health often improves. Many people feel better immediately after receiving the sacrament, and some recoveries are nothing less than miraculous.

Because the sacrament of Anointing of the Sick brings hope and comfort, an improvement in the psychological state of the elderly or ill person may contribute to one in the physical state. But even those people who do not recover, or who recover only to relapse again, draw strength and meaning from the sacrament. They can refocus their life on the essentials, to draw closer to God through the power of the Holy Spirit and to be more long-suffering and hopeful.

For the frail elderly and those with serious or terminal illnesses, death is an undeniable inevitability and a significant transition they must face sooner rather than later. And for many who develop cancer in midlife or who suffer a heart attack, serious illness is a reminder of their mortality. For such people, illness becomes a milestone in their lives; it is a transition with major psychological and emotional consequences. As a result, some people become bitter and full of self-pity, while others accept their illness and learn from it. The grace of the sacrament of Anointing of the Sick can help people with serious illnesses integrate what is happening to them into their spiritual lives to attain growth and understanding.

Ministries of Healing

In the New Testament, Christ healed by touch many people who were acknowledged to be hopeless cases. He did this as a demonstration of divine power and also out of compassion. However, he did not heal everyone. The Church teaches that sickness is related to the sinful state of mankind, but it is not directly related to an individual's sins and is not meant to be a punishment. People must accept their sickness and find meaning in their suffering as they find their own path to God.

FACT

In the Book of Acts of the Apostles, Peter and the other apostles anoint the sick. They act on the specific directive of Jesus, who tells them to heal in his name. In the early days of the Church, the sacrament of Anointing of the Sick was not focused on the dying, as it later came to be.

The Church teaches that all Catholics can be living, breathing sacraments of healing as they help those who need emotional, mental, or physical healing. Possibilities for this are endless, but they include some of the following:

- Visiting the sick
- Visiting the dying
- Volunteering in hospices or hospitals
- Volunteering to help the physically, mentally, or emotionally ailing.
- Volunteering to help the homeless and indigent
- Helping patients who are afflicted with AIDS, cancer, and other terminal illnesses

Chapter 18

Conversion to Catholicism

People who convert are seekers. Intellectually, spiritually, or emotionally, they are looking for a faith that satisfies a deep need within them. Conversion to Catholicism is a spiritual journey that many people have undertaken over hundreds of years. However, it is not an easy process. The Rite of Christian Initiation for Adults is an important process, and the Church has prepared guidelines for how it should be carried out.

Reasons for Conversion

People who convert have many reasons for their decision. Many say that something was missing in their lives until they discovered the fulfillment of faith through the Catholic Church. Some are influenced by Catholic friends and their lifestyle. Some come to admire Catholic heroes for their lives of service or other admirable qualities. Some are influenced by writers such as Thomas Merton or St. Augustine, both of whom detailed their own conversions in their writings.

Often it is an intellectual approach that leads converts to the Church. The Episcopalian and Anglican church followers who converted to Catholicism in the 1800s were biblical scholars who were disillusioned with their own faith and believed the Catholic Church had a better approach to Christianity. Today's evangelical and fundamentalist Protestants who convert often plumb the teachings of several Christian faiths before settling on Catholicism. Scholars who have studied the Bible and the history of Christianity are attracted to Catholicism because of its place at the very roots of Jesus' ministry.

Many converts are attracted to the moral structure of the Church and its demands that Catholics accept a Christian lifestyle and all of Catholic dogma. Some converts are attracted to the Church's teaching on family planning and sexual morality. Others seek out Catholicism because they agree with its emphasis on good works as a route to salvation.

The journey to the Catholic Church must be taken of your own free will. During Vatican II, the Church declared firmly that coerced conversion is wrong and is not supported by Catholic dogma.

Converts to Catholicism also cite emotional and spiritual reasons for their conversion. The beautiful rituals and mysteries of the Catholic Church appeal to many of the faithful and can lead to a deep commitment. Many of those who convert recall the role of a supportive church community or parish in helping them feel as if they were coming home.

Well-Known Converts

One of Christianity's most enduring images is Paul's conversion on the road to Damascus. A zealous Jew, Paul (who was then known as Saul) had just witnessed the stoning of Stephen. He was traveling to Damascus when he was struck down by a bright light. He heard the voice of Jesus telling him to stop the persecution of Christians and to take up ministry. The event left Saul blind for three days, until one of Jesus' followers laid hands on him and he could see again. With his new sight, Saul gained a new faith. He dropped his Jewish name in favor of the Romanized Paul and began preaching Christianity. The Catholic Church considers Paul one of the Twelve Apostles and one of the most prolific writers of the early Church.

Conversion of an Empire

One of the most important conversions in early Christianity was that of Constantine, who became the emperor of Rome in 312, at a time when Christians were being persecuted throughout the Roman Empire. Constantine prohibited the persecution of Christians in his Edict of Milan. He made a formal conversion to Christianity on his deathbed.

The second Roman emperor to exert great influence over Christian affairs was Theodosius the Great (346–395). Theodosius was baptized in 380, after he nearly died from an illness. He declared that all of Rome should be Christian and granted privileges to the Catholic clergy.

Conversion of a Sinner

One of Christianity's great philosophers, St. Augustine, was born in 354, in what is now Algeria, and studied in Carthage. Although his mother raised him as a Catholic, St. Augustine abandoned his faith in favor of philosophy and an easy, immoral lifestyle.

Augustine was a young professor of rhetoric in Milan when he discovered the philosophy of Plotinus and St. Paul. He then regained his long-lost Catholic faith and returned to North Africa, where he chose to adopt a monastic lifestyle. St. Augustine's meditations on the nature of grace and his books, *Confessions* and *City of God,* remain influential today.

Royalty and Religion

King Henry IV of France (1553–1610) was raised as a Huguenot and participated in the War of Religions that split France before his reign. He became heir to the throne in 1584, but the powerful Catholic League refused to accept a Protestant on the throne. Henry then converted to Catholicism, in one of history's more controversial conversions. Henry IV's reign was notable for his interest in the common people and the conciliatory approach he took to all faiths.

King Charles II of England (1630–1685) converted on his deathbed after a reign marked by efforts to win religious tolerance. The son of Charles I, who was killed by Cromwell, Charles II spent his youth on the Continent, where he became interested in Catholicism. He was called back to the throne in 1660, at a time when Anglicanism was the state religion in England. Parliament opposed his attempts to overturn laws against Catholicism.

The Oxford Movement

In the middle of the nineteenth century, many British thinkers and theologians converted to Catholicism under the influence of the Oxford, or Tractarian, movement. The Oxford movement was formed among scholars at Oxford University who decried the liberalism of the Anglican church and worried about political trends that threatened its influence on English society.

One of the leaders of the Oxford movement, John Henry Newman, wrote a series of tracts that criticized the Anglican Church and praised the newly formed evangelical movements that he hoped would restore more Christianity in everyday life. Newman converted to Catholicism in 1845 at age forty-four and later went on to become a cardinal in the Church.

The poet Gerard Manley Hopkins was influenced by the Oxford movement while he studied at Oxford. He converted in 1866 and joined the Jesuit Order. Hopkins worked among the poor of Liverpool and later became a preacher in London. He is best known for the original use of language in his religious poetry.

FACT

The Oxford movement was hotly debated in the United States. Episcopalian students were particularly interested. Many American theologians and thinkers converted, including Isaac Hecker, Orestes Brownson, and Clarence Walworth.

American Thinkers and Activists

As a young woman, Dorothy Day (1897–1980) was moved by the poverty of working people around her, and she became active in left-wing and labor movements. In 1927, after the birth of a daughter, she converted to Catholicism but was disappointed by the Church's lack of support for workers. She founded the *Catholic Worker*, an inexpensive paper covering labor news, during the Depression, while simultaneously operating a soup kitchen to help the thousands of unemployed.

The *Catholic Worker* took a pacifist stance during World War II, and it opposed the excesses of the Cold War. Unsurprisingly, Day was an early opponent of the Vietnam War and a supporter of Cesar Chavez's farm workers' movement. Her paper had a wide following among young activists and support from Church peace movements.

ESSENTIAL

Cardinal Spellman of New York disagreed with Dorothy Day over her support of left-wing and labor causes. One flashpoint was a strike of gravediggers at the Calvary cemetery, in which Day picketed the cardinal's office. The cardinal asked Day to take the word *Catholic* out of the title of her newspaper. When she did not comply, the cardinal backed down.

Thomas Merton is one of the most influential American spiritual writers of the twentieth century; in fact, he described the process of his conversion in *The Seven Storey Mountain*, a book that has been translated into twenty-eight languages. Merton has written more than sixty books. Many, including *The Silent Life*, are often studied at Catholic retreats. Merton was a Trappist monk, one of the most ascetic orders. He was influential in the peace movement of the 1960s and interested in Eastern religions, promoting dialogue between the East and the West.

Other Literary Figures

Many famous writers have converted to the Catholic Church. One of the best-known recent converts is Malcolm Muggeridge. Although he is known as a former editor of *Punch,* he was also a journalist and commentator. Furthermore, Muggeridge is credited with making Mother Teresa's work known to the world in his role as BBC producer of the 1968 documentary, *Something Beautiful for God.*

Here is a list of other distinguished literary figures who chose to accept the Catholic faith:

- **G. K. Chesterton (1874–1936)**: Great British writer, essayist, and social historian who wrote books, poetry, plays, and thousands of tight, cogent newspaper essays in a style that was his alone.
- **Alice Meynell (1847–1922)**: British poet and essayist, author of the *Rhythm of Life* and *Collected Poems,* Meynell converted in 1868. She was friend and confidante of Coventry Patmore (1823–1896), another British poet and convert to Catholicism.
- **Alfred Noyes (1880–1958)**: British poet, writer of *The Highwayman* and *The Lord of Misrule*, who converted in 1927. In the Catholic world, he is also known for his insightful essays on the relationship between Christianity and science.
- **Robert Lowell (1917–1977)**: American poet who converted in 1940. His interest in Roman Catholicism is a thread through earlier volumes such as *Land of Unlikeness* and his Pulitzer Prize winner, *Lord Weary's Castle.*
- **Graham Greene (1904–1991)**: Novelist who was notable for having

Catholic characters in his writing. His novel *Brighton Rock* is a study of modern evil.

- **Evelyn Waugh (1903–1966)**: Novelist whose *Brideshead Revisited* is concerned with religion without sounding like a morality tale.

Modern Converts

Prominent people continue to seek out the Catholic Church. Among American converts, there is a tradition of confessional literature, in which writers tell of their own struggles with faith and their reasons for settling on Catholicism.

FACT

Dr. Bernard Nathanson, a former atheist and abortionist, reversed his position on abortion and joined the church in 1970. He once helped draft the laws liberalizing abortion. He is now a pro-life advocate.

Scott Hahn chronicles his personal journey to the church in *Rome Sweet Home*. David Currie, a former preacher's son from a fundamentalist family, tells his conversion story in *Born Fundamentalist, Born Again Catholic*. In *Surprised by Truth*, Patrick Madrid, himself a convert to Catholicism, tells the stories of eleven Americans, of all differing backgrounds, who decided that the Church was the true way. Many of these seekers came from evangelical traditions. Some came from mainstream churches, and others had little religious education at all.

Requirements of Conversion

The Church has the right and an obligation to receive any convert who professes the Catholic faith, regardless of religion, age, sex, or background, but it lays down some conditions. Those who are interested in converting to Catholicism must first learn about the religion, profess the faith, and make a commitment to live in accordance with Catholic teaching.

The first step to becoming a Catholic or investigating the Catholic Church is contacting the nearest Catholic parish. A pastor or religious educator will meet with those interested in converting and advise them of the steps to becoming Catholic. Parishes usually offer a Rite of Christian Initiation for Adults (or RCIA), a process by which adults can convert to Catholicism.

Most adults begin their conversion with a period of intense study to gain a sufficient understanding of Catholicism. In addition, after they have received the permission of a local bishop, new converts participate in three important rites:

1. Rite of Acceptance
2. Rite of Election
3. Sacraments of Initiation

In most parishes, the RCIA begins in September and ends during Holy Week. Throughout the initial period of study, seekers are expected to ask hard questions about Christianity and Catholic dogma. Adults may be paired with mentors who are usually other adults living in the faith who can help answer their questions. The informal discussions during the inquiry period help the seekers determine whether they can live with the rules and teachings of the Catholic community. Many have no formal Christian education and are new to the ideas and traditions of the Church.

Rites of Acceptance and Election

The first major rite of the RCIA process, the Rite of Acceptance, is held several times each year at Sunday Mass. At this ceremony, inquirers are marked with the sign of the cross on the ears, eyes, lips, heart, shoulders, hands, and feet—a symbol of both the joys and the costs of Christian discipleship. This ritual begins their period of catechumenate.

ALERT!

The word *catechumenate* means "time of serious study." Unbaptized Christians studying to be Catholics become catechumens. There is a different term for Christians baptized as Protestants who want to join the Catholic Church. They are called candidates.

Catechumenates join Sunday Mass during the Liturgy of the Word, after which they move to another place to continue reflecting on the Scriptures. The length of this period of study varies according to individual need. Catholic children are expected to have at least two years of study in preparation for their Confirmation. The norm for adults is a year or more.

The catechumenate period ends with the Rite of Election. This rite is held on the first Sunday in Lent. In a ceremony performed by the bishop of the diocese, catechumens receive the Call to Continuing Conversion. The bishop formally acknowledges the readiness of the catechumens and calls them to the Sacraments of Initiation. They respond by expressing their desire for these sacraments.

Preparing for the Sacraments

Before the Sacraments of Initiation can be administered, the catechumens (now known as the Elect) undergo a final period of purification and enlightenment. The Elect spend this period, which falls during the forty days of Lent, in intense prayer and preparation. They are expected to repent of past sins and to reflect on their character and on their readiness to join the Church.

The Elect participate in several further rituals, called scrutinies, on Sundays throughout Lent. The scrutinies are rites for self-searching and repentance whose aim is to heal qualities that are weak or sinful while strengthening those that are positive and strong. During this period, the Elect are also formally presented with the Apostles' Creed and the Lord's Prayer, both of which they recite on the night they are initiated.

Sacraments of Initiation

The Sacraments of Initiation integrate the formal process by which adults are finally admitted to the Catholic Church. Usually performed at the Easter Vigil on Holy Saturday, they include Baptism, Confirmation, and receiving the Eucharist. Only people who have never been baptized in a

Christian church undergo all three sacraments.

The rite of Baptism symbolizes the death of the old sinful person and the creation of a new person in Christ. The convert must renounce Satan and make a profession of faith. Then, he or she is baptized "in the name of the Father and of the Son and of the Holy Spirit." The baptized are dressed in white to symbolize their rebirth and purity.

The second rite, Confirmation, completes the renewal experienced in Baptism. Anointing with sacred chrism seals and strengthens the newly baptized Christians. The Church prays that the Spirit be poured forth upon the new Christians to anoint them to be more like Christ.

The final act that makes the adult convert a full member of the Church is the taking of the Eucharist. Faithful and active participation at the Eucharistic table of the Lord as apostles and witnesses is the goal of Christian initiation. In sharing the bread and wine, which Catholics believe becomes the Body and Blood of Christ, each person becomes one with the Christian community and the Church.

Period of Mystagogy

In the fifty days following the celebration of Christian initiation, newly baptized converts continue their program of Christian formation. They can participate fully with the faithful in Eucharist and in the mission of the Church for justice and peace. This period of *mystagogy* normally lasts until Pentecost Sunday and reminds everyone that growth in faith is ongoing and lifelong.

FACT

For the first year after they are accepted to the Church, newly baptized Christians are called "neophytes." The term derives from the Greek word *neophutos* and is used in the New Testament (1 Timothy 3:6) by Paul to describe a recent convert. Around the eleventh century, the word *neophyte* emerged in English to mean "new convert" or novice.

Converting from Another Church

People who have already been baptized at another Christian church must undertake a different kind of preparation for the Sacraments of Initiation. The Church may insist on separation of these people from the catechumens. The needs of mature, practicing Christians from other faith traditions are considered on an individual basis. Those who have lived as Christians and who only need instruction in the Catholic tradition do not undergo the full program required by catechumens. The parish may propose a period of individual instruction or create a program based on the degree of their familiarity with Christian doctrine.

QUESTION?

How can lapsed Catholics return to the Church?
Catholics who have left the faith and worshiped in another church can return to the fold by going to confession and being reconciled. This process is generally arranged by the parish priest.

Christians from other religious backgrounds who want to convert are called candidates. Since candidates are already baptized, the liturgical rites that mark the steps of the formation process are different from those of catechumens. Their journey begins with rites of welcoming by the parish community and recognition by the bishop. Rather than the Rite of Acceptance, they undergo a sacrament of Penance (confession). Like catechumens, candidates undergo a period of training and inquiry, joining services for the Liturgy of the Word. On the first Sunday in Lent, when catechumens are undergoing the Rite of Election, the candidates participate in the Celebration of the Call to Continuing Conversion.

During the period of purification and enlightenment, candidates are expected to participate in a penitential rite as well as a period of reflection. Since candidates will have committed sins since their baptism, they must confess their mortal sins before receiving Confirmation. Reception into full communion in the Catholic Church takes place with the profession of faith, Confirmation, and Eucharist. However, the candidates are not normally admitted to Church life on Holy Saturday. Their first communion will be in a Sunday Eucharist with their local parish.

Chapter 19

Catholics in the Greater Society

Catholics—as well as Catholic institutions—are a large presence in our society. Catholic schools, colleges, and universities offer religious as well as secular education, preparing students to go out into the world as politicians, businesspeople, teachers, and so on. Catholic hospitals provide medical care to believers and nonbelievers alike. This chapter examines how Catholicism influences the secular lives of Catholics and their stances on political, environmental, and social issues.

The Grassroots Parish

In the United States, many Catholic communities were originally formed by immigrants from the Old World who settled in the same neighborhoods as their former countrymen. They raised their children in tight communities that reflected their values. At the center of these communities was the parish, a reliable support mechanism that, in turn, centered on a priest and a church. Often, the parish formed its own social institutions—charity organizations, schools, and hospitals.

FACT

Today, the parish remains the anchor of the Catholic community, but it is no longer heterogeneous. A priest, a church, and a school are still at the center, but expectations of what the parish could do and who would do it are changing.

The Church begins its work in the world at the parish level through programs for youth, charitable work, and pastoral care. Catholic sociologist Andrew Greeley, a priest and research associate at the National Opinion Research Center in Chicago, calls the parish "a sacrament of God's presence." He believes that parishes evolved naturally because Catholics like to be close to a church. Catholics value community in part because it is one of the tools God uses to work for good in the world. Various overlapping networks that link people together have evolved out of parish life, not just religious organizations but also social, civil, fraternal, and political groups.

Catholics turn to their parish for support in their spiritual life and to establish strong personal relationships that carry them through times of trouble. They want their children to be part of a community that shares the same values. The parish is a vehicle for getting involved in charitable work, but it is also increasingly a place to get involved in organizations that back a moral cause, such as pro-life, social-justice, or environmental groups. Inner-city parishes are still dealing with problems of poverty and congregations of recent immigrants, but many Catholics now live in the suburbs, and their parishes are challenged to deal with the problems that accompany affluence.

The parish is where people live and die, marry and baptize their babies, educate their children and make lifelong friends. A good sermon or conversations with a nun, a supportive priest, or a teacher who serves as a role model are significant factors in deciding whether young people stick with their religious life. The latest news from the Vatican or the position papers of the bishops are of less significance, even among Catholics who follow political events closely. Even the birth-control encyclical, which significantly reduced church attendance and donations, can be dismissed by Catholics who disagree with it if they feel at home in their parish.

The parish priest is the heart of a successful parish and a key to the quality of both pastoral care and religious instruction. A priest who gives an excellent sermon is highly valued. But the laypeople who keep things going in a parish usually outlast their priests. They have built and operated the parish, made decisions and invested time and money. They are willing to wait out a priest whose ideas are out of sync or whose sermons are indifferent, because they know the next one may be better.

New Pressures on the Parish

As the number of priests in the United States declines, the role of the laity in parish life increases in importance. Laypeople help distribute communion and prepare for worship, get involved with local schools, visit members of the congregation who are ill, and operate Catholic charities. As the role of women in the society has changed, Catholic women have insisted on doing more than making coffee and running bake sales. They play leadership roles in worship, charitable organizations, and school councils.

There is pressure to experiment with more modern styles of worship within middle-class communities. Some parishes have tried worship in small groups. Some are pressing their priest for sermons more rooted in the world. Some parishes are heavily involved in political issues such as homelessness, poverty, and minority rights. Active parishes are pushing against the strictures of a conservative Church that has not abandoned its traditional hierarchical structure.

Some parishes that are losing the numbers game have been forced to merge with neighboring parishes as the number in the congregation dips. But the closing of a parish can destroy important community relationships, even if it is no longer financially viable. The Church has made a commitment to remain open in some inner-city parishes, despite financial pressures, because there is a need for the work the Church can do with children and youth. For most Catholics, the parish remains an accepting community and represents the close relationship most Catholics have with the Church.

Charity Work

The Church has offered some form of charity ever since its early days, when Paul urged Christian communities to take care of the widows and put them to useful work. For centuries, Catholic religious orders and groups have been operating schools, hospitals, orphanages, and homes for the elderly.

In 1633, St. Vincent de Paul established a charity to work among slaves, serfs, and the laborers. The Sisters of the Good Shepherd devoted themselves to the reformation of wayward girls. Countless other charities have also evolved in the framework of the Catholic Church.

There has been a blossoming of Catholic charities into numerous areas of work. In the Western world, Catholic charities are working among minority, immigrant, and refugee groups, trying to give a voice to the poor in the legal system. Catholic charities still run hospitals and many are involved in family support.

In the United States and Canada, groups such as FoodShare operate community kitchens, hostels for the homeless, drop-in centers, and food banks. Catholic charities devoted to food aid internationally include Canadian Food for Children and Save a Family Plan, organizations that help the poor of India and Haiti on the road to self-reliance. Catholics also work within larger organizations, such as the Red Cross, United Way, and World Vision.

Catholic Education

Catholic families continue to send their children to Catholic schools in record numbers, with some schools in suburban areas having waiting lists. Catholic parochial schools generally have a reputation for high academic achievement at both the elementary and high-school levels. Catholic education appears to make a significant difference in religious and moral behavior, with Catholic-educated young adults more likely to continue attending church and to be more sexually conservative.

The first Catholic schools in North America were founded by religious orders to train the young in reading and religion and to select candidates for the seminary. Parishes took over the task of establishing schools in the 1800s as Catholic immigrants streamed into American cities. In the United States, Catholic parochial schools remained under the control of the Church, and they have never attained full access to public funding. Catholic parochial schools do qualify for federal funding for enhancement of science and technology programs. States with charter school or voucher programs may approve credits to parents who pay tuition at Catholic schools.

FACT

In Canada, public funding for Catholic schools varies by province, from full funding in Ontario to a voucher system for religious schools in Alberta. Elected Catholic school boards run publicly funded Catholic schools. Public funding comes with complications as governments may insist on an approved curriculum, nondiscriminatory hiring policies, and liberal policies that may not concur with Catholic teaching.

Catholic schools play an important role in integrating children into the parish community. That's not just the result of the hours spent on religious instruction. The basketball courts and football fields are equally important in connecting young people to the parish. Students who go to school with other Catholics are more likely to have a network of Catholic friends as they grow older. Preparing for a First Communion or helping as an altar server among a group of peers makes the experience more memorable.

The Church views Catholic education as an important tool for setting a moral foundation for the young. Religious education and lessons on applying Catholic faith in daily life are important parts of the curriculum. Catholic schools offer instruction in sexual morality, the sanctity of family life, and the meaning of the sacraments. At the same time, there is an emphasis on academic excellence as many students continue their education at colleges and universities.

The Confraternity of Christian Doctrine (or CCD), founded in the sixteenth century, is a group dedicated to promoting devotion. In most parishes in North America, the CCD is a program where children come for a few hours a week to be educated in the Catholic faith and moral values. Belonging to the CCD is especially beneficial for those who attend public school.

Colleges and Universities

The earliest universities in Europe operated under papal charter, among them the University of Paris, Oxford University, and the University of Bologna. The University of Paris was an influential school of theology that attracted clergy from throughout Europe. In the eleventh and twelfth centuries, there was a rise in interest in learning, resulting in groups of scholars or clergy in the large cities gathering together to exchange ideas. In the thirteenth century, these centers of learning sought papal charters or royal charters, so both civil and religious authorities played a role in the founding of the great universities. These places of learning taught the law, the arts and philosophy, medicine, and theology.

In the New World, the earliest Catholic colleges were established as a way of training priests and female religious in their vocations. But after 1900, higher education started gaining momentum as Catholics began to recognize the power education had to encourage upward mobility. Catholic colleges and universities were created to compete with secular and Protestant institutions and to continue the work of the parochial schools in forming young men and women as "citizens for the city of God." The colleges were under the control of religious orders and staffed by priests or nuns. The teaching approach was conservative, emphasizing Catholic doctrine and limiting opportunities for women to teaching, nursing, social work, and home economy.

Following World War II, many young men flowed into the universities on the G.I. Bill. These former soldiers were interested in earning academic credentials that would improve their career prospects. Pressured to provide superior education, Catholic colleges and universities sought to improve the quality of Catholic education. Laypeople were brought in to teach secular subjects like science and technology.

During the 1960s, there was a revolution in Catholic academia as universities and colleges sought separate incorporation. Independent boards of trustees were set up to run the colleges and universities, and religious orders turned over property and charters to these new boards. The tight control exercised by the Church was broken, and boards began building institutions such as University of Notre Dame and Fordham University into the some of the best schools in the country. In the 1970s, the universities gained access to federal funding on the same basis as other institutions of higher learning.

FACT

Charles Curran, a well-respected Catholic theologian at Catholic University, opposed the Church's stand against birth control. A 1966 strike by fellow faculty members over academic freedom forced the university to keep him on. It was 1989 before the Congregation on the Doctrine of the Faith forced Curran's removal from his post as a teacher of theology.

The creation of a more secular environment left campuses struggling with secular issues—such as who to hire and whether Catholic faith should be a prerequisite, how to improve the opportunities for minority groups in higher education and how to handle academic freedom. Many lay professors who joined these institutions assumed the right to academic freedom. Yet professors who spoke freely, especially on issues such as contraception and abortion, found themselves on a collision course with the Vatican.

The Vatican moved to reassert some kind of control, demanding that professors who teach theological studies be appointed with approval of the local bishops. Pope John Paul II's 1990 document on the relationship between universities and the Church, *Ex Corde Ecclesiae,* renewed this demand but left this tension between the academic community and the Vatican unresolved.

Many of the students who streamed into Catholic universities throughout the 1970s are now affluent alumni who can support their alma maters. The United States now has 238 Catholic colleges and universities providing higher education to more than 600,000 students. They are located in forty of the fifty states and include—among many—the University of Saint Louis, the University of New Rochelle, and Georgetown University.

Many of the nineteen Catholic colleges of Canada have merged with the public university system, including St. Michael's College, now part of the University of Toronto; St. Jerome's at University of Waterloo; and St. Paul's at the University of Manitoba. Only St. Francis Xavier University in Antigonish, Nova Scotia, and St. Thomas University in Fredericton, New Brunswick, remain separate universities. Some have evolved into theological schools, including the faculty of theology at *Cité Universitaire* in Quebec City; Newman Theological College in Edmonton; and *Collège Dominicain* in Ottawa.

Catholic intellectuals still struggle with the question of how much the North American universities remain Catholic. There are pro-abortion and homosexual rights organizations on campus. Faculties are not universally Catholic, nor do all the teachings reflect the position of the Church. Students at these colleges meet and befriend other Catholic students, but, immersed in a secular college environment, they are also part of a much wider circle. Debate rages even inside the departments of theology, where outspoken faculty members question the direction of the Church.

Catholics and the Environment

Catholics believe that God expects humankind to exercise stewardship over the earth. As God's highest creation, human beings have a responsibility to use their knowledge to preserve and protect the environment. Both the

Holy See and the U.S. Conference of Catholic Bishops have pressed for action in response to global warming and have urged governments to move toward models of sustainable development. In North America, the Church operates an "environmental justice" grants program that gives money for environmental education, research, and action. The Church's environmentalist stance is tied to its support for developing nations, as their growth hinges on an equitable sharing of the earth's resources.

There is also fledgling lay movement for individual action to preserve the environment. This movement urges Catholics to live with respect for the rest of creation by practicing organic gardening, supporting organic farming, reducing automobile use, and consciously reducing consumption of material goods.

Catholic Catechism emphasizes the interdependence of all things as part of God's plan. When individuals take too many of the world's resources for themselves, they upset the natural order. Each plant and animal has its own particular goodness and perfection and should be respected as a work of creation. Making use of creation for our own livelihood is part of mankind's role, but each tree or plant or animal must be taken with good reason and in a way that would not lead to disorder in the environment.

Scientific Beliefs

The Church keeps a close watch on scientific discoveries through its committee on Science and Human Values. The role of the committee is to identify areas where ethical discussion is necessary to advance the common good. The committee enters into dialogue with scientists to understand new developments and isolate ethical issues and has issued public statements about topics such as global population, genetic testing, genetic screening, death and dying, cloning, stem cell research, genetic modification in plants, evolution, and the relationship of brain, mind, and spirit. As new reproductive and genetic technologies develop, the Church is continually challenged to define the moral course of the Catholic community.

For instance, the Vatican has spoken out against human cloning and euthanasia. It says the use of stem cells from aborted fetuses and human embryos is clearly wrong, but it endorses the use of stem cells from adults for medical advances. It urges caution in xenotransplantation—the use of animal organs to prolong human life. In regard to genetic engineering and modification, the Church warns against concentrating the patents for the gene pools of plants and animals in the hands of a few rich nations. It also states that genetic modification should not proceed until we can establish that it will not harm God's creation.

Catholics in Business

Pope John Paul II often criticizes American culture, saying it puts financial profits ahead of all other values. This poses an ethical dilemma for Catholics in business. Conservative Catholics may also find themselves at odds with letters from the bishops calling for better treatment of workers and advocating measures to limit the excesses of the free market system. Jesus' own detachment from wealth and material possessions and his love of the poor are powerful themes of Christian life.

ALERT!

Pope John Paul II's encyclical, *Laborem Exercens,* released in 1981, is a meditation on human work. It traces the relationship between the poor Third-World worker and his often indirect employer, the multinational firm. The encyclical also argues that people are entitled to benefits such as unemployment compensation and medical coverage, and defends the right of the worker to unionize and to emigrate in search of meaningful work.

Yet the drive to succeed financially and to build a better life for one's family is a staple of North American life. Among the Irish Catholics who filled the cities at the turn of the century, there were plenty with entrepreneurial talent. In 1836, Patrick Donahoe of Boston founded the *Boston Pilot,* an influential Catholic newspaper, and went on to prosper as a banker. Joseph P. Kennedy ran a bank at age twenty-five and amassed a fortune as a stockbroker during the 1920s. The Polish Catholics and the Hispanic Catholics who came to the New World in the twentieth century were equally able to make the most of the opportunities that a capitalist democracy presents.

By the 1960s, Catholics were as affluent as any religious group in North America, and some were extremely successful in business. There was very little discussion of business ethics during the Sunday sermon. Instead, wealthy Catholics were urged to give generously to charity and to express their faith through good works. Discussions of ethical conduct for Catholics in business occur mainly within educational institutions, where few in business can hear them.

Ethics experts such as Father Mark Miller of Edmonton, Alberta, say that ethical conduct isn't a shortcut to bankruptcy. Often the more ethical choice—being honest with shareholders, treating workers well, or keeping a straightforward set of books—is also the better business practice. But in plenty of situations, a business is operating in a way that is legally right yet morally questionable. Business organizations such as Legatus (an international organization for Catholic businesspeople begun in Detroit); Business Leaders for Excellence, Ethics, and Judgment in Chicago; and Civitas Dei in Indianapolis are bringing more talk about living the faith into the workplace.

FACT

A second papal encyclical on the social concerns of the Church, *Sollicitudo Rei Socialis*, was issued in 1987. The pope again confronted the American capitalist system, criticizing the "all-consuming desire for profit" and its ties to imperialism in weaker countries, and challenged the West's rapacious consumption of goods and services.

Catholics and Secular Politics

With Vatican II, the Church outlined a new role in its relations with political systems everywhere. It called for a more humane society built on justice and animated by Christ's love. Laypeople play a role in developing the society they live in by being politically active and working toward world development and peace.

Vatican II called on Christian politicians to protect the welfare of the people and to discharge their duties for the common good. The role of the Church itself is to direct society in moral understanding.

In the United States, the Catholic vote is far from predictable. Although it used to be a truism that Irish Catholics vote Democrat, it's also true that William F. Buckley, editor of the right-wing *National Review,* is a Catholic. Catholics are not uniform in their political views. Some are socially conservative and concerned about public morality, others campaign hard for social justice, and yet others would place themselves somewhere in the middle of the political spectrum. In the United States, Church leaders have a policy of not endorsing any candidate or party, even though they clearly support some political proposals and oppose others.

Before Vatican II, priests confined the political messages in their sermons to decrying the godlessness of communism and warning Catholics to avoid the secularism and materialism of American life. But the Church has slowly created a more public and powerful role for itself. Catholic bishops have addressed concerns of interest to all Americans, including defense, the U.S. role in Latin America, economic justice, health care, child welfare, and human rights. Priests also play a role in interpreting the bishop's position within their parishes.

Prominent Catholics in Office

Anti-Catholic laws, along with an insistence on the separation of Church and state, kept priests and religious women out of office in early

American history. A thread of anti-Catholic sentiment ran through American life. These sentiments were most strongly represented in the presidential campaign of Catholic Alfred Smith in 1928. Prominent Protestant writers asserted that Catholics owed their allegiance to Rome and not to the United States, and argued that Catholics should not be allowed to play a more prominent role in politics.

Nevertheless, anti-Catholic sentiment did not prevent Catholics from taking on public roles, beginning with municipal politics in the predominantly Catholic cities of Boston and Chicago. In 1884, Hugh O'Brien was the first Catholic elected as mayor of Boston, to be followed by John Fitzgerald (who was Rose Kennedy's ambitious and powerful father) and James Michael Curley. Richard Daley and his son, Richard Daley Jr., both served as mayor in Chicago.

Illinois also elected a large number of Catholics to state and congressional office including Edward F. Dunne, who was governor, and Melvin Price, who served as Illinois representative in Congress from 1945 to 1988. Catholics began to be widely represented at the state level and in Congress in the 1950s. Many saw the election of a Catholic president, John F. Kennedy, as a hallmark of political maturity.

Left-wing Catholics took a leading role in protesting the Vietnam War throughout the 1960s and early 1970s. Daniel and Philip Berrigan were Catholic priests and leaders in the anti-war movement. In 1968, they removed records from the draft office in Catonsville, Maryland, and were convicted on charges of conspiracy and destruction of government property.

Increasing political activism even led some clerics and nuns into office. Sister Clare Dunn, an activist for social justice, was elected to serve as a representative in the Arizona State legislature in 1975. Father Roland St. Pierre was a three-term mayor of Plattsburgh, New York. Robert Drinan sat in Congress from 1970 as a representative of Massachusetts until the Vatican asked him in 1980 to resign. A new Code of Canon Law from 1983 forbids both clerics and members of religious orders from taking public office. However, bishops have the authority to grant an exception.

Behind the Scenes

The Holy See has a representative in Washington, D.C., and at the United Nations in New York. The U.S. bishops take prominent stands on public issues and make presentations to government committees on topics as diverse as reproductive technology, the economy, the environment, and the arms race. In the 1970s and 1980s, the abortion issue dominated the Church's public agenda as it fulfilled its role of directing society in moral understanding. The Church even went as far as to criticize Catholic officials in office, including former U.S. Secretary of Health Joseph Califano and Democratic vice-presidential candidate Geraldine Ferraro, who did not work toward its pro-life agenda.

The Church's opposition to reproductive choice led to its stance against legislation to improve the equality of women, including the Equal Rights Amendments. Political conservatives have found a ready ear in the Vatican of John Paul II. However, lay Catholic organizations have not hesitated to press the feminist cause and other liberal causes. Lay organizations represent a range of political views and lobby in a wider spectrum of issues than the bishops. The causes they champion include rights for homosexuals, the peace movement, racial equality, social justice, and international development.

Chapter 20

Looking into the Future

The message of Jesus and of the Gospels that tell his story will always remain the same. However, the interpretation of Christ's message changes along with developments in human understanding. The Holy Spirit, acting through the Church, can take a new and unexpected direction, continually renewing the Catholic faith. The Church is not stagnant in its thinking—it is constantly transforming, as it grows in its understanding of Christ's love.

Toward Democratization and Diversity

Recently, the Church has been engaging with the secular world on many issues—moral, social, and political—and it does not shrink away from taking controversial stands.

The focus of the Church generally reflects the style of the papacy. Pope John Paul II had a reputation as a conservative leader who approves of the hierarchical structure of the Catholic institution and prefers a small group of cardinals to set the agenda for discussion and the tone of debate, which are then passed down to the bishops and parishes. Priests working among people at the parish level are expected to teach and implement Church policies.

However, Vatican II did rule that the laity has a role in accepting the teachings of the Church. This is because, in essence, the Church *is* the whole people of God. Pope John Paul II made little progress in implementing this new direction for the Church, leading to tension between the Church hierarchy and the laity. There is pressure for democratization of the Church, particularly from people living in Western-style democracies who understand that it is beneficial for power to be shared. Most are not asking for a kind of institution where majority rules but for a way of expressing their concerns and jointly developing solutions that work in the real world they live in.

Pressure for Democratization

In the United States in particular, there has been a disconnection between the institutional Church and its people. In the past thirty-five years, the idea of obedience to the Church has fallen into disregard. People walk their own paths over sexual mores, prohibitions on using birth control, and the Church's approach to poverty and health care. While it's not hard to find people who call themselves Catholic, it is harder to find those who obey the Church in every aspect. Many people today accept the faith, but they are not comfortable with the structure of the Church.

FACT

Catholic Organizations for Renewal is a group of more than thirty Catholic groups from the United States and Canada pushing for reform and renewal in the Church, in the spirit of Vatican II. They strongly oppose Church positions on ordination of women and birth control, and their mission statement includes a call for "bringing about a world of justice and peace, reflecting the sacredness of all creation."

Today, dissent is still strongly discouraged, and those who openly discuss controversial issues like the ordination of women are disciplined. Theologians in independent universities need a contract from the bishops to continue with their teaching, and these contracts may be revoked if the scholars investigate new ways of thinking. Married couples who see sex as a way of reaffirming their love, rather than a mere necessity for procreation, are told they are sinful. These are problems of a Church whose teaching is dictated from the top, with little reference to the parish priest or lay believer. However, it seems that the gradual democratization of the Church is a strong possibility, given the commitment of many lay Catholics and their growing presence in the workings of the Church. Many Catholics hope that the Holy Spirit will help guide the Church toward a more inclusive attitude toward its laity and a review of the Church hierarchy and its position and role.

A More Diverse Church

The Church is no longer predominately Western, European, and white. As it moves away from its European traditions, it is pressed to be more multicultural and diverse in its practices and liturgies. The concerns of the Church and the leadership may also change to reflect the strength of the Latin American and African clergy. The concerns of Africa and Latin America, including poverty, AIDS, human rights, and the exploitation of resources may loom larger on the Church agenda.

About 62 million Americans, or 22 percent of the American population, are Catholics; Canada is home to 13 million Catholics. There are 118 million Catholics in Africa and 280 million Catholics in Latin America (from information gathered at ✑ *www.catholic-hierarchy.org*).

The need for greater cultural diversity, particularly in Africa, where more than sixty languages are spoken, is likely to push the Church in new directions. As it grows, it seeks ways to honor traditional African customs and ways of thinking within the Church community. Already more of the priesthood is indigenous, as a result of a push in the 1980s to educate and recruit young people. The most challenging aspect of the mission of the Church in Africa is how to serve society in the face of human rights violations, war, famine, and disease.

On other continents, the need to innovate is equally strong. In the Western world, great affluence and a decline in religious thinking has created an atmosphere where people feel spiritually lost. New models of worship are pulling in groups such as divorced Catholics who thought they no longer had a place within the Church. European and American churches are experimenting with small faith groups, prayer circles, and innovative liturgies and services.

A Quest for Peace and Justice

For a long time, many Catholic thinkers called for greater Catholic involvement in issues of peace, justice, and human rights. Jacques Maritain, a French theologist exiled to the United States during World War II, urged the Church to play a larger role in the political world. He saw God as a prime source of natural law and saw working for human rights as part of the natural order for man. Emmanuel Mounier, an influential Catholic thinker of the first half of the twentieth century, criticized the capitalist system, particularly American interests, and called on priests to ally themselves with workers.

Vatican II set the Church's path to creating the conditions for Christ's reign on earth. It would seek salvation for its members, not only through their faith, but through their human development. Many of the papal encyclicals of the last thirty years have emphasized this course of action—urging Catholics to temper their drive for material gain and work toward justice for all.

FACT

Since the late 1970s, when U.S. Supreme Court decisions led to the resumption of executions in many U.S. states, the nation's Catholic bishops have shown strong opposition to the death penalty. The bishops' position is that, "in the conditions of contemporary American society, the legitimate purposes of punishment do not justify the imposition of the death penalty."

Theology of Liberation

A group of clerics from Peru, Uruguay, and Brazil, Latin American countries with a dramatic gap between rich and poor, developed liberation theology in the 1970s. Liberation theology sees the Word of God mediated through the poor and oppressed. Only by participating in the struggles of these people can Christians truly understand the message of the Gospels. This theology was embraced by many priests in Latin America and led to their support of trade union movements, political struggles, and protests that aided the poor.

Not all priests of Latin America embraced liberation theology; some retained their traditional ties to the power elite of these countries. They confined themselves to the more usual charity work: serving in soup kitchens, educating the young, and working with poor families. However, others took the more radical approach, despite the threats and the danger. Many of the clergy who were active in the fight to improve the conditions of the poor became victims of right-wing death squads, including Oscar Romero, archbishop of El Salvador. These courageous people did not die in vain; their deaths helped galvanize support among Catholics interested in human rights all over the world.

There are charities devoted to peacemaking, both internationally and within specific communities. Development and Peace, an international Catholic organization, works in war-ravaged areas such as Afghanistan, East Timor, and the Congo. The U.S. bishops issued a Call to Solidarity with Africa to focus attention on the problems of the continent and have also made statements on Israeli-Palestinian violence. The Catholic Campaign for Human Development is conducting an awareness campaign about poverty in America.

A Whole People of God

The role of the individual Catholic is to devote time and money to these causes. A portion of church tithes is offered to some charities, while others fund-raise separately. Good works are part of the requirement of Catholic life, and a route to unity with Jesus. For the most motivated, there is the opportunity to work for justice and equality on a political stage.

This obligation to give comes back to message of the Gospels. Jesus tells us to treat our neighbors as we ourselves would like to be treated. The Church holds this message in mind as it lobbies in political forums, publishes encyclicals, and sends its charities out to work in the world. The Church recognizes that this is a time of crisis, when there is rapid change in every area. It seeks the unity of humankind through both a union of the spirit and the cultivation of equality for all people.

What's Next for the Catholic Church?

Having accepted its new role of intervening in secular affairs, the Church is defining its stand on the moral and ethical issues and trends sweeping the world in science, ecology, business, and human rights. These stands are not always popular with secular society or even with some Catholics.

Recent encyclicals on abortion and reproductive technologies reveal the Church's ability to stay on top of the latest social and scientific developments. It has issued frequent commentaries on the state of the world, praising the value of human work, and criticizing both Western capitalists and old-style Communists for contributing to poverty in the developing world. The American bishops have developed position papers about the U.S. economy, the American role in Central America, and the U.S. government's environmental policies. Pope John Paul II worked behind the scenes with Jewish leaders, an initiative that culminated in his tour of the Holy Land in 2000. He also made overtures toward the Eastern Church, holding out hope of finally healing the Great Schism.

ALERT!

Part of the Vatican's world role is to set a course through ethical quagmires created by new science and technology. The Vatican plays a valuable role in stating its opposition to the death penalty or trying to define the ethical issues surrounding new reproductive technologies.

A Shortage of Priests

Some of issues that dog the American church are also of concern in Latin America and Africa, both regions that boast a growing number of Catholics. The status of women, the celibacy of priests, and Church stands on sexuality are issues that could come to the fore in the twenty-first century. While the concerns may be the same, the underlying conditions that give rise to these concerns are very different. And none is more pressing than the shortage of priests.

In the United States, the shortage of priests has led to parishes merging or putting up with mediocre ministry. One of the most pressing issues is that priests cannot marry. The issue of celibacy has contributed to the shortage of priests in Latin America, and there is also a shortage of men to provide ministry as they often must work outside their community. Yet there is no shortage of women willing to take up these tasks.

Additional problems in the United States include the issues of contraception and the treatment of homosexuals. In Africa, the controversy is over the spread of AIDS. African women are still fighting to improve their status within their own cultures and have asked the Church to back them in attempts to stop female circumcision, early marriage, and the shunning of widows. They have not demanded ordination of women, in part because there is no shortage of priests there. Many African men have been drawn to the priesthood.

Few Catholic thinkers want the church to give in to prevailing attitudes. Most want to seek an ethical choice that is responsive to the needs of local congregations. That would involve some kind of mechanism for each diocese or national Church to listen to its people. Again, there is the pressure for structural change and for ministry that adapts to local conditions. Whether such a change happens, whether there will be a Vatican III that sets a new course for the Church, may rest on the men chosen to be pope over the next 100 years.

The Future of the Papacy

The current office of the Bishop of Rome still retains the trappings of a feudal monarchy. No matter how hard the pope and the cardinals try to engage with the world, they are limited by a strict notion of hierarchy. The most responsive faith experiences are initiated first among the priests and the laity. They reach the ears of the bishops only later and only when the Spirit opens their hearts to change.

Vatican II set trends in motion that have already changed the role of the papacy, beginning with a redefinition of infallibility. Infallibility is expressed by the belief of the people of the Church who are in union with the popes and bishops. The people have to believe and accept a teaching for it to be a true belief. In his role as the visible head of the Church, the pope is infallible in teaching Christ's message and in his moral rulings, but it has been acknowledged that he can err.

The idea that the pope can sin and make mistakes in governing the Church or ruling on temporal matters opens the door to a different kind of papacy. Even moral and religious teachings of the past can be reformed, if they are not taught by a consensus of theologians and received by the people of the Church. This may lighten the heavy load of tradition within the Church and allow later popes to lead the Church in a new direction.

Potential Reforms of the Structure of the Church

This change would have to rest on a reformed Church structure in which the voices of the laity reach the top more quickly. The laity is already playing a stronger role in the Church because of the shortage of new priests. If they succeed in creating structures at the national Church level that are more responsive to lay concerns, they could begin to dissolve the hierarchy. The pope would remain a spiritual leader, reinterpreting Christ's message for every age with the help of the Holy Spirit, but Church structures would be decided and operated by laypeople.

The concerns of a parish in Boston are unlikely to be the same as the concerns of a Catholic community in El Salvador. Each country or region might choose its own course, creating its own style of leadership. The institutional structure of today's Vatican would be largely unnecessary. Leaders of national Churches would consult together regularly, but there would be no need for central control.

The papacy might be a movable office under this new regime. Perhaps national Church leaders would elect popes for a fixed term of five or ten years. The seat of the Holy See itself could shift around the world with the nationality of the current pope, becoming a movable Vatican. The role of the pope would be that of a peacemaker, mediator, and ethical counselor who fosters dialogue and keeps communication lines open among different parts of the world.

The character and convictions of the pope have enormous influence on the direction the Church takes. Any adult male Roman Catholic is a potential candidate for the papacy, but in the last 450 years, only cardinals have been elected. The 123 cardinals elect the pope in a twenty-day period after the death of the previous pope. The changing background of the cardinals can therefore affect what kind of pope is elected.

Other Christian churches have models for more democratic leadership, but none has a spiritual leader of the stature of the pope. One of the Church's goals is unity among Christians. This could be the task of a reformed papacy. As of now, no one has yet suggested a course that would bring all Christians together.

In a less reform-oriented Church, there is a different danger for the papacy—the widening rift between the liberal Western democratic ideals of

Europe and the increasingly dominant representatives of developing countries. This could split the Catholic world, with the Western Church rejecting the authority of Rome, if not in words, at least in action. The papacy would then lose its spiritual hold over the hemisphere that dominates world economies and become less influential in its teachings.

The Role of the Laity

Laymen and women are taking increasingly sophisticated jobs within the Church, jobs that used to be performed by priests and members of religious orders. Often, these laypeople have professional training in nursing, social work, or counseling. Priests are getting burned out and are retiring early, and the Church is having difficulty finding young men who can step in to replace them. Fewer men and women are seeking life as monks or nuns. Consequently, laypeople are stepping up to fill the void.

In the liturgy, laypeople take on the role of cantors, music directors, readers, altar servers, and Eucharistic ministers. Some even lead Sunday worship in absence of a priest. They teach youth and adults and participate in marriage preparations, bereavement programs, and ministry with divorced or separated Catholics. Some are involved in Catholic charities, peace and justice networks, soup kitchens, and shelters. They work in Catholic health care and social service institutions.

Often these laypeople are responding to a vocation of their own. They feel the call to serve Christ and the Church and to live the Christian message. The Church sometimes pays poorly for jobs that require years of training, and many people are serving in volunteer positions. In those areas where laypeople serve on parish councils that attempt to make decisions for all, the work is often a difficult meeting of minds as traditional and reformist laypeople learn to work together.

Lay Involvement Is Limited

Although some have objected to receiving the Eucharist from a layperson or getting a pastoral visit from someone other than the priest, most Catholics accept these practices and realize that the clergy cannot accommodate all of the parishioners. Acceptance is more widespread when a pastor has clearly communicated that he is delegating his responsibilities.

ALERT!

Catholic laypeople frequently complain that they are not heard at upper levels of the Church. They regard the structure of other Christian congregations, such as the Methodists or Episcopalians, as potential models for a more democratic Church.

The area that is understandably off limits for laypeople is consecration of the host and administering of sacraments. Another area that may or may not be controlled by laypeople is the decision-making necessary to run parishes, churches, and other Catholic institutions. In some cases, the scope for decision-making is restricted by the parish priest, local bishop, or even the Church officials at the national level.

Will Women Ever Be Ordained?

The Church position that women cannot be ordained is a point of contention in Europe and the Americas, where Catholic women have seen other Christian churches accept female ministry. Catholics in these parts of the world are alarmed at the dearth of young men willing to train for the priesthood. Many women are willing to take on the ministry, and some have become better trained than many priests.

Women played important roles in the Church throughout its early history as martyrs for the Christian faith, saints, and members of religious orders. However, they appear to have lost their leadership positions in the Church around the sixth century.

FACT

In the early Church, women did take on significant roles as deaconesses who ministered to other women; furthermore, older widows and single women were consulted in church decisions. The Bible makes mention of several prominent female leaders of the early Church, including Lydia and Priscilla.

Women began to ask for a more prominent role in the Church in the 1960s, with the advent of the women's liberation movement. In 1976, the Pontifical Biblical Commission reported that it could find no support in the biblical evidence for the exclusion of women from the ordained priesthood. The Bible provides no ready answer to the role of women. Both the pope and the American bishops have written letters saying the ordination of women is not justified. The issue continues to be hotly debated.

Changing Attitudes

The Church has already shifted its perception of women and their roles. Women are seen as equal in human dignity with men. They are no longer subject to men, nor are they expected to obey male authority. In 1995, Pope John Paul II said there was an urgent need to achieve equality in every area, including equal pay for equal work, protection for working mothers, fairness in career advancement, and access to the rights of citizenship. He further wrote that the process of women's liberation has been substantially positive.

As lay ministers, women are already taking on tasks that were once limited to men. They contribute to pastoral teams, administer in parishes where there are no priests, and take jobs as chaplains in hospitals and prisons. They run Catholic schools and charities, do legal work, and minister to the poor. They serve as ministers of the Eucharist, lectors, servers, and chancery and tribunal officials. Women take training in theology and other aspects of ministry right up to the point where laws against ordination prevent them from continuing further.

There are already widespread examples of ordained women in the

Protestant churches, including the Anglican and Episcopalian, which are the closest in beliefs and liturgy to the Catholic Church. Feminist theology is now part of the curriculum in Catholic academia, and women may even teach in seminaries. Female theologians re-examine the Scriptures with fresh insights, reflecting how Jesus himself rejected the narrow subservient role of women that was the norm in his day, and how he treated women with great respect and compassion.

The Main Arguments

The argument the Church makes against ordination of women is that Jesus did not select any women to serve among his Twelve Apostles. Since the hierarchy of the Church draws its authority from being the spiritual descendants of the apostles, it follows that like the apostles, the clergy should be male. When serving the Eucharist, the priest acts as the representative of Christ. A woman cannot fill this role because Jesus was not a woman. Any movement to ordain women would meet deep opposition among laypeople as well as the clergy.

The counterargument is that Christ did not ordain anyone to be a priest, man or woman. Furthermore, he had many women among his followers; after his resurrection, he appeared first to Mary Magdalene. Many Catholics say that priests suffer in their understanding of the world by being cut off from close relationships with women, because they cannot marry, are trained separately, and work in a collegial atmosphere mainly with other priests. While many parish priests develop an understanding of the problems of women's lives by ministering to women within their congregation, those who rise highest in the Church are much more isolated, a condition that some say leads to condescending and antifeminist attitudes.

The exclusively male hierarchy of the Church leads to decisions being made without any discussion from a female point of view, and this tends to work against the ordination of women. The Vatican II charge that the Church should become the whole people of God is contributing to a push for new understanding. If people are the Church, they might be able to affect a change, as long as they continue to seek ministry among women. If Christ calls everyone to use his or her skills to serve the Church, then women must follow this call as faithfully as men.

This quote from Paul's letter to the Galatians is often used to argue in favor of ordination of women: "For through faith you are all children of God in Christ Jesus. For all of you who were baptized into Christ have clothed yourselves with Christ. There is neither Jew nor Greek, there is neither slave nor free person, there is not male and female; for you are all one in Christ Jesus" (Galatians 3:26–28).

Relations with Other Religions

Over the centuries, the one Christian Church underwent a series of splits and schisms, the most important of which were the split that created the Eastern Orthodox and the Roman Catholic churches and the separation of Protestant faiths from the Catholic Church during the Reformation. The Catholic Church has recently acknowledged its own faults in creating these divisions, and it has taken on as one of its important missions the task of moving toward unity. The Decree on Ecumenism, passed by Vatican II, urges fellow Christians to have brotherly generosity toward one another.

Unity will be accomplished through prayer, discussion, and new understandings among the Christian churches. Almost all Christian churches are in fact participating in this movement toward ecumenism. The shared Gospel of Jesus Christ already unites Christians. In practice, they have come together in Christian charities, peace, and social justice movements to work toward a common cause. But there is still a long way to go toward a time when all Christians can share communion.

Ecumenical discussions over the last thirty years have led to many areas of agreement. The Eastern Orthodox churches are very similar to the Catholic Church in rites and liturgy, but they do not accept the authority of Rome. The Anglican or Episcopalian church is also close in its belief, sacraments, and Church structure, though it differs with the Catholic Church over ordination of women. The Catholic Church considers Lutheran, Presbyterian, and Methodist churches, which have bishops, Baptism, and the Eucharist, to be apostolic, though there are greater differences in belief and practice. The many and varied Protestant denominations are valued for their fidelity to the message of the Gospels.

Official dialogues among churches are taking place all over the world. Students for the ministry of various denominations study together, and theologians of different backgrounds compare insights. Where they disagree, the message of ecumenism is to keep talking. If unity is to be achieved, it will be a result of taking spiritual insight from many traditions. The Church has acknowledged that no single Church dogma can express the whole truth of Christianity.

Dialogue with Non-Christians

Respect and love must also be shown to non-Christians and their faiths. Those who serve one God, such as Muslims and Jews, have much in common with Christians. From Buddhism and Hinduism, Christians can learn techniques of meditation and other skills that will bring them closer to God. The institutional Church has official dialogues set up with leaders of these religions. It even has a mandate to talk with nonbelievers.

The Church has already identified areas in which it can work together with other faiths on issues of justice and peace. Even those without faith agree with some of the issues that concern the Catholic Church.

Appendices

Appendix A
Liturgical Calendar

In the cycle of the liturgical year, the Church commemorates the mysteries from the life of Christ and the feasts of Mary and the saints. The following is the Church calendar of feast days, saint memorial days, and solemnities celebrated by Catholics around the world. (Please note that some of the saint days listed here are only celebrated in some parts of the world and are no longer universal Catholic holidays.)

January	
1	Mary, Mother of God
2	St. Basil the Great; St. Adalhard; Gregory Nazianzen, Doctor of the Church
3	St. Genevieve
4	Elizabeth Ann Seton
5	St. John Nepomucene Neumann; St. Simeon Stylites
6	Epiphany; Blessed André Bessette
13	St. Hilary
15	St. Paul the Hermit
17	St. Devota, St. Anthony of Egypt
19	St. Canute, St. Henry of Uppsala
20	St. Sebastian; St. Fabian
21	St. Agnes
22	St. Vincent of Saragossa
24	St. Francis de Sales
25	The Conversion of Paul the Apostle
26	St. Paula; St. Timothy; St. Titus
27	St. Angela Merici
28	St. Thomas Aquinas
31	St. John Bosco

February

1	St. Brigid
2	The Presentation of the Lord
3	St. Blaise; St. Ansgar
5	St. Agatha
6	St. Amand; St. Peter Baptist; St. Dorothy; Paul Miki and his companions
8	St. Jerome Emiliani
9	St. Apollonia
10	St. Scholastica
11	Our Lady of Lourdes
12	St. Julian the Innkeeper
14	St. Valentine; St. Cyril; St. Methodius
17	Seven Founders of the Order of Servites
21	St. Peter Damian; John Henry Newman
22	Chair of Saint Peter
23	St. Polycarp
25	St. Walburga

March

1	St. David
3	Blessed Katharine Drexel; St. Cunegund
4	St. Casimir
7	St. Perpetua; St. Felicity
8	St. John of God
9	St. Frances of Rome; St. Dominic Savio; St. Catherine of Bologna
13	St. Ansovinus
15	St. Louise de Marillac
17	St. Agricola of Avignon; St. Gertrude of Nivelles; St. Joseph of Arimathea; St. Patrick
18	St. Cyril of Jerusalem
19	St. Joseph (husband of Mary)
20	St. Cuthbert
21	St. Benedict
23	St. Toribio Alfonso Mogrovejo
25	Annunciation; St. Dismas

April

2	St. Francis of Paola
3	St. Adjutor
4	St. Isidore of Seville
5	St. Vincent Ferrer
7	St. Jean-Baptiste de la Salle
11	St. Gemma Galani; St. Stanislaus of Cracow
13	St. Martin I
14	St. Peter González; St. Lidwina
16	St. Benedict Joseph Labre
21	St. Anselm
23	St. George
24	St. Fidelis of Sigmaringen
25	St. Mark
27	St. Zita
28	St. Peter Chanel
29	St. Catherine of Siena
30	St. Pius V

May

1	St. Joseph the Worker
2	St. Athanasius
3	St. Philip; St. James
4	St. Florian
8	St. Plechelm
10	St. John of Ávila, St. Antonius of Florence; St. Catald
12	St. Nereus; St. Achilleus; St. Pancras
13	St. Julian of Norwich
14	St. Matthias
15	St. Isidore the Farmer; St. Dymphna
16	St. John of Nepomuk, St. Honoratus, St. Brendan of Clonfert; St. Peregrine of Auxerre

18	St. John I
19	St. Dunstan; St. Ivo; St. Celestine V
20	St. Bernardino of Siena
22	St. Rita; St. Julia of Corsica
25	St. Gregory VII; St. Mary Magdalene de Pazzi; St. Bede the Venerable
26	St. Philip Neri
27	St. Augustine of Canterbury
28	St. Bernard of Montjoux
29	St. Bona
30	St. Joan of Arc; St. Ferdinand
31	The Visitation of the Blessed Virgin Mary

June	
1	St. Justin; St. Theobald
2	St. Marcellinus; St. Peter; St. Elmo
3	Charles Lwanga and companions; St. Kevin of Glendalough; St. Morand
5	St. Boniface
6	St. Norbert
8	St. Medard
9	St. Ephrem; St. Columba of Iona
11	St. Barnabas
13	St. Anthony of Padua
15	St. Vitus
19	St. Romuald
21	St. Aloysius Gonzaga
22	St. Paulinus of Nola; St. John Fisher; St. Thomas More; St. Nicetas
23	St. Joseph Cafasso
24	The Birth of St. John the Baptist
27	St. Cyril of Alexandria
28	St. Irenaeus
29	Solemnity of St. Peter and St. Paul
30	First Martyrs of the Church of Rome

July	
1	Blessed Junipero Serra
3	St. Thomas
4	St. Elizabeth of Portugal
5	St. Anthony Zaccaria
6	St. Maria Goretti
7	St. Cyril; St. Methodius
8	St. Kilian
11	St. Benedict II
12	St. John Gualbert
14	Blessed Kateri Tekakwitha; St. Camillus de Lellis
15	St. Bonaventure; St. Swithun; St. Vladimir
16	Our Lady of Mount Carmel
19	St. Justa; St. Rufina
21	St. Lawrence of Brindisi
22	St. Mary Magdalene
23	St. Bridget of Sweden
25	St. James the Greater
26	St. Joachim and St. Anne (parents of Mary)
27	St. Pantaleon
29	St. Martha; St. Olaf
30	St. Peter Chrysologus
31	St. Ignatius of Loyola

August	
1	St. Alphonsus de Liguori; St. Friard
2	St. Eusebius of Vercelli
3	St. Hippolytus
4	St. John Vianney
5	Dedication of the Basilica of Saint Mary Major; St. Addai
6	The Transfiguration of the Lord

7	Pope St. Sixtus II and his companions; St. Cajetan
8	St. Dominic
10	St. Lawrence
13	St. Pontian; St. Hippolytus
14	St. Maximilian Kolbe
15	The Assumption of the Blessed Virgin Mary
16	St. Stephen of Hungary; St. Roch
18	St. Jane Frances de Chantal
19	St. John Eudes; St. Sebald
20	St. Bernard of Clairvaux
21	St. Pius X
22	Queenship of Mary
23	St. Rose of Lima
24	St. Bartholomew; St. Ouen
25	St. Joseph Calasanctius; St. Genesius the Actor
27	St. Monica
28	St. Augustine of Hippo; St. Moses the Ethiopian
29	The Beheading of St. John the Baptist
31	St. Raymond Nonnatus

September

1	St. Fiacre; St. Giles
3	St. Gregory I (the Great)
7	St. Gratis of Aosta
8	Birth of Mary; St. Hadrian
9	St. Peter Claver
10	St. Nicholas Tolentine
11	St. Hyacinth
13	St. John Chrysostom
14	Triumph of the Cross
15	Our Lady of Sorrows
16	St. Cornelius; St. Cyprian; St. Ludmilla
17	St. Robert Bellarmine; St. Hildegard of Bingen

18	St. Joseph of Cupertino
19	St. Januarius
20	Andrew Kim Taegon, Paul Chong Hasang, and their companions
21	St. Matthew
22	St. Phocas
23	St. Adamnan
26	St. Cosmas; St. Damian
27	St. Vincent de Paul
28	St. Wenceslaus; St. Lawrence Ruiz and companions
29	Archangels Michael, Gabriel, and Raphael
30	St. Jerome; St. Gregory the Illuminator

October

1	St. Thérèse of the Child Jesus (of Lisieux)
2	Guardian Angels
4	St. Francis of Assisi
6	Blessed Marie Rose Durocher; St. Bruno
7	Our Lady of the Rosary
9	St. Denis and his companions; St. John Leonardi; St. Louis Betrand
10	St. Francis Borgia; St. Gereon
14	St. Callistus I
15	St. Teresa of Jesus (of Ávila)
16	St. Hedwig; St. Margaret Mary Alacoque; St. Gall; St. Gerard Majella
17	St. Ignatius of Antioch
18	St. Luke
19	St. John de Brébeuf, St. Isaac Jogues, and their companions
20	St. Paul of the Cross; Blessed Contardo Ferrini
22	St. Peter of Alcántara
23	St. John of Capistrano
24	St. Anthony Claret
25	St. Crispin; St. Crispinian
27	St. Frumentius
28	St. Simon; St. Jude

November

1	All Saints
2	All Souls
3	St. Martin de Porres; St. Hubert of Liège
4	St. Charles Borromeo
5	St. Kea
6	St. Leonard of Noblac
7	St. Willibrord
8	Four Crowned Martyrs
9	Dedication of the St. John Lateran Basilica
10	St. Leo the Great; St. Aedh Mac Bricc; St. Gertrude the Great
11	St. Martin of Tours
12	St. Josaphat
13	St. Frances Xavier Cabrini; St. Brice; St. Homobonus; St. Stanislaus Kostka
15	St. Albert the Great (Albertus Magnus)
16	St. Margaret of Scotland; St. Gertrude
17	St. Elizabeth of Hungary; St. Gregory the Woodworker
18	St. Rose Philippine Duchesne; St. Odo of Cluny; Dedication of the Churches of Peter and Paul
21	The Presentation of Mary
22	St. Cecilia
23	Blessed Miguel Agustín Pro; St. Clement I; St. Columbanus
24	St. Andrew Dung-Lac and his companions
26	St. Leonard Casanova; St. John Berchmans
30	St. Andrew

December

1	St. Eligius
2	St. Bibiana
3	St. Francis Xavier
4	St. John Damascene; St. Osmund; St. Barbara
6	St. Nicholas of Myra
7	St. Ambrose
8	The Immaculate Conception of the Blessed Virgin Mary
9	Blessed Juan Diego
11	St. Damasus I
12	Our Lady of Guadalupe; St. Jane Frances de Chantal
13	St. Lucy; St. Odilia
14	St. John of the Cross
21	St. Peter Canisius
23	St. John of Kenty; St. Thorlac; St. John Cantius
25	Christmas
26	St. Stephen
27	St. John the Evangelist
28	The Holy Innocents
29	St. Thomas à Becket
30	Holy Family
31	St. Sylvester I

In addition to these fixed-date feasts, the Catholic Church celebrates a number of floating feasts.

Sunday after Christmas—The Feast of the Holy Family (Jesus, Mary, Joseph)

Third Sunday after Christmas—Feast of the Baptism of Jesus by John the Baptist

First Sunday after Pentecost—Holy Trinity

Thursday after Holy Trinity—Body and Blood of Christ

Friday following the second Sunday after Pentecost—Sacred Heart

Saturday following the second Sunday after Pentecost—Immaculate Heart of Mary

Last Sunday of Ordinary Time—Christ the King

Appendix B

A Timeline of Notable Events

Catholic history spans over 2,000 years, and has touched the lives of millions of people. This timeline highlights a few major points that help set the progression of the Catholic Church in perspective. Please note that some dates here are approximate.

Timeline: An Overview	
2090 B.C.–A.D. 30	Biblical times
4–30	Jesus' life
30–600	The early Church
35–312	Age of Martyrs
600–1300	Papal rule
1054	Great Schism
1350–1700	European Renaissance
1377–1407	Great Papal Schism (struggle between Rome and Avignon)
1517–1648	Protestant Reformation
1542–1648	Catholic Counter-Reformation
1697–1790	The Enlightenment
1760–1914	The Industrial Revolution

Timeline of Events	
2090 B.C.	God calls out to Abraham
1487 B.C.	Moses leads the Israelites out of bondage
1004 B.C.	King David rules Israel
858 B.C.	Elijah becomes a prophet of God
739 B.C.	Isaiah is a prophet of God
509 B.C.	Israel and Judah fall under control of the Roman Empire
37 B.C.	Herod captures Jerusalem
4 B.C.	Jesus is born
27	Jesus begins his ministry
30	Jesus is crucified; the Church is born at Pentecost
35	Conversion of Saul, who becomes St. Paul
42	Antioch is the center of Christian activity
70	Rome replaces Antioch as the center of Christian activity

Timeline of Events

99	Death of St. Clement, first Bishop of Rome and successor to St. Peter
100	Christianity becomes illegal in the Roman Empire
312	Constantine becomes emperor of Rome; his Edict of Milan stops persecution of Christians
325	The Nicene Creed is created at the Council of Bishops at Nicaea
381	Emperor Theodosius declares Christianity the official religion of the Roman Empire
397	New Testament is formalized by bishops at Carthage
410	Rome falls
440–461	Pope Leo the Great steps into the power vacuum, providing both religious and political leadership
451	Council of Chalcedon; Pontiff at Rome asserts supreme authority
480	Establishment of the Benedictine order, which gives rise to other monastic orders
590	Pope Gregory I
751	Papal States are established and the pope is placed to rule over these territories
800	Charlemagne, King of France, is named Emperor of Romans
1054	Split between Latin-speaking Catholic Church and Eastern Orthodox Church
1073	Pope Gregory VII centralizes control of Church with new theory of papal infallibility
1098–1099	First Crusade regains control of Jerusalem
1147–1187	Jerusalem is lost in Second Crusade
1189–1192	Third Crusade
1202–1204	Fourth Crusade
1212	St. Francis creates the first of the mendicant orders, the Franciscans. The Dominicans, Carmelites, and Augustinians also arise in the 1200s
1224–1274	Life of St. Thomas Aquinas
1231	University in Paris gets papal charter; universities are set up throughout Europe
1232–1300	Pope Gregory IX attempts to counteract heresy by beginning the Inquisition
1301	King of France arrests the pope
1305–1378	Pope Clement V moves seat of papal power to Avignon
1377	Papacy returns to Rome, but a second pope is elected at Avignon
1417	Council of Constance ends Great Schism, Martin V is elected pope
1486	Start of the Spanish Inquisition
1517	Augustinian monk Martin Luther begins fighting the corruption of the Church
1540	Formation of the Jesuits

Timeline of Events

1543	Copernicus asserts that the Earth revolves around the sun
1544	Jesuit missionary work begins among pagan people of Japan, Africa, and North America
1545–1563	The Council of Trent
1559	John Calvin sends missionaries throughout Europe to convert Catholics to the new faith of Protestantism
1566	Pope Pius V standardizes Latin Mass
1632	Galileo supports Copernicus based on his observations through a telescope
1648	Jesuits Antony Daniel, Jean de Brebéuf, and Gabriel Lalemont become first martyrs in North America
1663	Monsignor François de Montmorency Laval is named Catholic bishop at Quebec
1789	French Revolution fractures the Church
1789	John Carrol becomes the first Bishop in the United States and creates the first diocese, the See of Baltimore
1814–1820	Second Spanish Inquisition
1869	Pope Pius IX calls the Vatican I Council, which strengthens the Church and rejects modernization
1891	Pope Leo XIII issues *Rerum Novarum*, an important encyclical on workers' rights
1959	Pope John XXIII announces he will call an ecumenical council
1962–1965	Second Vatican Council
1963	Pope John XXIII dies; Pope Paul VI is elected
1968	Pope Paul VI publishes encyclical on *Humanae Vitae*, birth control
1978	Pope Paul VI dies; Pope John Paul I is elected and dies shortly after; Pope John Paul II is elected
1981	Pope John Paul II publishes *Laborem Exercens*, on human work
1986	U.S. Catholic Bishops publish a pastoral letter "Economic Justice for All: Catholic Social Teaching and the U.S. Economy"
1987	Pope John Paul II publishes *Sollicitudo Rei Socialis* on the social concerns of the Church
1995	Pope John Paul II publishes *Evanelium Vitae*, reiterating his stand on abortion, and *Ut Unum Sint*, renewing the Church's commitment to ecumenism
2000	Year of Jubilee

Appendix C
Q&A: The Eucharist

The Eucharist is not just one of the sacraments but the pre-eminent sacrament in the Church. It is a matter of mystery and faith, a miracle worked by Christ for his people that is repeated every day throughout every Catholic community in the world. For the individual, the Eucharist is a renewal of the covenant with the Church and with other Christians around the world.

Q: What is transubstantiation?
A: The Catholic Church teaches that Christ is really present in the consecrated elements of bread and wine. Transubstantiation is the transformation that the bread and wine undergo during Mass to become the actual Body and Blood of Christ. However, during communion, Christ is also present in the community gathered for worship, in the Word of God read from the Bible, and in the person of the priest who presides in his name.

Q: Who can take communion?
A: Only Catholics confirmed as members of the Catholic Church may take communion in a Catholic Church. However, there are times when individual non-Catholic Christians may share in Eucharist with Catholics. Local bishops have the jurisdiction to establish guidelines for particular occasions like interfaith marriage, First Communion, or anniversaries. Priests may also serve the Eucharist to non-Catholics if they are dying and if they request the sacraments and share the Church's faith regarding the Eucharist.

Q: Who can administer communion?
A: In the Catholic Church, only the priest may consecrate the bread and the wine of the Eucharist. The priest has the power by virtue of his ordination to make Christ present and to reveal his death and resurrection. This power is passed on to him by the Church itself through the sacrament of Holy Orders, linking Church, priest, and laity in the Eucharistic sacrament.

In the modern Catholic Church, deacons may hold the cup during consecration, and deacons or lay ministers may distribute the communion to the congregation.

Q: What is the Eucharist made of?
A: Catholic churches serve a special wafer, unleavened bread that must be made only of wheat flour (white or brown) and water. The wine must be a natural wine made of grapes. Drops of water are mixed with the wine to symbolize Christ's humanity and divinity combined.

Q: When do the bread and wine become the Body and Blood of Christ?
A: Consecration by a priest turns the Eucharist into Christ's body and blood. Consecration takes place when the priest says the words, "This is my body, broken for you. This is my blood."

Q: How is the communion administered?
A: Before Vatican II, the priest placed the host into the mouths of the parishioners. Now Catholics may receive communion in their hands. Congregants usually come forward to the front of the church or to stations in the aisles manned by ministers to receive communion. The priest or minister places the host in their hand. Then they may drink from the cup.

Some churches serve Eucharist by the process of intinction, in which the priest breaks the bread and dips it in wine before giving it to the communicant. However, many Catholics only take the bread, a practice that is acceptable because both the bread and the wine incorporate the whole of Christ's presence. Only sick people may take the wine alone.

Q: How often should Catholics take communion?
A: The Catholic Church requires that the Eucharist be taken once a year—during Easter time—and before death. However, Catholics may take it as often as once a day, during daily Mass.

Q: Does Eucharist have to be given in a church?
A: The Eucharist can be served in a home or hospital, on the battlefield or in the street—anywhere there is a need. It is the ritual, rather than the place, that creates the covenant with Jesus.

Q: What do Catholics need to do to prepare for communion?
A: The Church asks that Catholics fast for at least an hour before they receive the Eucharist. This is done out of reverence for the Body and Blood of Christ. This means no food or drink, except for water. People who are ill may reduce their fast to fifteen minutes.

To receive Holy Communion worthily, the believer must be free from mortal sin. That means it is necessary to confess and receive absolution from a priest before receiving the Eucharist.

Q: Why do Catholics genuflect toward the host?
A: The genuflection is made toward the monstrance that holds the communion bread and wine. It is a way of honoring Christ's presence in the Church.

Q: What happens after the meal is over?
A: Catholics hold that the Body and Blood of Christ remain in the consecrated elements after the communion service. The best way to show respect for the Eucharist is for a congregation to consume it. If some Eucharist is not used during a service, it should be offered to the sick and those who are absent. The Catholic Church stores the host in monstrance, or ostensorium. Any wine that has not been drunk during the service is consumed by the priest, ministers, or deacons.

Index

A

Abortion, 191, 233, 252, 258
Advent, 145
Afterlife, 163–74
    Anointing of the Sick and, 20, 21, 100, 102–4, 165, 224–26
    death and, 164–65
    heaven and, 167–70
    hell and, 163, 172–74
    judgment in, 163, 165–67
    Purgatory and, 163, 164, 170–72
    reincarnation and, 164
Alexander VI, Pope, 52
Altar, 123, 130
Analogy, 7
Angel Gabriel, 11, 78
Angels, 8
Angelus, 89
Anglican Church, 62, 266
Annulment, 223
Annunciation, 11
Anointing of the Sick, 20, 21, 100, 102–4, 165, 224–26
Anointing with oil, 70, 76, 96
Apostasy, 112
Apostles, 14–15
    defined, 14
    Holy Spirit and, 19–20
    letters of, 14, 24–25, 153
    names of, 14
    Paul, x, 14, 24–25, 26, 27, 153
    Peter, x, 15, 27
    preaching of, 19–20
Apostolic succession, 5
Apostolic tradition, 106–8, 156
Aquinas, Thomas, Saint, x, 5, 43
Arianism, 31
Ascension, 74
Ash Wednesday, 146
Augustine of Hippo, Saint, x, 7, 34–35, 229
Augustinians, 50, 185
Authority, shift, 58, 59–60
Avignon, France, 45

B

Baptism, 93–95, 214–15
    ceremony, 93–94, 214–15

for children, 94–95, 214–15
Christian initiation and, 92, 214, 235–36
defined, 93
Holy Spirit and, 74
of Jesus Christ, 12, 16
Nicene Creed and, 114–15
origin of, 21
Protestantism and, 4
as sacrament, 20, 21, 40, 92, 93–95
water symbolism in, 76
See also Confirmation
Beatific vision, 167–68
Beatitudes, 13–14, 208
Beliefs, 109–36
    apostasy and, 112
    canon law and, 110–12, 176, 177–78
    Catechism of, 52, 115–17
    charity and, 117–18, 203–4, 221, 242
    daily life and, 117–20, 202–4
    excommunication and, 113
    fasting and, 122
    heresy and, 31, 43–44, 112
    limbo and, 122–23
    Nicene Creed and, 30, 64, 74, 114–15
    saints, veneration of, 124, 207–8
    schisms and, 3, 45–46, 113, 155, 338–39
    scriptures and, 119–20
    Ten Commandments and, 118–19
    See also Prayer
Bellarmine, Robert, 198
Bells, 132
Benedictine order, 184
Benedict of Umbria, Saint, 35
Benedict XV, Pope, 57
Bible
    analogy and, 7
    creation of, 152–54
    Gospels and, 7, 12, 14, 25, 69, 152
    as history, 158–59
    interpretation of, 4, 7, 155–56, 161
    Jesus' birth and, 10–12
    as literature, 160–61
    metaphors of, 159–60
    New Testament, 14, 24–25, 151, 152, 153–54
    Old Testament, 69, 98, 99, 151, 152–54
    Protestantism and, 4, 49–50

    study of, 156–57
    symbols of, 159–60
    tradition and, 6
    translations of, 157–58, 161
    understanding, 7, 157–61
    as Word of God, 156, 157
    See also Scriptures
Birth control, 59–60, 187, 191
Bishops, 178–80
    defined, 178–79
    hierarchy of, 179
    Holy Orders and, 102, 106, 107, 108
    laity and, 194–95, 263
    role of, 180
Black Death, 44, 48
Blaise, Saint, 127
Blessing of Throats, 127
Blessings, 126–27
Blood of Christ, 4, 18, 98
Body of Christ, 4, 18, 98
Body-of-Christ model, 198–99
Boniface (monk), 33
Boniface VIII, Pope, 45
Breviary, 52
Brothers, 184
Business, 248–49
Byzantium, 31, 38–39

C

Calendar, liturgical, 144–45, 148–49, 270–78
Calixtus II, Pope, 40
Call, receiving. *See* Ministry
Calvin, John, 50, 81
Candles, 131–32
Canon law, 110–12, 176, 177–78
Canon of Scripture, 152
Capuchin order, 50, 53
Cardinals, 176, 177
Carmelite order, 51, 53
Carthage, 25
Catechesis, 156–57
Catechism, 52, 115–17
Catechumenate period, 234–35
Cathedrals, 41
Catherine of Siena, Saint, 45
Catholicism
    challenges of, 186–88, 224, 258–60

THE EVERYTHING SERIES!

BUSINESS & PERSONAL FINANCE

Everything® Accounting Book
Everything® Budgeting Book
Everything® Business Planning Book
Everything® Coaching and Mentoring Book
Everything® Fundraising Book
Everything® Get Out of Debt Book
Everything® Grant Writing Book
Everything® Home-Based Business Book, 2nd Ed.
Everything® Homebuying Book, 2nd Ed.
Everything® Homeselling Book, 2nd Ed.
Everything® Investing Book, 2nd Ed.
Everything® Landlording Book
Everything® Leadership Book
Everything® Managing People Book, 2nd Ed.
Everything® Negotiating Book
Everything® Online Auctions Book
Everything® Online Business Book
Everything® Personal Finance Book
Everything® Personal Finance in Your 20s and 30s Book
Everything® Project Management Book
Everything® Real Estate Investing Book
Everything® Robert's Rules Book, $7.95
Everything® Selling Book
Everything® Start Your Own Business Book, 2nd Ed.
Everything® Wills & Estate Planning Book

COOKING

Everything® Barbecue Cookbook
Everything® Bartender's Book, $9.95
Everything® Chinese Cookbook
Everything® Classic Recipes Book
Everything® Cocktail Parties and Drinks Book
Everything® College Cookbook
Everything® Cooking for Baby and Toddler Book
Everything® Cooking for Two Cookbook
Everything® Diabetes Cookbook
Everything® Easy Gourmet Cookbook
Everything® Fondue Cookbook
Everything® Fondue Party Book
Everything® Gluten-Free Cookbook
Everything® Glycemic Index Cookbook
Everything® Grilling Cookbook

Everything® Healthy Meals in Minutes Cookbook
Everything® Holiday Cookbook
Everything® Indian Cookbook
Everything® Italian Cookbook
Everything® Low-Carb Cookbook
Everything® Low-Fat High-Flavor Cookbook
Everything® Low-Salt Cookbook
Everything® Meals for a Month Cookbook
Everything® Mediterranean Cookbook
Everything® Mexican Cookbook
Everything® One-Pot Cookbook
Everything® Quick and Easy 30-Minute, 5-Ingredient Cookbook
Everything® Quick Meals Cookbook
Everything® Slow Cooker Cookbook
Everything® Slow Cooking for a Crowd Cookbook
Everything® Soup Cookbook
Everything® Tex-Mex Cookbook
Everything® Thai Cookbook
Everything® Vegetarian Cookbook
Everything® Wild Game Cookbook
Everything® Wine Book, 2nd Ed.

GAMES

Everything® 15-Minute Sudoku Book, $9.95
Everything® 30-Minute Sudoku Book, $9.95
Everything® Blackjack Strategy Book
Everything® Brain Strain Book, $9.95
Everything® Bridge Book
Everything® Card Games Book
Everything® Card Tricks Book, $9.95
Everything® Casino Gambling Book, 2nd Ed.
Everything® Chess Basics Book
Everything® Craps Strategy Book
Everything® Crossword and Puzzle Book
Everything® Crossword Challenge Book
Everything® Cryptograms Book, $9.95
Everything® Easy Crosswords Book
Everything® Easy Kakuro Book, $9.95
Everything® Games Book, 2nd Ed.
Everything® Giant Sudoku Book, $9.95
Everything® Kakuro Challenge Book, $9.95
Everything® Large-Print Crossword Challenge Book
Everything® Large-Print Crosswords Book
Everything® Lateral Thinking Puzzles Book, $9.95
Everything® Mazes Book

Everything® Pencil Puzzles Book, $9.95
Everything® Poker Strategy Book
Everything® Pool & Billiards Book
Everything® Test Your IQ Book, $9.95
Everything® Texas Hold 'Em Book, $9.95
Everything® Travel Crosswords Book, $9.95
Everything® Word Games Challenge Book
Everything® Word Search Book

HEALTH

Everything® Alzheimer's Book
Everything® Diabetes Book
Everything® Health Guide to Adult Bipolar Disorder
Everything® Health Guide to Controlling Anxiety
Everything® Health Guide to Fibromyalgia
Everything® Health Guide to Thyroid Disease
Everything® Hypnosis Book
Everything® Low Cholesterol Book
Everything® Massage Book
Everything® Menopause Book
Everything® Nutrition Book
Everything® Reflexology Book
Everything® Stress Management Book

HISTORY

Everything® American Government Book
Everything® American History Book
Everything® Civil War Book
Everything® Freemasons Book
Everything® Irish History & Heritage Book
Everything® Middle East Book

HOBBIES

Everything® Candlemaking Book
Everything® Cartooning Book
Everything® Coin Collecting Book
Everything® Drawing Book
Everything® Family Tree Book, 2nd Ed.
Everything® Knitting Book
Everything® Knots Book
Everything® Photography Book
Everything® Quilting Book
Everything® Scrapbooking Book
Everything® Sewing Book
Everything® Woodworking Book

Bolded titles are new additions to the series.
All Everything® books are priced at $12.95 or $14.95, unless otherwise stated. Prices subject to change without notice.

HOME IMPROVEMENT

Everything® Feng Shui Book
Everything® Feng Shui Decluttering Book, $9.95
Everything® Fix-It Book
Everything® Home Decorating Book
Everything® Home Storage Solutions Book
Everything® Homebuilding Book
Everything® Lawn Care Book
Everything® Organize Your Home Book

KIDS' BOOKS

All titles are $7.95

Everything® Kids' Animal Puzzle & Activity Book
Everything® Kids' Baseball Book, 4th Ed.
Everything® Kids' Bible Trivia Book
Everything® Kids' Bugs Book
Everything® Kids' Cars and Trucks Puzzle & Activity Book
Everything® Kids' Christmas Puzzle & Activity Book
Everything® Kids' Cookbook
Everything® Kids' Crazy Puzzles Book
Everything® Kids' Dinosaurs Book
Everything® Kids' First Spanish Puzzle and Activity Book
Everything® Kids' Gross Hidden Pictures Book
Everything® Kids' Gross Jokes Book
Everything® Kids' Gross Mazes Book
Everything® Kids' Gross Puzzle and Activity Book
Everything® Kids' Halloween Puzzle & Activity Book
Everything® Kids' Hidden Pictures Book
Everything® Kids' Horses Book
Everything® Kids' Joke Book
Everything® Kids' Knock Knock Book
Everything® Kids' Learning Spanish Book
Everything® Kids' Math Puzzles Book
Everything® Kids' Mazes Book
Everything® Kids' Money Book
Everything® Kids' Nature Book
Everything® Kids' Pirates Puzzle and Activity Book
Everything® Kids' Princess Puzzle and Activity Book
Everything® Kids' Puzzle Book
Everything® Kids' Riddles & Brain Teasers Book
Everything® Kids' Science Experiments Book
Everything® Kids' Sharks Book
Everything® Kids' Soccer Book
Everything® Kids' Travel Activity Book

KIDS' STORY BOOKS

Everything® Fairy Tales Book

LANGUAGE

Everything® Conversational Chinese Book with CD, $19.95
Everything® Conversational Japanese Book with CD, $19.95
Everything® French Grammar Book
Everything® French Phrase Book, $9.95
Everything® French Verb Book, $9.95
Everything® German Practice Book with CD, $19.95
Everything® Inglés Book
Everything® Learning French Book
Everything® Learning German Book
Everything® Learning Italian Book
Everything® Learning Latin Book
Everything® Learning Spanish Book
Everything® Russian Practice Book with CD, $19.95
Everything® Sign Language Book
Everything® Spanish Grammar Book
Everything® Spanish Phrase Book, $9.95
Everything® Spanish Practice Book with CD, $19.95
Everything® Spanish Verb Book, $9.95

MUSIC

Everything® Drums Book with CD, $19.95
Everything® Guitar Book
Everything® Guitar Chords Book with CD, $19.95
Everything® Home Recording Book
Everything® Music Theory Book with CD, $19.95
Everything® Reading Music Book with CD, $19.95
Everything® Rock & Blues Guitar Book (with CD), $19.95
Everything® Songwriting Book

NEW AGE

Everything® Astrology Book, 2nd Ed.
Everything® Birthday Personology Book
Everything® Dreams Book, 2nd Ed.
Everything® Love Signs Book, $9.95
Everything® Numerology Book
Everything® Paganism Book
Everything® Palmistry Book
Everything® Psychic Book
Everything® Reiki Book
Everything® Sex Signs Book, $9.95
Everything® Tarot Book, 2nd Ed.
Everything® Wicca and Witchcraft Book

PARENTING

Everything® Baby Names Book, 2nd Ed.
Everything® Baby Shower Book
Everything® Baby's First Food Book
Everything® Baby's First Year Book
Everything® Birthing Book
Everything® Breastfeeding Book
Everything® Father-to-Be Book
Everything® Father's First Year Book
Everything® Get Ready for Baby Book
Everything® Get Your Baby to Sleep Book, $9.95
Everything® Getting Pregnant Book
Everything® Guide to Raising a One-Year-Old
Everything® Guide to Raising a Two-Year-Old
Everything® Homeschooling Book
Everything® Mother's First Year Book
Everything® Parent's Guide to Children and Divorce
Everything® Parent's Guide to Children with ADD/ADHD
Everything® Parent's Guide to Children with Asperger's Syndrome
Everything® Parent's Guide to Children with Autism
Everything® Parent's Guide to Children with Bipolar Disorder
Everything® Parent's Guide to Children with Dyslexia
Everything® Parent's Guide to Positive Discipline
Everything® Parent's Guide to Raising a Successful Child
Everything® Parent's Guide to Raising Boys
Everything® Parent's Guide to Raising Siblings
Everything® Parent's Guide to Sensory Integration Disorder
Everything® Parent's Guide to Tantrums
Everything® Parent's Guide to the Overweight Child
Everything® Parent's Guide to the Strong-Willed Child
Everything® Parenting a Teenager Book
Everything® Potty Training Book, $9.95
Everything® Pregnancy Book, 2nd Ed.
Everything® Pregnancy Fitness Book
Everything® Pregnancy Nutrition Book
Everything® Pregnancy Organizer, 2nd Ed., $16.95
Everything® Toddler Activities Book
Everything® Toddler Book
Everything® Tween Book
Everything® Twins, Triplets, and More Book

PETS

Everything® **Aquarium Book**
Everything® Boxer Book
Everything® Cat Book, 2nd Ed.
Everything® Chihuahua Book
Everything® Dachshund Book
Everything® Dog Book
Everything® Dog Health Book
Everything® **Dog Owner's Organizer,**
$16.95
Everything® Dog Training and Tricks Book
Everything® German Shepherd Book
Everything® Golden Retriever Book
Everything® Horse Book
Everything® Horse Care Book
Everything® Horseback Riding Book
Everything® Labrador Retriever Book
Everything® Poodle Book
Everything® Pug Book
Everything® Puppy Book
Everything® Rottweiler Book
Everything® Small Dogs Book
Everything® Tropical Fish Book
Everything® Yorkshire Terrier Book

REFERENCE

Everything® Blogging Book
Everything® **Build Your Vocabulary Book**
Everything® Car Care Book
Everything® Classical Mythology Book
Everything® Da Vinci Book
Everything® Divorce Book
Everything® Einstein Book
Everything® Etiquette Book, 2nd Ed.
Everything® Inventions and Patents Book
Everything® Mafia Book
Everything® Philosophy Book
Everything® Psychology Book
Everything® Shakespeare Book

RELIGION

Everything® Angels Book
Everything® Bible Book
Everything® Buddhism Book
Everything® Catholicism Book
Everything® Christianity Book
Everything® History of the Bible Book
Everything® **Jesus Book**
Everything® Jewish History & Heritage Book
Everything® Judaism Book
Everything® Kabbalah Book
Everything® Koran Book
Everything® **Mary Book**

Everything® Mary Magdalene Book
Everything® Prayer Book
Everything® Saints Book
Everything® Torah Book
Everything® Understanding Islam Book
Everything® World's Religions Book
Everything® Zen Book

SCHOOL & CAREERS

Everything® Alternative Careers Book
Everything® **Career Tests Book**
Everything® College Major Test Book
Everything® College Survival Book, 2nd Ed.
Everything® Cover Letter Book, 2nd Ed.
Everything® **Filmmaking Book**
Everything® Get-a-Job Book
Everything® Guide to Being a Paralegal
Everything® Guide to Being a Real Estate
Agent
Everything® **Guide to Being a Sales Rep**
Everything® **Guide to Careers in Health**
Care
Everything® **Guide to Careers in Law**
Enforcement
Everything® **Guide to Government Jobs**
Everything® Guide to Starting and Running
a Restaurant
Everything® Job Interview Book
Everything® New Nurse Book
Everything® New Teacher Book
Everything® Paying for College Book
Everything® Practice Interview Book
Everything® Resume Book, 2nd Ed.
Everything® Study Book

SELF-HELP

Everything® Dating Book, 2nd Ed.
Everything® Great Sex Book
Everything® Kama Sutra Book
Everything® Self-Esteem Book

SPORTS & FITNESS

Everything® **Easy Fitness Book**
Everything® Fishing Book
Everything® Golf Instruction Book
Everything® Pilates Book
Everything® Running Book
Everything® Weight Training Book
Everything® Yoga Book

TRAVEL

Everything® Family Guide to Cruise Vacations
Everything® Family Guide to Hawaii

Everything® Family Guide to Las Vegas,
2nd Ed.
Everything® **Family Guide to Mexico**
Everything® Family Guide to New York City,
2nd Ed.
Everything® Family Guide to RV Travel &
Campgrounds
Everything® Family Guide to the Caribbean
Everything® Family Guide to the Walt Disney
World Resort®, Universal Studios®,
and Greater Orlando, 4th Ed.
Everything® **Family Guide to Timeshares**
Everything® Family Guide to Washington
D.C., 2nd Ed.
Everything® Guide to New England

WEDDINGS

Everything® Bachelorette Party Book, $9.95
Everything® Bridesmaid Book, $9.95
Everything® **Destination Wedding Book**
Everything® Elopement Book, $9.95
Everything® Father of the Bride Book, $9.95
Everything® Groom Book, $9.95
Everything® Mother of the Bride Book, $9.95
Everything® Outdoor Wedding Book
Everything® Wedding Book, 3rd Ed.
Everything® Wedding Checklist, $9.95
Everything® Wedding Etiquette Book, $9.95
Everything® **Wedding Organizer, 2nd Ed.,**
$16.95
Everything® Wedding Shower Book, $9.95
Everything® Wedding Vows Book, $9.95
Everything® **Wedding Workout Book**
Everything® Weddings on a Budget Book,
$9.95

WRITING

Everything® Creative Writing Book
Everything® Get Published Book, 2nd Ed.
Everything® Grammar and Style Book
Everything® Guide to Writing a Book
Proposal
Everything® Guide to Writing a Novel
Everything® Guide to Writing Children's
Books
Everything® Guide to Writing Research
Papers
Everything® Screenwriting Book
Everything® Writing Poetry Book
Everything® Writing Well Book

Available wherever books are sold!
To order, call 800-258-0929, or visit us at *www.everything.com*
Everything® and everything.com® are registered trademarks of F+W Publications, Inc.